Fifty Years of Yoknapatawpha:
Faulkner and Yoknapatawpha,
1979

Fifty Years
of Yoknapatawpha

FAULKNER AND YOKNAPATAWPHA
1979

EDITED BY
DOREEN FOWLER
AND
ANN J. ABADIE

UNIVERSITY PRESS OF MISSISSIPPI
JACKSON • 1980

*This volume is authorized & sponsored by the
University of Mississippi*

Library of Congress Cataloging in Publication Data
Main entry under title:

Fifty years of Yoknapatawpha.

1. Faulkner, William, 1897–1962——Congresses.
2. Novelists, American—20th century—Biography—
Congresses. I. Fowler, Doreen. II. Abadie, Ann J.
PS3511.A86Z78324   813'.52 [B]   80–12255
ISBN 0–87805–121–X
ISBN 0–87805–122–8 (pbk.)

Contents

Contents

Introduction

In 1929 a virtually unknown writer, William Faulkner, published *Sartoris*, his third novel, and Faulkner's mythical Yoknapatawpha County, the locale of his greatest works, was born. Fifty years later, in 1979, William Faulkner is considered by many the greatest twentieth-century American novelist, and thousands come to Oxford, Mississippi to see the reality after which Faulkner's Yoknapatawpha was modeled. In Oxford, for the past six years, the University of Mississippi has sponsored a Faulkner and Yoknapatawpha conference as a forum for Faulkner scholarship. This year the annual conference took for its theme the fiftieth anniversary of the creation of Yoknapatawpha, and on July 29 through August 3, on the Oxford campus of the University of Mississippi, scholars gathered to explore and celebrate Faulkner's unforgettable fictional world.

Appropriately, Joseph Blotner, Faulkner's biographer and friend, spoke first and last. Blotner opened the conference with an impression of Faulkner, the man. Faulkner emerges from this account as an infinitely unknowable man, whose own life proved the thesis of many of his novels: the inviolable isolation of the individual consciousness. Blotner recalls a man armored in reserve and fortressed in silence (Faulkner never allowed a television or a radio in his home), who spoke somewhat infrequently and always carefully. For the most part, Faulkner avoided social interactions, distancing himself from others; yet, Blotner insists,

Faulkner was unfailingly courteous, even courtly. Blotner's description stresses an essential core of insecurity which explains some of Faulkner's occasionally contradictory behavior. Shy, short (five feet six inches tall), and convinced of his own physical unattractiveness (Faulkner's face, in all of his self-portraits, is dominated by a disproportionately large nose), Faulkner was apparently always troubled by feelings of inferiority, although at the same time aware of his genius.

Faulkner's genius is the subject of Joseph Blotner's second paper, which concluded the conference. In this essay, "The Sources of Faulkner's Genius," Blotner attempts to identify the elements in Faulkner's nature which together constituted genius. Faulkner was apparently baffled by his own gift and spoke of himself as a "vessel" through which his novels were made: "I dont know where it came from. I dont know why God or gods or whoever it was, selected me to be the vessel." It is precisely this question that Blotner addresses—why Faulkner? Why was such talent vested in this particular individual? Blotner's first answer is heredity. A survey of Faulkner's ancestors and family reveals an abundance of artistic and literary talent. Next, Blotner points to Faulkner's astonishing memory (Faulkner once said: "As far as I know I have never done one page of research. Also, I doubt if I've ever forgotten anything I ever read too.") and suggests that Faulkner's novels could never have been written if Faulkner had not the ability to recall at will everything he'd ever seen, read, or heard. Blotner then considers the question Why did Faulkner write?—and points out that, for Faulkner, almost as if he had no choice about it, writing always came first. Faulkner frequently referred to himself as "demon-driven" and doomed to the writer's trade. To earn money, especially during the early years of his literary career, Faulkner was sometimes forced to labor at other trades, but he always wrote. While working in the university post office and at the university power house, while selling books, and even while painting houses, Faulkner wrote. Faulkner's uncle, John, spoke more truly than he knew when he complained that Faulkner *"wouldn't* work . . . he never was nothin' but a writer," for Faulkner always fully understood the necessity for total dedication to his art and allowed nothing to interfere: "The writer's only responsibility is to his art. . . . Everything goes by the board: honor, pride, decency, security, happiness, all, to get the book written. If a writer has to rob his mother, he will not hesitate; the 'Ode on a Grecian Urn' is worth any number of old ladies." There were, of course, other motivations: the desire to achieve a kind of immortality through writing, or, as Faulkner put it, to leave "a scratch on the wall of oblivion"; and, in his later years, another motivation—a feeling of responsibility, the writer's responsibility, as one whose voice is heard by millions, to encourage and direct mankind.

Whereas Blotner, in both his essays, tries to analyze Faulkner's nature, the other conference participants look rather to Faulkner's art. In his essay "Faulkner's First Trilogy: *Sartoris, Sanctuary,* and *Requiem for a Nun,*" Michael Milligate broaches a relatively untapped area of Faulkner research—the patterns of relationship among Faulkner's novels. Millgate first explains in what sense *Sartoris, Sanctuary,* and *Requiem for a Nun* form a trilogy. *Requiem* is, of course, the sequel to *Sanctuary,* but what right has *Sartoris* to figure in this trilogy? Millgate points out that the original version of *Sartoris, Flags in the Dust,* bore a close relationship to the original version of *Sanctuary,* a relationship which revision obscured. Both novels, in their unrevised forms, were Horace Benbow narratives. Thus, the original *Sartoris,* the original *Sanctuary,* and *Requiem* are intimately connected, forming an "ad hoc trilogy." Having uncovered a previously unexplored grouping of novels, Millgate goes on to investigate the effects of using similar characters and situations in these three novels, in an attempt to answer the question How are we meant to read Faulkner's interconnected fiction? Millgate's examination yields a number of tentative conclusions.

Introduction

First, there may be a number of as yet unexplored "paired novels, trilogies, abortive trilogies, or significant groupings" among
Faulkner's discrete texts, and, second, although every Faulkner
novel demands to be read as "unique and self-sufficient," no
Faulkner novel is entirely self-contained. Finally, Millgate explains that Faulkner's use of recurrent characters is an instructional technique. Faulkner makes his meanings clearer by recalling similar meanings in his other novels.

Another essay which, like Millgate's, analyzes relationships
among Faulkner's works is John Pilkington's paper, "'Strange
Times' in Yoknapatawpha." Focusing primarily on "Skirmish at
Sartoris," Pilkington examines three versions of the same story
in three separate Faulkner works. The three narratives have in
common this much: the time is the Reconstruction; two carpetbaggers, who were purportedly buying Negro votes, are killed
(the circumstances of these deaths vary slightly with each telling) by Colonel Sartoris. The story is told first by old man Falls
in *Sartoris*, again by Joanna Burden in *Light in August*, and
finally by Bayard Sartoris in "Skirmish at Sartoris." Pilkington
concludes that Faulkner's last version of the story, which contains "important changes," may represent "Faulkner's final
thinking about certain aspects of Reconstruction."

Several of the conference speakers chose to discuss topics
suggested by the fiftieth anniversary of the founding of Yoknapatawpha. For example, Michael Millgate, in his other discussion, comments on the development of Faulkner's mythical
county. In "'A Cosmos of My Own': the Evolution of Yoknapatawpha," Millgate offers an explanation for inexactitudes and
even inconsistencies in Faulkner's created world. According to
Millgate, Faulkner learned from his creative experience that life
is motion, or, in other words, as Faulkner wrote, he matured as
an artist and his characters and fictive world grew beyond the
bounds he had originally set for them. In order to allow for this
growth, Faulkner's Yoknapatawpha had to be capacious and flex-

ible, capable of accommodating diversity, change, and even contradiction. As an example, Millgate singles out Quentin Compson. Millgate conjectures that Quentin may have originally been
meant to function as the recording and evaluative consciousness
in several Yoknapatawpha novels—a plan which foundered
when, in the course of writing *The Sound and the Fury*, Quentin's suicide became inevitable. In such cases, Faulkner was always ready to start again, rethink, and recreate, for Faulkner's
first responsibility was always to the truth and coherence of the
individual novel and only secondly to the overall consistency of
the system.

Whereas Michael Millgate considers the development of
Yoknapatawpha, Merle Keiser addresses its founding. In her essay "*Flags in the Dust* and *Sartoris*," Keiser reviews the bibliographical history of the book published fifty years ago as *Sartoris*, the first novel in Faulkner's Yoknapatawpha sequence. The
story Keiser tells proves Faulkner's ability to revise with endless
patience. Making frequent references to two bibliographical dissertations which examine the making of *Sartoris*, Keiser distin-
guishes six major stages of revision preceding the publication of
Sartoris. It was presumably the fifth typescript version (since
lost) that, in 1928, Harcourt Brace agreed to publish—if the
novel were reduced in length to one hundred thousand words
and resubmitted in sixteen days. The novel which Ben Wasson
and Faulkner then cut to the specified length was published in
1929 as *Sartoris*. In 1973, Random House published *Flags in the
Dust*, the fourth typescript version of the novel. According to
Keiser, a comparison of *Flags in the Dust* and *Sartoris* reveals
Faulkner's growth as an artist. In the cut version of the novel,
action takes the place of statement, and telling gives way to
showing.

Noel Polk observed the fiftieth anniversary of Yoknapatawpha by considering two venerable Yoknapatawphan institutions—
respectability and the law. In "Faulkner and Respectability"

Polk challenges the popular notion that respectability is flatly condemned in Faulkner's fiction. Polk demonstrates that Faulkner's attitude toward respectability is complex and double-edged. Respectability can foster mediocrity and quell individualism; but responsibility also establishes a common standard of behavior without which community relations would be difficult, perhaps impossible. To corroborate his point, Polk focuses on three Faulkner works in which respectability figures prominently. In the short story "Uncle Willy," in *The Town*, and in *The Mansion*, Faulkner's attitude toward respectability is ambivalent: respectability is both a powerful, even necessary, stabilizing force and a dead weight obstructing the free flow of human thought and endeavor.

In his second essay, Noel Polk surveys Faulkner's depiction of another fundamental Yoknapatawphan institution—the law. Once again, Faulkner's attitude is complex and not easily pigeonholed. In some novels (*Requiem for a Nun*, *Intruder in the Dust*, and *The Town*), Faulkner lampoons lawyers, courts, and related legal paraphernalia; in other novels, most notably *Sanctuary*, the legal system is pitted against human evil in a tragically unequal contest. However, after weighing all the evidence, Polk concludes that Faulkner takes a basically hopeful view of the law. Lawmen like Butch Lovemaiden, who abuse the power vested in them, are the exception; a far more typical representative of the legal system in Faulkner's world is Gavin Stevens—occasionally ineffectual, sometimes mistaken, but always well-meaning.

Another topic suggested by the fiftieth anniversary of Yoknapatawpha is James Watson's essay, "Faulkner: The House of Fiction." Faulkner makes his imaginary Yoknapatawpha visually available to his reader by describing this world in minute detail. Watson selects one of these details—the houses that line the Yoknapatawphan landscape—and shows how these houses "nearly as many, as varied, and as unique in form and function as the individuals who dwell in them," not only contribute to our sense of place, but also function as "complex and expressive symbolic figures," invoking content through form.

James Watson's second article, "Faulkner's Short Stories and the Making of Yoknapatawpha County," also commemorates the founding of Faulkner's Yoknapatawpha. In this essay, Watson connects the creation of Faulkner's short stories with the growth of Faulkner's carefully designed community. Watson contends that the development of Yoknapatawpha was, and had to be, a gradual process, accomplished in a "piecemeal" fashion and that the publication of *These Thirteen* (referred to by Faulkner as "stories of my townspeople") marks a "significant stage" of development in that process. Because the stories in *These Thirteen* move backward and forward in time within individual stories and between stories, they anchor Faulkner's mythical community temporally as well as spatially. In discussing the making of Yoknapatawpha County, Watson also points to the large body of American small town literature which may have served as a model for Faulkner's mythical county. To this list of possible sources, Watson adds two previously unmentioned works: Edwin Arlington Robinson's 1916 volume of poems, *The Man Against the Sky*, and F. Scott Fitzgerald's 1924 story, "Absolution."

Whereas James Watson identifies writers who may have influenced Faulkner, Thomas McHaney reverses Watson's practice and examines the influence Faulkner has had on generations of writers. In "Faulkner's Impact Upon the Creative Writer," McHaney insists that the word "impact" most accurately describes Faulkner's influence on other writers—so striking, powerful, and lasting has been Faulkner's effect. McHaney begins with the year 1926 (the year of the publication of Faulkner's first novel, *Soldiers' Pay*) and works his way through to the present, surveying the responses of creative writers to Faulkner's novels. His findings call into question the widely accepted theory that

Faulkner's works were not seriously considered or appreciated in this country prior to 1939. McHaney shows that although professional reviewers, for the most part, failed to appreciate Faulkner, responding more frequently to "where Faulkner lived than what or how he wrote," creative writers invariably received Faulkner's work with praise and even "wonderment."

In his other essay, "Faulkner's Curious Tools," Thomas McHaney attempts to shed some light on Faulkner's controversial later novels, which have sometimes been described as polemical—concerned more with ideas and opinions than with the old truths of the human heart. McHaney argues that the truths which Faulkner stressed in his early works are also evident in the later novels, but in the later fiction extremely unlikely characters are the exponents of these truths. These characters, who in "the most unpropitious circumstances and sometimes unawares speak to our hearts," are Faulkner's "curious tools." Examples of such incongruous standard-bearers of truth are Nub Gowrie, the "one-armed reprobate" in *Intruder in the Dust*, Mink Snopes, that "bush-whacking murdering bastard" in *The Mansion*, Harry, "the obscene vicious groom" in *A Fable*, and Nancy Mannigoe, "the nigger dope-fiend whore" in *Requiem for a Nun*. McHaney concludes by suggesting that Faulkner may have regarded himself as a kind of "curious tool." Like the other "curious tools," Faulkner was an unlikely figure—"a small-statured, quiet-voiced ne'er do well from a simple town in a poor state"—who nevertheless speaks to the hearts of millions.

The conference celebrating the fiftieth anniversary of Faulkner's creation of Yoknapatawpha featured the lectures printed here as well as tours of Oxford and Lafayette County, discussions of Faulkner by his friends and family, a slide presentation by J. M. Faulkner and Jo Marshall, dramatic readings entitled *Voices from Yoknapatawpha*, an exhibition of watercolors by William C. Baggett, Jr., several displays, and three films. The Yoknapatawpha Arts Council displayed paintings and photographs of Oxford collected by Chester A. McLarty, a local physician, and Valerie Braybrooke, director of the university museums. The university's John Davis Williams Library exhibited Faulkner books, photographs, and memorabilia. The University Press of Mississippi hosted an exhibit of Faulkner books submitted by various university presses throughout the United States. Conference participants saw previews of three films: *William Faulkner: A Life on Paper*, produced by the Mississippi Authority for Educational Television through a grant from the National Endowment for the Humanities; *Barn Burning*, part of the American Short Story Series, also sponsored by NEH, and made available at the conference through the efforts of John Leslie, mayor of Oxford, and director Peter Werner; and *Artist at Home*, directed and produced by Kent Moorhead. *Barn Burning* and *Artist at Home* were filmed in Oxford, as was part of *William Faulkner: A Life on Paper*.

The editors gratefully acknowledge the efforts of many people who contributed to the conference, among them, members of the Faulkner and Yoknapatawpha Committee, faculty and students of the English Department, staff members of the Division of Continuing Education and the Center for the Study of Southern Culture, and, most especially, Evans Harrington, chairman of the Department of English and director of the conference since its inception.

DOREEN FOWLER
UNIVERSITY OF MISSISSIPPI
OXFORD, MISSISSIPPI

Fifty Years of Yoknapatawpha:
Faulkner and Yoknapatawpha,
1979

Did You See Him Plain?

JOSEPH BLOTNER

It is one of those anecdotes that lodge in the memory and grow more vivid with time. Browning is standing in the bookshop listening as a customer begins a conversation with the proprietor about Shelley, whom Browning adored. He had seen Shelley, he had spoken to him, the customer says. Turning, he sees Browning "staring at him with a blanched face," and laughs. That scene and that emotion Browning would try to recapture years later in "Memorabilia":

> Ah, did you once see Shelley plain,
>> And did he stop and speak to you,
> And did you speak to him again?
>> How strange it seems and new![1]

It is seldom that we have the chance to meet the writers we care most about, even at one remove, as did Browning. We are lucky if it is at two removes. I remember one evening, nearly a quarter of a century ago now, when I heard James Southall Wilson say, "I am going to give you one octogenarian's recollections

---

1. When I began writing this talk I thought I had thought of the Browning-Shelley reference all by myself. Rereading the "Welcome Address" to the participants in the 1977 conference as it appeared in *The Maker and the Myth: Faulkner and Yoknapatawpha, 1977*, ed. Evans Harrington and Ann J. Abadie (Jackson: University Press of Mississippi, 1978), xi–xiv, I realized that the connection must have been lodged in my unconscious, or my unconscious memory by the welcomer, Associate Vice-Chancellor Noyes.

of another octogenarian's memory of having dinner with Edgar Allan Poe." Poe was not my favorite poet, but I remember a sense of excitement almost, at hearing of that candlelit room, and then seeing the pale face of the poet as it flushed with the wine.

It was my extraordinary privilege, shared by some of you here, to know William Faulkner. I still marvel at it. I think he is America's greatest novelist. When I consider the number of writers who can truly be called great, and when I think of all the people who lived during the lifetimes of those writers, it seems to me that the odds against knowing any of them, let alone the one who seems to me the greatest, must be astronomical. The question that is put to me most often about Faulkner is, "What was he like?" I always try my best to answer it in a few moments of conversation, feeling the futility of the attempt when I have already written two thousand pages trying to do that very thing. But thinking back to James Southall Wilson's story, I wonder, if I were to live to be an octogenarian, could I try then to tell someone what Faulkner was like? Could I remember much about him at all? And when I knew him, how much of him did I know? And I ask myself, as Browning asked in the poem that recalled the man in the bookshop who had seen Shelley, Did you see him plain?

The need to capture fleeting memory and set it down imperishably was one that Faulkner felt and expressed poignantly when he wrote about the impulses that led him to the composition of *Flags in the Dust*. Two years after it had appeared in compressed and revised form as *Sartoris*, he wrote a little under a thousand words for his literary agent describing the composition of *Flags* and his reaction to its rejection by his publisher and the events that followed. He began:

One day about 2 years ago I was speculating idly upon time and death when the thought occurred to me that doubtless as my flesh acquiesced more and more to the standardized compulsions of breath, there would come a day on which the palate of my soul would no longer react to the simple bread and salt of the world as I had found it in the finding years. . . .

All that I really desired was a touchstone simply . . . but . . . nothing served but that I try by main strength to recreate between the covers of a book the world as I was already preparing to lose and regret.[2]

We have most of us felt this emotion at some time in our lives. What I want to try to do now is to set down more coherently than I have before, if I can, what he was like. I do not mean the psychodynamics of the artist, William Faulkner, of the inner man. I shall try, perhaps foolhardily, to do something of that in my second talk to you. What I mean to try to do now is to say—thinking of another Browning poem, "How It Strikes a Contemporary"—how he seemed during the brief half-dozen years that I knew him in the last tenth of his life.[3]

From the time he gained prominence, people were always trying to give a sense of what this man was like—in part because of the disjunction and contrast, especially when he was young, between his often unprepossessing appearance and the nature of his gift and the force of his work. Seven years ago Andrew H. Pfeiffer compiled a large number of these impressions in a useful essay he called "Eye of the Storm: The Observers' Image of the Man Who Was Faulkner."[4] It is interesting to see how many,

2. Joseph Blotner, "William Faulkner's Essay on the Composition of *Sartoris*," *Yale University Library Gazette*, XLVII (January, 1973), 121–24.

3. Reading Browning's poem about the nameless poet of Valladolid, really the archetypal artist, I am struck by his resemblance to Faulkner: the way he observed life: "You'd come upon his scrutinizing hat, / Making a peaked shade blacker than itself / Against the single window spared some house / Intact yet with its moldered Moorish work"; the way he looked: ". . . such a brow / His eyes had to live under!—clear as flint / On either side the formidable nose / Curved, cut, and colored like an eagle's claw," and the magnitude of his achievement: " . . . the general-in-chief, / Through a whole campaign of the world's life and death."

4. Andrew Pfeiffer, "Eye of the Storm: The Observers' Image of the Man Who Was Faulkner," *Southern Review*, VIII (October, 1972), 763–73.

how varied, and how often contradictory these images are. At the time when I was trying to get some coherent sense of everything I had been reading, for some years, about Faulkner, I was struck by the metamorphosis he went through. (I don't mean the series of roles that took him from wounded veteran to bohemian aesthete to gentleman farmer.) The sense of this physical change was very different from what I saw in the pictures Carlos Baker included in his outstanding biography of Ernest Hemingway: the winsome and sturdy child, the fine-featured teenager, the handsome and ruddy-cheeked young man, the powerful figure in maturity, and the majestic one before the deterioration at the end. In Faulkner's case, there was the elfin and bright-eyed infant, the short and silent boy who was the least well-favored of the four brothers, the dapper young man with the thin moustache—but then gradually the metamorphosis as the very features seemed to change: the strong jaw balancing the large nose, the mustache gradually growing fuller, the piercing eyes revealing, it seemed, a wider range of perception and emotion. Then at the end there was the handsome and imposing, the noble countenance that seemed so appropriate to the noble achievement. Fortunately for all of us, the whole process is superbly recorded in *William Faulkner: The Cofield Collection*, published, appropriately, by the Yoknapatawpha Press of Oxford.[5]

From this physical phase of full maturity come two descriptions that I think I like best. Malcolm Cowley had already put together and published *The Portable Faulkner* for the Viking Press before he ever met the author. When he did meet him, nearly two and a half years later in October of 1948, he set down this description:

Faulkner is a small man (5 ft. 5, I should judge), very neatly put together, slim and muscular. Small, beautifully shaped hands. His face

5. Jack Cofield, *William Faulkner: The Cofield Collection*, ed. Lawrence Wells with an introduction by Carvel Collins (Oxford, Miss.: Yoknapatawpha Press, 1978).

has an expression like Poe's in photographs, crooked and melancholy. But his forehead is low, his nose Roman, and his gray hair forms a low wreath around his forehead, so that he also looks like a Roman emperor. Bushy eyebrows; eyes deeply set and with a droop at the outer corners; a bristly mustache. He stands or walks with an air of great dignity and talks—tells stories—in a strong Mississippi accent.[6]

Almost three years later, in the aftermath of the worldwide fame enlarged by Faulkner's receipt of the Nobel Prize, Robert Coughlan came to Oxford. After Faulkner's reluctant cooperation which turned to vehement objection, he wrote the two-part series for *Life* magazine which gave the most extensive view yet available into the life of this very private writer. Coughlan looked at the region, the books and their sources, the family, the man:

William Faulkner is a small, wiry man with closely cropped iron-gray hair; an upswept mustache of a darker color; a thin, high-bridged aquiline nose; heavy-lidded and deeply set brown eyes in which melancholy, calculation and humor variously are reflected; and a face tanned and webbed, especially near the eyes, with the creases and lines and tiny tracings of advancing middle age and the erosion of many days spent in the open in all weathers. He is entirely self-possessed, with a manner easy, courteous, speculative, and deadly. He is a quiet man; yet when he is at ease, with his short legs outstretched and a blackened pipe in his thin lips, and perhaps a drink at his elbow, he is like a somnolent cat who still in the wink of an eye could kill a mouse. Faulkner does not look or act like what he is. He acts like a farmer who had studied Plato and looks like a river gambler. In the way he looks there is something old-fashioned, even archaic.[7]

Here, then, are two descriptions by different observers. Before entertaining another one, we should perhaps consider what

6. Malcolm Cowley, *The Faulkner-Cowley File: Letters and Memories 1944–62* (New York: Viking Press, 1966), 103–104.
7. Robert Coughlan, *The Private World of William Faulkner* (New York: Harper & Brothers, 1954), 21.

the man said about himself. In keeping with the total pattern of his personality, he said very little. There are a half-dozen utterances, however, drawn from a thirty-year span in his life, which give some hint of the way he thought of himself. Writing home to his mother in early September of 1925 from Paris, where he was briefly living the life of the expatriate writer, he told her that he was growing a beard. "Makes me look sort of distinguished," he wrote, "like someone you'd care to know." A few days later, though, writing to his Aunt 'Bama McLean, he mentioned a story he had written about a girl in the Luxembourg Gardens. It was so beautiful, he said, "that when I finished it I went to look at myself in a mirror. And I thought, Did that ugly, ratty-looking face, that mixture of childishness and unreliability and sublime vanity, imagine that?"[8] A little more than a year and a half later, when he published his second novel, *Mosquitoes*, he would include in it a brief description of himself by Jenny, the shopgirl on the yachting party: "he was a white man, except he was awful sunburned and kind of shabby dressed—no necktie and hat."[9] It was about ten years after that, in Hollywood, "one afternoon," Faulkner would recall, "when I felt rotten with a terrible hangover," that he wrote a story that amused him. It was called "Afternoon of a Cow," and it was ostensibly by his amanuensis, a rather prissy man named Ernest V. Trueblood who said that it was actually he who, at Faulkner's direction, wrote the novels and stories that bore Faulkner's name. In this story of compounded misfortunes, Trueblood described his employer as "a man of what might be called almost violently sedentary habit by nature." When one of a series of catastrophes, fire, occurred, Trueblood was therefore amazed to see Faulkner jump a pasture fence, "not only because of his natural lethargic humor . . . but because of that shape and figure which ordinarily accompanies

---

8. Joseph Blotner (ed.), *Selected Letters of William Faulkner* (New York: Random House, 1977), 18, 20.
9. William Faulkner, *Mosquitoes* (New York: Boni & Liveright, 1927), 145.

it." The climax of Trueblood's story brought out momentarily what he took to be an amazing gentleness which he wanted to see at the heart of Faulkner's characters. But in the last vignette, as Faulkner sat holding a julep, clothed only in a horse blanket after a saddle soap cleansing from the effects of the cow, Beulah's, terror, Trueblood wrote, "He just drank, with that static violence which was his familiar character, and so I knew that he was himself once more and that the real Mr. Faulkner which had appeared momentarily to Oliver and myself in the pasture had already retreated to that inaccessible bourne from which only the cow, Beulah, had ever evoked it, and that doubtless we would never see it again."[10] When Faulkner read the piece to guests he was surprised and disappointed that they received it with reverent silence rather than the laughter he expected.

The last reference is only vaguely physical, but it is worth quoting. A little over four months after the publication of *Intruder in the Dust*, Faulkner sent to Robert Haas at Random House a passage he wanted included in any future edition of the novel. In it Gavin Stevens prophesied the ultimate disappearance of the Negro race through assimilation. Without using their names or the title of the book, he alluded to Shreve McCannon's prediction to Quentin Compson in what he called "the tag line" of *Absalom, Absalom!* that "in time the Jim Bonds are going to conquer the western hemisphere." In one of the lines in the new two-page interpolation Stevens said that the tag line came from "a novel of about twenty years ago by another Mississippian, a mild retiring little man over yonder at Oxford."[11]

There is one other kind of utterance, more graphic literally than these that we should examine: Faulkner's self-portraits.

---

10. Joseph Blotner (ed.) *Uncollected Stories of William Faulkner* (New York: Random House, 1979), 426, 434.

11. *William Faulkner, Absalom, Absalom!* (New York: Modern Library, 1951), 378; Patrick Samway, S.J., "New Material for Faulkner's *Intruder in the Dust*," in *A Faulkner Miscellany*, ed. James B. Meriwether (Jackson: University Press of Mississippi, 1974), 111.

They were actually sketches, sometimes caricatures, and they show a surprising consistency. Perhaps the most interesting is a pencil sketch he did in 1923, when he was twenty-five, of himself and his friend, Lottie Vernon White, dancing. Both figures are elongated and rather stylized. Faulkner is nattily dressed in a herringbone-tweed suit with wide-bottomed trousers. Though he is in profile, it is clear that he has a thin face under curling hair. The eyes are narrow, the chin pointed, the mustache thin over small lips, and dominating all the features is the large, long, pointed nose. There is no self-flattery there. When he followed the direction in which this sketch pointed and moved to direct caricature, he employed the standard technique: find a distinguishing feature and exaggerate it. Whether he drew himself for his little daughter as he prepared to return from an early Hollywood trip in the 1930s, or whether he drew himself for a friend thirty years later in New York, the sketch was the same. It was clear and economical, employing only a few firmly drawn lines. Again he was in profile. The hair was neat and the moustache still small. Dominating all was the massive beaked and hooked nose. The last time Malcolm Cowley saw him, six weeks before his death, he could say, "That day he had a country look, his face bronzed under the white hair and apparently glowing with health." And Cowley's wife, Muriel, recalled to a friend that "his magnificent dark eyes had the clarity that young children's often have."[12]

Despite the impression he made on others, his own self-image was marked still, it seemed, by that sense of facial disproportion. In his novel *Mosquitoes* the sculptor, Gordon, hears the name of young Pat Robyn and thinks to himself, "your name is like a little golden bell hung in my heart."[13] Faulkner would use this simile, in varied forms, in love relationships of his own extending over a thirty-year period. The source is by now well-

12. Cowley, *Faulkner-Cowley File*, 148.
13. *Mosquitoes*, 267–68.

known: the words of Edmond Rostand's Cyrano de Bergerac to his love Roxanne—Cyrano, the hero, the man of many parts, the most obvious of which makes it impossible for him to gain his beloved, so that the words of love resonating with that bell hung in his heart are spoken for someone else. Some sense of affinity or identification Faulkner must surely have felt.[14]

Where most of us might respond to caricature by someone else with embarrassment or hurt, he was capable of a marvelous response of detachment and amusement. Not long after he came to the University of Virginia, the student humor magazine, *The Virginia Spectator*, brought out a "Writer-in-Residence Issue." The art editor provided the cover. It showed the artist in a genial moment—long-nosed and spindly-legged, his cuffs over his knuckles, a book under his arm, a rose in his lapel. He rested one hand on a broken Greek column and looked smiling ahead. We watched as the editor handed him his copy. The mustache twitched. Then his face flushed, and he began to shake with soundless laughter. He laughed until he was overcome with coughing. Then he wiped his eyes and thanked the editor for his copy of the magazine.

One of the reasons why Faulkner had such a protean appearance in the collective recollections of his observers is that he did look so different from the time people began observing him. He was clean-shaven, he grew a mustache, let it become a beard, reduced it to a neatly clipped mustache again, and finally allowed it to grow into a fit adornment for a swashbuckling cavalryman. He dressed in tailored dinner jackets and tatterdemalion tweeds. He was photographed genial and granite-faced, alert and bemused, in health and in hangover. But almost all the observers agreed on one thing: he was a small man.

William Faulkner's Royal Air Force Certificate of Service gave his height as five feet, five and a half inches and his chest

14. See Cleanth Brooks, *Toward Yoknapatawpha and Beyond* (New Haven: Yale University Press, 1978), 55–57.

measurement as thirty-three inches. His hair was described as dark brown, his eyes as hazel, and his complexion as dark. These vital statistics were presumably entered when he volunteered in New York in mid-June of 1918 or in early July when he reported for duty in Toronto. His weight was not listed, but less than a month later he wrote his mother that he had gained so much that his uniforms were tight even without the extra clothing he wore beneath them to keep out the Canadian cold. Even so, his cadet photographs show a very slim young man. Passports issued to him in the 1950s give his height as five feet, six inches, and now his hair is grey and his eyes are black. When he had visited Cowley in 1948, Cowley recorded that at fifty-one Faulkner weighed 148 pounds but that his waist was so slim he could wear trousers that Cowley's thirteen-year-old son had outgrown.[15] Where was the weight then, on that short frame? He had small shapely feet of which he sometimes seemed inordinately proud. He had well-formed hands, which were if anything a bit large for his size, with smooth, slightly raised, rectangular, neatly trimmed nails—a right hand that did not simply shake yours but gripped it, hard and firmly, a hand-clasp that seemed right for a man who drove a tractor, fired shotguns and rifles, and grasped the reins of strapping strong horses. The weight was near his center of gravity: he was deep-chested, the only noticeable asymmetry of his body observable in the upper back. He made me think of Anse Bundren in *As I Lay Dying*. Later I learned that he suffered from rather more than the average arthritic spinal process that our species seems prone to with the accreting years. With him it was very pronounced, a sort of male equivalent of what used to be called "dowager's hump."

How did he move? Slowly and with dignity—that seems

---

15. See Joseph Blotner, *Faulkner: A Biography* (New York: Random House, 1974), *passim.*, and Cowley, *Faulkner-Cowley File*, 104–5. Material not footnoted in this essay can usually be located in Blotner, *Faulkner: A Biography* through the index.

agreed. I think that sometimes he moved slowly, just as he sometimes sat gingerly, because he was in pain. In the spring of 1952 it had been discovered that at some point he had suffered a broken back. Subsequent x-rays revealed compression fractures of at least four vertebrae and possibly a fifth: surely enough to make anyone walk stiffly. But that posture and gait were in part inherited. He was like his grandfather, whose distinctive carriage black people called "rear-backted." There was also something else. As a boy he had moved fast when he was a pitcher, a shortstop, and a quarterback. In his thirties he still enjoyed tennis. In his forties he could move fast when he had to, leaping across a room to catch a friend's child as he toppled from his highchair. As he grew older he would welcome the exertion of riding and training horses, but he disdained most exercise. He seems to have moved slowly and sometimes sedately because he liked to. I think that he moved that way sometimes because his mind was miles away from the steps his feet were taking. A friend, one of his doctors, chuckled as he recalled them. "He was so slew-footed," he said, "that sometimes I wondered how he could walk at all."

Whether he was walking or sitting, a kind of nimbus surrounded him. With some of us, it doubtless resided in the eye of the beholder, because we knew that he was the genius, the legendary artist, whose works moved us so. This is a well-known, all-too-common phenomenon in its baser forms. The idolatry that greets the scruffy rock singer or the hulking athlete derives not so much from the innate nobility of the object— Washington first comes to mind as one typifying those who do possess *innate* qualities to elicit the adoration—as the qualities ascribed to him by the admirer. I know how subjective and vulnerable this argument is, but I do insist that there was a quality in his person that was in the truest sense extraordinary.

When I first saw him in 1953 his hair was grey-white. A few years later, it was almost entirely white. It was fine-textured and

13

usually neatly cut. Later he wore it fuller, like the mustache. Though he was indeed shy, he had, as a photographer once remarked, a sense of composition and presentation. In a group shot, the photographer said, he would always distance himself slightly from the others somehow, and rather than gazing at the lens, he would look away, though he did unbend from this practice in candid shots when he was writer-in-residence at the University of Virginia. And he was far from indifferent to grooming. One afternoon at his house, at drink time, I said to his wife and daughter and son-in-law, "I know one reason why the Chief looks so good at these sessions we've been having: he shampoos his hair just before them." He cast me a quick sidelong look. "Now you're catchin' on," he said.

But the dominant feature was the eyes, a brown so dark they looked black, so that you could scarcely distinguish the iris from the pupil. Because of the fold of skin which started over the inner portion of the upper eyelid and curved down covering the outer portion, he had a hooded look. The eyes were enormously expressive. His brothers remarked how like his mother's they were when both were angry. They would almost seem to spark, they said. (His nephew, Jimmy, noticed another warning sign of anger: the hair would stand straight out at the back of his neck.) Those eyes could express a deep melancholy. (Both his brothers felt he was never a really happy man.) They could also express delight at wit and humor, showing not just merriment but sometimes even a wicked twinkle. It seemed to me that he looked directly at others less often than anyone I have ever known. There was one exception: when his daughter, Jill, spoke she usually had his complete attention. Her father followed her words and expressions not just with attention but with open and unmistakable love. With most others, though, he would look down as he listened, at his pipe, his matchbox, or just the floor. But then he might look up, fixing the speaker or hearer with that quick piercing gaze, and then it would flick away.

14

The stories are legion, and genuine, about his absorption in thoughts so deep that with abstracted gaze he might walk across the square in Oxford looking, unseeing, right through a member of his own family. This was a kind of corollary to his enormous concentration when he was at his desk. When on occasion he briefly shared the office of a Random House editor, he could work on utterly oblivious to the ringing phones and chattering visitors. But when he directed that powerful mind and vision upon a scene, that effect too was extraordinary. Visiting his friend Phil Stone shortly after Stone's wedding, Faulkner complimented his bride, Emily, on the way she had decorated their rooms in the Stone home. "Why, Bill," she responded, "I didn't think you saw things like that." He fixed her with that glance. "I see everything," he said.

The eyes may have been so dominant partly because those surer conveyers of emotion—the mouth and lips and teeth—were for the most part concealed. He was thin-lipped to begin with, as pictures from his youth make clear. Later, of course, the mustache covered virtually all of his upper lip and most of the lower one. I think that normally only his dentist saw his teeth. But I do recall one exception. After a horseback riding mishap he needed a new, four-tooth bridge for his left upper jaw. When I asked him if the work had been completed satisfactorily, he said it had and added, "I decided if I ever got some store teeth they were really going to look like false teeth, just like china." That sounded to me like an invitation to a question. "Do they?" I asked. "Yes," he said, turning his face slightly and lifting his lip with a forefinger. "See?" I saw pearly teeth gleaming, set off by a tobacco-stained neighbor and the suntanned skin. He smiled in amusement at his private joke.

Those eyes were so like his mother's that for years I thought he resembled her to the exclusion of the male Faulkners—with the exception, of course, of the nose with the hump at the bridge and the curve just below, where it had been broken. As I saw more photographs, years later, I realized that he also resembled not only his great-grandfather, the old Colonel, but even his father, from whom he was so different in stature and temperament. Now I could see the resemblance. They were strong faces. His showed the marks of living, not just the old fracture but a small deep scar too, at the point of his chin. More than that, there were the signs of the skin weathered by the out-of-doors. And there were the etchings: the wrinkles around the eyes with the good laugh lines, and then the further furrows, the ones graven by his own and others' sorrows. One physician who had treated him said, "He was so sensitive that life must have been very painful for him. He had such receptiveness for other people that their problems hurt him." His nephew said that was one reason he let few people get close to him: he knew how vulnerable he was. Once, when he had let down most of his defenses in a relationship that he rued, he thought of his characteristic role: "the cat that walks by himself" was the way he put it. I think those qualities helped to give him the lines, and reflexively, the lines showed them. Near the end of *The Mansion* Mink Snopes feels the pull of the earth as his end nears. We all feel the pull of gravity as the years go on, and once out of youth, our muscles and other tissues show it. Of all the men of his age I have known, I think he was the one whose face resisted that inexorable pull most strongly.

Of course he did not always look well. Once when I thought he looked particularly well and acted most convivial, it was because, as I would shortly learn, he had begun a session of drinking that would go on for some time. And when he was ill, he was one of the sickest-looking people I have ever known, with the deep circles of debilitation and a weariness that partook, it seemed, as much of the spirit as of the body. But when he did look well, no one looked better, dressed formally or informally, on stage or at ease.

As he sat there in the neatly tailored tweeds, the rich aroma

16

from his tobacco pouch impressing a mark upon the very air, one that would linger after he was gone, there was about him an ambiance of silence and reserve. He would seem utterly withdrawn, as he sat in your office or in his own living room over after-dinner coffee and liqueurs. He would gaze, seemingly, at the wall through slitted eyes, or he would look through it. And when his wife said, "Don't you think that's true, Bill?" there would be a moment of awkward silence as the guests' heads turned and his mind was penetrated by the awareness that he was being addressed and must respond. He would almost shake himself like a swimmer rising from the depths or a dreamer from the mists of sleep. With a slight raising of the head, like some subtle response of defense or defiance, he replied that night, "I'm sorry. I wasn't listening. What did you say?" There would be the times, in small groups composed usually of family and perhaps intimate friends, when he would be easy and conversational, following the give-and-take, interjecting his own comments freely. But if he felt put on display by a careless host or a tactless guest, a stony silence, palpable as a wall, would descend over his voice, his face, his whole person. When he was tired or bored after dinner he might simply doze. In his defense, he slept but poorly, rose early, and napped throughout the day. One night, in a comfortable arm chair, he just drifted off. We kept the conversation flowing around him. He revived in fifteen minutes or so. Feeling someone's gaze, he said to my wife, "I'm sorry. I'm just like a field hand. After supper I fall asleep." And not long afterwards he was engaged in animated conversation which he left only reluctantly when the driver of the family car had to depart against an early engagement the next morning.

To be with him alone, to talk with him alone, was to learn a new mode of communication. He felt no need whatever to engage in talk just for the sake of talk. He was a master of avoidance. Even the most gregarious of us experiences moments when he simply does not want to talk with the friendly stranger in the elevator who though wordless is pregnant with some well-meant and trivial conversational gambit. It was as though Faulkner by a subtle act of will or legerdemain compressed his ectoplasm and retreated within himself. A glance showed that he was unreachable. And if an unwary adventurer missed these signals, he might encounter no word, no gesture, but instead a glance like a rapier, which would flick out, that rapid motion succeeded in the next millisecond again by the glacial remoteness. It sounds cold, almost cruel, but for him it was a matter of necessity as well as preference. He was genuinely shy. Personal relations were more often than not a trial to him, and his body language showed it. He combined instinct and calculation. One of the things he taught me by example was the value of silence as a tactic. If you wish to be quiet, if you wish to be uninvolved, at least nine times out of ten you can trust to the garrulity of others, given half a chance, to gain this end for you.

Liking him and admiring him, thinking that he liked you too, what did you do about talking to him? Sometimes you found yourself thinking of a whole conversational gambit, knowing that if it interested him as it did you, there would not only be the contact you wanted with this valued friend but there would also be the unpredictable workings of that extraordinary brain. This must be very like, it seems to me, the thoughts and feelings of an anxious student before he put a question to Plato, or the concerns that moved a follower before he ventured an opinion to Goethe. He might answer shortly or briefly, but he never answered carelessly. He paid you the compliment of thinking about what you had said. Sometimes there would be a pause before the answer came, one that was brief by actual measurement but long by relative standards. I remember one night at dinner when the talk had ranged far afield. We were halfway through the entrée. Suddenly I heard myself asking, "What do you think of Grant's qualities as a general?" The minute the question was out of my mouth and the silence descended, I was

18

appalled. I thought, "You fool, how could you do that?" After three full beats came the measured answer: "He had courage. It took courage to cut himself off from his base of operations and make his way through hostile country down to Vicksburg." I had not only stopped eating; I had virtually stopped breathing. Now I resumed. A Yankee, I had asked this Confederate about the conqueror of Lee, and he had answered me not only with honesty but with forbearance.

And so you would share a moment's contact on one level among a series of varying intensity. When you learned the value and uses of silence (this was a man who never allowed a radio or television set in his home), the time would come when it would be he who would initiate the conversation. And it would never be trivial. It would have a quality somehow thought-out, as if he had rehearsed it silently before he asked you the question or made the comment. This is the hardest thing to describe about him. In some situations there was ease and spontaneity, as when you told stories together or drank together. But all the rest of the time you felt that this good friend operated in his daily life out of a reserve of privacy and sensitivity and perhaps even insecurity that made his intercourse with others a series of forays out into the dubious world from the fortress which was his psyche, his inner self. There was a bond which you felt, but if it was true—as Matthew Arnold and Thomas Wolfe and so many other writers and psychoanalysts and philosophers have said—that free and fundamental contact between human beings on the deepest level is almost impossible, here was a powerful and exquisitely sensitive human being who seemed clearly to verify it in some way almost every waking hour of his life.

But there were the precious times when, breaching your own reserve, you might tell him your troubles. And then that silence was all sympathy. And when you ran dry or ran down, there would be the familiar pause, followed usually by a firm statement embodying all at once perspective, good sense, and sympathy. And if you were truly fortunate, another time the roles would be reversed and you would have the chance to try to respond in kind.

What I have just been saying is, I think, a necessary corrective to the impression, naturally but mistakenly gained, of a man consistently silent and dour. If he could indeed act that way much of the time, there were the other times when he was completely different, the times when he talked easily and with interest, not just with children or companions at fox hunts and horse shows, but even with people such as writers and teachers. And when the mood was on him he would sing songs, tell stories, recite poems—I remember even one bawdy limerick—and could be convulsed at a story that tickled him. There would come that wonderful laugh, his eyes crinkling, his face reddening—a laugh soundless until the paroxysm ended in the veteran pipe-smoker's fit of coughing.

I must mention something else that sticks in the memory: the voice. People would say he spoke with a Mississippi accent, but that is of no help, really, unless you know *which* Mississippi accent. His speech pattern had much in common with what is taken to be the "southern accent," with familiar vowel changes and omissions of consonants, as when the phrase "I was tired" becomes "Ah was tahd." There were other familiar and expected pronunciations. "Yes, sir, he sure caught fourteen fish" would become "Yes, suh, he show caught foeteen fish." Sometimes "Sir" would be shaded from "suh" to "sah." The omitted consonant *r* would make "forever" into "foe-evah." But to my ear, his accent became more distinctively regional when a phrase such as "his heart had scars" became "his hawt had scaws." Equally distinctive was the pronunciation "woik" for "work," "coise" for "curse," and "inoit" for "inert." That is putting is just a shade broadly, for what I mean is closer to an accent of New Orleans than of Brooklyn. And sometimes the quality of the vowel would vary slightly. But heard quickly, "learn" would sound like "loin."

In another process "New Orleans" would be rendered "Ny-alyuns," just as "endure" would become "endyoo-uh." One variant that interested me was his schwa vowel sound, the indeterminate sound of most unstressed vowels in English. For "dedication" I have heard him say "dedicashahn," and yet more interesting, to me at least, is this one: for "plantation" he would use this the variant of the normal schwa sound and also attach the first t of the word to the end of the first syllable rather than to the beginning of the second, so that the word as he uttered it had a fine rolling sound—"plant-a-shahn." He had a rich Mississippi accent indeed.

The quality of his voice itself was high and thin, and when he spoke he did not drawl. I always thought he spoke rather rapidly. This was particularly true when he read from prepared material. He would speak quite rapidly then, as if to get it over with as fast as possible, with very little breath control. He was susceptible to colds and sore throats, and he had a tender throat no doubt made more so by the constant smoking of the rich, heavy tobacco mixture he loved. When he reached the end of a sentence, the place where the voice normally drops to a lower tone, a lower part of the normal register, his would sometimes seem almost to vanish momentarily. He tended to read too with the up-and-down intonation and rhythm of the old-fashioned preacher. Near the end of *The Sound and the Fury*, when Dilsey takes Luster, Frony, and Benjy to church with her, Frony is at first disappointed by the unprepossessing appearance of the guest minister, Reverend Shegog, who has come all the way from St. Louis. But when he begins to preach, the congregation is astonished at the voice of this small wizened man; it is a marvelously versatile instrument, sonorous, rich, and moving. Faulkner's own voice was nowhere near that impressive (though I once heard him read from that sermon very effectively). But to hear him read from his own work was a moving experience, and his everyday speech, once one was tuned in to its varied inflections and nuances, was to hear a voice so unique that one would never forget it.

Is there, then, any dominant, overall image that remains? Yes and No. He was too varied for a single image and at the same time too strong to fail to leave a powerful impression behind. That short, straight figure with its body language of aloofness at one time and of the courtesy and genuine courtliness at other times was utterly unique, like the voice. Many times, nearby or at a distance, most of us see in one figure almost a double of another that we know. This has never happened to me in all the years since I first saw William Faulkner. But I can speak only for myself. Each saw him in his own way. When Sherwood Anderson first saw Faulkner he was wearing one of the trenchcoats he favored all his life. The big coat so swallowed him that it reminded Anderson of Abraham Lincoln's remark about Confederate Vice-President Alexander Stephens: "Did you ever see so much shuck for so little nubbin?" Almost exactly thirty years later a Japanese reporter would write, "He did not look like an American, rather his physiognomy was that of a familiar Japanese old man. And yet his features were deep, with sculptural beauty."

I began with a question from Browning. My answer to it is, Yes, I saw him plain—the William Faulkner I knew, at those times, and in those places. Browning was right: "How strange it seems and new!" I hope that I have helped some of you to see him again, if not more clearly, perhaps at least differently. This journey into the past leaves me with many different emotions. One of them prompts me to recall not Browning now, but Tennyson:

> . . . O for the touch of a vanish'd hand,
> And the sound of a voice that is still!

"A Cosmos of My Own"
The Evolution of Yoknapatawpha

MICHAEL MILLGATE

At the University of Virginia in the 1950s Faulkner recalled his original conception of his fictional world as a moment of instantaneous revelation: "I thought of the whole story at once like a bolt of lightning lights up a landscape and you see everything."[1] That seems to me a most important statement in its insistence upon the primacy of a landscape as well as upon the suddenness and comprehensiveness of the vision itself, and I want to explore its implications a little further, to consider the origins of Yoknapatawpha in both general and specific terms, and to try and determine in what ways and with what consequences it changed in conception and realization during the course of Faulkner's subsequent career.

We do not yet know—we may never know—just when Faulkner had that first vision of what was to become Yoknapatawpha County. In a prefatory note to *The Mansion*, first published in 1959, he spoke of that novel as the conclusion and summation of "a work conceived and begun in 1925."[2] Faulkner was never very precise about dates—they seem to have ranked high among those facts which, as he so often declared, didn't much interest him—but this date is twice insisted upon within the one

1. Frederick L. Gwynn and Joseph L. Blotner (eds.), *Faulkner in the University: Class Conferences at the University of Virginia 1957–1958* (Charlottesville, Va., 1959), 90. Faulkner was specifically answering a question about the origins of *The Hamlet*.
2. William Faulkner, *The Mansion* (New York, 1959), n.p.

brief note and seems worth pondering a little. It is true that there seems to be no evidence of the Snopeses, who were absolutely central to his vision, having been invented earlier than "Father Abraham," that unpublished early version of the spotted horses material, written, at the very earliest, in 1926. James B. Meriwether has argued very interestingly in a recent lecture, however, that the Snopeses had their origin in the Al Jackson tall tales which Faulkner swapped with Sherwood Anderson in New Orleans in 1925,[3] and I would myself venture the guess that in bringing the story of the Snopeses to an end in *The Mansion*, Faulkner was anxious to pay tribute not only to his friend and early supporter Phil Stone—to whom all three of the Snopes novels are dedicated—but also to Sherwood Anderson, to whom he had dedicated *Sartoris*, the first work in which the Snopeses had appeared. (That dedication, incidentally, is a characteristic Faulknerian mixture of compliment and arrogance: "To Sherwood Anderson through whose kindness I was first published, with the belief that this book will give him no reason to regret that fact."[4] Though one has, I think, to entertain the possibility that Faulkner who had parodied Anderson before was making gentle fun of Anderson's own somewhat self-regarding dedication to *Winesburg, Ohio*: "To the memory of my mother Emma Smith Anderson Whose keen observations on the life about her first awoke in me the hunger to see beneath the surface of lives, this book is dedicated.")[5]

That Faulkner was deeply aware of the part Anderson had played in showing him the way to his own literary ground is indicated by a number of close correspondences between the familiar passage on Yoknapatawpha in the *Paris Review* inter-

3. James B. Meriwether, "The Beginning of the Snopeses"; I am grateful to Professor Meriwether for allowing me to read this unpublished paper. Also relevant here is his "Faulkner's Essays on Anderson" in George H. Wolfe (ed.), *Faulkner: Fifty Years After "The Marble Faun"* (University, Alabama, 1976), 159–81.
4. William Faulkner, *Sartoris* (New York, 1929), n.p.
5. Sherwood Anderson, *Winesburg, Ohio* (New York, 1919), n.p.

view of 1955 and the essay on Anderson which Faulkner had written for the *Atlantic Monthly* just a year or so previously. Faulkner recalled in that essay the excellent advice Anderson had given him back in 1925:

"You have to have somewhere to start from: then you begin to learn," he told me. "It dont matter where it was, just so you remember it and aint ashamed of it. Because one place to start from is just as important as any other. You're a country boy; all you know is that little patch up there in Mississippi where you started from. But that's all right too. It's America too; pull it out, as little and unknown as it is, and the whole thing will collapse, like when you prize a brick out of a wall."[6]

Here, clearly, are the origins of those famous Faulknerian phrases about the little postage stamp of native soil and the created world that he liked to think of "as being a kind of keystone in the Universe; that, as small as that keystone is, if it were ever taken away, the universe itself would collapse."[7] Characteristically, Faulkner quarrelled at the time with Anderson's image of the brick pulled out of the wall—"'Not a cemented, plastered wall,' I said"[8]—and he improved upon that image by using the keystone idea when speaking of his own work later on. But I take this to be a perfectly conscious acknowledgment of indebtedness to Anderson, less perhaps for his advice—which Faulkner arguably didn't really need—than for his example, especially in *Winesburg, Ohio*.

It certainly seems relevant that *Winesburg* is subtitled *A Group of Tales of Ohio Small Town Life*, that it focuses on a small rural community, and that it treats of that community's life in a series of episodes which, while sufficiently independent for some of them to have been separately published, are neverthe-

6. James B. Meriwether (ed.), *William Faulkner: Essays, Speeches and Public Letters* (New York, 1965), 8.
7. James B. Meriwether and Michael Millgate (eds.), *Lion in the Garden: Interviews with William Faulkner 1926–1962* (New York, 1968), 255.
8. Meriwether (ed.), *Essays, Speeches and Public Letters*, 8.

less interrelated both as vignettes of Winesburg life and as juxtaposed parables, chapters in the Book of the Grotesque. Nor can Faulkner have missed the presence, on the inside front cover of the first edition, of a sketch-map of the fictional town. That map—together, no doubt, with maps of Hardy's Wessex, Stevenson's Treasure Island, and so on—was perhaps as important to Faulkner as anything else. It is a typical approach of the regionalist to work with existing geography but make it his own through the invention of new names and the relocation of places and buildings in order to suit his artistic convenience. So Hardy superimposes his fictional Wessex upon the actual geography of southwestern England, making up names for the towns and villages in which the action of his stories takes place but retaining the real names of places on the periphery of his region as a way of establishing a generalized sense of location and authenticity. So, too, Faulkner refers to Memphis, New Orleans, and so on as places to which it is possible to go from Yoknapatawpha, even though you will recall that the inhabitants of Frenchman's Bend are unable to answer the Texan's inquiry as to the short way to New York.

Faulkner's realization in print of the potentialities of his own region began, as he says in the *Paris Review* interview, with *Sartoris*, that abbreviation of *Flags in the Dust* which was first published in 1929. There was no Yoknapatawpha map published at that time—that was not to come until *Absalom, Absalom!*, when Faulkner was a more established figure—but the author clearly had a map in his mind, perhaps even on paper on the table beside him as he wrote. (To be accurate, Faulkner at this point still seems to have been calling it Yocona County.[9]) A strong visual image of the region is created in *Sartoris*, distances are given, towns and houses are described in a good deal of detail. We are told about the agriculture of the region, its climate

9. See, for example, Faulkner, *Flags in the Dust* (New York, 1973), 87.

through the course of the full annual cycle, its social, economic, and racial structure, something of its history and characteristic activities. Faulkner was staking out his territorial claim, and with such deliberateness and at such length that he would not need to do the job again, at least so far as Jefferson and the surrounding area were concerned. There is, indeed, a sense in which such early novels as *The Sound and the Fury* and *Sanctuary* depend to some considerable extent upon the reader's assumed familiarity with the earlier work.

Immediately at issue here, of course, is the whole question of the relationship of Faulkner's Yoknapatawpha novels one to another. "I found out," said Faulkner, "that not only each book had to have a design but the whole output or sum of an artist's work had to have a design."[10] Evidently he had appreciated early on the need for something more complex than Hardy's rather two-dimensional Wessex design—of which I strongly suspect that he was fully aware: he seems to have read at least *The Mayor of Casterbridge*,[11] and the centrality of Jefferson in his scheme is closely similar to that of Casterbridge in Hardy's.[12] Evidently, too, his mind was running much on Balzac's example at this period—indeed, he had mentioned two of Balzac's recurring characters in the course of the article on Sherwood Anderson he wrote for the *Dallas Morning News* in April, 1925. His comments on Balzac in later years are always appreciative, and in the *Paris Review* interview he speaks, in an especially revealing phrase, of Balzac's having "created an intact world of his own, a bloodstream running through twenty books."[13] The oddity of that figure "twenty," a significant underestimate of Balzac's total production, perhaps had more than a little to do with the

10. Meriwether and Millgate (eds.), *Lion in the Garden*, 255.
11. Joseph Blotner (comp.), *William Faulkner's Library: A Catalogue* (Charlottesville, Va., 1964), 67.
12. For a more extended comparison of Wessex and Yoknapatawpha, see Michael Millgate, *Thomas Hardy: His Career as a Novelist* (London, 1971), 345–51.
13. Meriwether and Millgate (eds.), *Lion in the Garden*, 251.

fact that Faulkner himself, at the time of the interview, had published precisely twenty volumes of fiction. Ambitious as he obviously was for an intact world, a bloodstream running through all his own work, Faulkner must have contemplated very early on the Balzacian concept of a systematically organized fictional world, with novels of Parisian life, novels of provincial life, and so on, intertwined with a multiplicity of recurring characters, deliberately designed to demonstrate the complex interlocking of all classes of society and the pervasiveness throughout them all of the same pattern of human folly. And while Faulkner did not in fact adopt such a design, its traces may still be discernible in the social structuring of *Sartoris/Flags in the Dust*, in the intricately sordid interconnections—political, economic, sexual—which exist among the different social layers of *Sanctuary*, in the thematic and possibly even narrative continuities which were evidently intended to run from *Flags in the Dust* to *Sanctuary* and on into *Requiem for a Nun*, projected at that time though not brought to completion until 1951. (It seems likely that the material now contained in the short story "There Was a Queen" had its original place as an ironic counterpoint to Narcissa Benbow's principled persecution of Ruby Lamar, who had given herself sexually to a lawyer in a somewhat better cause.) Add to this the extended backward glance of *The Unvanquished*. Add, too, the fact that all of these texts are infested in differing degrees with Snopeses, strongly suggesting that the whole body of Snopeslore was once perceived as forming part of the total design. Add all these elements and one begins to get some sense of the ambitiousness of Faulkner's original Yoknapatawpha conception.

Only the beginning, however, since the summary I have just given leaves almost entirely out of account the wide-ranging body of material centered, at least in technical terms, upon the figure of Quentin Compson. Quentin, you will recall, is the narrator not only of the Compson story, "That Evening Sun," and also of "Lion," one of the principal starting points of what eventually became *Go Down, Moses*, and of "A Justice," in which he hears from Sam Fathers the tale of Indian times which relates specifically to Sam's own birth. Though he is not identified by name, Quentin may at some stage have been imagined as the narrator, too, of some of those early stories in which the voice of the town, of the local community, is invoked—"A Rose for Emily," for example, and "Death Drag." He was certainly to have been the residual narrator, so to speak, the recording hearer, of the story about Ab Snopes's defeat by the horse-trader Pat Stamper, which was published in *Scribner's Magazine* as "Fool About a Horse," a V. K. Suratt story, and incorporated into *The Hamlet* as an extended anecdote told by V. K. Ratliff—Suratt renamed and to some extent reconceived. Two other Suratt/Ratliff stories, "Spotted Horses," absorbed in *The Hamlet* as the omnisciently told episode of the auction of the Texas horses, and "A Bear Hunt," another story on the fringes of *Go Down, Moses* territory, must also have been Quentin Compson narratives.[14]

Faulkner's use of the device of the framed narrative, the story within a story or at least as transmitted through a particular recording consciousness or point of view, is understandable enough in itself. His imagination had from boyhood been seized by the stories of hunting, of Indians, of the Civil War, of Reconstruction, of the deeds of local heroes and villains, including members of his own family, which he had heard over and over again from the lips of his elders, both white and black, and there can be no question but that such tales were a major element in the growth of his awareness of the potentialities of his own region as a subject for fiction. If that awareness came, as I have suggested, in the form of a single overwhelming shock of recog-

14. Quentin's ubiquitousness, first drawn to my attention by Professor James B. Meriwether, has recently been commented upon by Estella Schoenberg, *Old Tales and Talking: Quentin Compson in William Faulkner's "Absalom, Absalom!" and Related Works* (Jackson, Miss., 1977), 16–29.

nition, then such tales and their usability were precisely what was recognized; they were salient features of that suddenly illuminated landscape. One of Faulkner's earliest instincts as a writer, even before Yoknapatawpha, was to exploit the tale, and especially the traditional tall tale, as a basis for written narrative, as he can be seen doing in the Al Jackson stories and in that original Snopes narrative, the unpublished "Father Abraham," which contained not only the first working out of the "Spotted Horses" material but also the outline of Flem Snopes's whole career. But while such a method served well enough for primarily humorous purposes, it was less adaptable to those wider, richer, and often more somber implications which Faulkner soon learned to see in many of the tales he wanted to tell. By inserting a hearer or intervener such as Quentin, however, someone whose assumptions, instincts, and sensitivities were quite different from those of the tale-teller himself, it was immediately possible to bring out the tale's other aspects, or at least to alert the reader to the possibility of responding to it in alternative ways. In "A Justice," for example, the story of Sam Fathers's birth is told in comic terms, but the presence of Quentin, brooding upon something he would understand only when he had grown older ("passed on and through and beyond the suspension of twilight"[15] is the phrase actually used), effectively brings home to the reader some sense of what the events narrated must have meant in human terms to those involved, what they must still mean, in personal and racial terms, to Sam himself.

Faulkner's reasons for using a narrator such as Quentin are not therefore difficult to appreciate. But in making Quentin the recipient of so many tales from so many different sources, he clearly had something additional in mind. Earlier novelists who had used framing devices had often used them for sequences of

15. William Faulkner, *Collected Stories* (New York, 1950), 360.

narratives rather than for single works, and Faulkner, who would certainly have been familiar with the precedents established by, for example, Scott and Hawthorne, seems clearly to have intended Quentin to fill some structural and indeed specifically regional role. In "A Justice" Quentin is accompanied by a family group made up of his sister and brother, Caddy and Jason Compson, his grandfather, General Compson, and one of the family's black servants, Roskus; as in "That Evening Sun" there is no mention of Benjy. In surviving manuscript and typescript versions of the "Fool About a Horse" material, Quentin listens to Suratt's tale as one of a group consisting of General Compson, Roskus, and Doc Peabody. The latter, of course, provides a link with the worlds of *Sartoris/Flags in the Dust* and of *As I Lay Dying*, and his presence in this particular context tends to confirm one's sense of the tight interrelatedness of Faulkner's initial design. So far as Quentin himself is concerned, it is my assumption or hypothesis that he was at one stage intended to function as the essential recording figure within variant forms of this same framing situation deployed through a whole series of otherwise separate narratives. In looking back from the perspective of adulthood upon the tales he had heard as a child, he was presumably to have learned to appreciate not only their intrinsic human significance but also their particular meaning for him as a boy and man of his place and time—to recognize, in short, that they were quintessential expressions of that regional world, past and present, which had made him what he was.

In this respect it is, I think, quite proper to suggest, as some critics have already done, that Quentin is in some sense and in at least some texts a semi-autobiographical figure whose listening to the tales of the past has its basis in Faulkner's own experience. Just what structural role was once envisioned for him it is now hard to determine. It is, of course, possible that he was never intended to be anything more than a convenient device for grouping together, making a loosely unified volume out of, a series of miscellaneous stories—such as the "collections of short stories of my townspeople" Faulkner mentioned to Horace Liveright in February, 1927.[16] But I think the available evidence is sufficient to suggest that Quentin was once perceived as a focal point–though not necessarily the only one–for the Compson material, the Surratt/Snopes material (the idea had already evaporated by the time Ratliff appeared), and for what subsequently became the Sam Fathers/hunting/McCaslin material. The Sartoris/Benbow material seems to have been kept quite separate, though linked within the overall Yoknapatawpha pattern by means of such overlapping characters as Doc Peabody and some of the Snopeses. It seems probable, in fact, that when (in 1926 or thereabouts) Faulkner first embarked on a Sartoris novel and a Snopes novel more or less simultaneously, he deliberately chose quite different narrative methods for the two projects. In *Sartoris/Flags in the Dust* as in the later, closely connected *Sanctuary*, the point of view was omniscient; though discrete narrative episodes such as the tales told by Will Falls and the Memphis adventures of Vergil and Fonzo were by no means excluded, they were consistently absorbed within the prevailing narrative flow. With the Snopes material, on the other hand, Faulkner seems to have decided, if not at the very beginning then shortly afterwards, to allow the separate narratives not only to retain but to proclaim their individuality, to have them told in self-contained units and in specifically regional and often dialectal voices, and to tie them together in terms of their common and no doubt cumulative impact upon the sensitive imagination and educated mind of Quentin Compson, who was at once (like Faulkner himself) ineluctably of the South and yet capable of seeing it, or of trying to see it, in wider, nonregional perspectives.

16. Joseph Blotner (ed.), *Selected Letters of William Faulkner* (New York, 1977), 34.

Before I leave Quentin I want to indulge my speculative appetites a little further by pondering upon the possible implications of Faulkner's having once given the title "As I Lay Dying" to a short story version (never published) of the closing stages of the Spotted Horses episode,[17] the sequel to the auction itself. It seems on the face of it an absurdly inappropriate title, much better (if still somewhat confusingly) applied to the novel for which Faulkner used it a little later on. But if it is possible to understand his once calling "Spotted Horses" itself "Aria con amore"[18] as a gesture of love and commitment on his own or (what may be much the same thing) the narrator's part towards his regional material or towards the horses themselves as embodiments of energy, sexuality, and above all creativity, then it is surely possible to look for some explanation for that "As I Lay Dying" title as well. We know, of course, that the phrase "As I Lay Dying" can be traced to a translation of the *Odyssey*, and one could, I suppose, speculate that Faulkner, already looking forward to the death of Flem Snopes (an ironic Agamemnon?), thought of him as looking back with remorse upon his past misdeeds—among them his contemptuous treatment of Mrs. Armstid when she seeks restitution of the money her husband has paid for one of the Texas ponies. According to Professor Blotner, that "As I lay dying" phrase formed part of a longer quotation from the *Odyssey* that Faulkner was fond of reciting: "As I lay dying the woman with the dog's eyes would not close my eyelids for me as I descended into Hades."[19] He does not identify a specific translation that Faulkner was using—or adapting—but what is interesting for my present purposes is the fact that a

17. Joseph Blotner, *Faulkner: A Biography* (New York, 1974), 596–97; see also James B. Meriwether, "Faulkner's Correspondence with *Scribner's Magazine*," *Proof*, III (1973), 257.

18. Blotner, *Faulkner*, 684; Meriwether, "Faulkner's Correspondence," 264.

19. Blotner, *Faulkner*, 634–35; see also Carvel Collins, "The Pairing of *The Sound and the Fury* and *As I Lay Dying*," *Princeton University Library Chronicle*, XVIII (1957), 123.

fragment of that same quotation ("the woman with the dog's eyes") appears in "Carcassonne," a story about creative vision and inspiration which was obviously of special private significance for Faulkner–and which is also related to the Spotted Horses material in that it uses a buckskin pony as a Pegasus-image, a symbol of creative aspiration. The poet-narrator of "Carcassonne" is evidently dying himself, and I think it is reasonable to infer that Faulkner at some point had the idea of Quentin as a dying narrator before whose eyes his whole world would pass in almost instantaneous review, as is said to be the experience of those who drown, and hence reflect or reenact his own instantaneous and comprehensive vision of Yoknapatawpha. Technically, that review would consist of a series of regional narrations linked by Quentin's presence as auditor and recorder.

Quentin does, of course, drown in *The Sound and the Fury*, and his whole section could be, has been, spoken of as just such a dying flashback. Interestingly, it is a flashback full of voices, of remembered conversation and speech, chiefly Mr. Compson's but also Caddy's and Shreve's and several others'. In *Absalom, Absalom!*, indeed, Quentin is torn apart by the various conflicting voices juxtaposed within his memory, and it is possible to see in that novel the ultimate realization, what Faulkner himself might have called the apotheosis, of just the kind of retrospective, re-evaluating role that Quentin was originally invented to perform—though made much more complex, and much more somber, as a consequence of Faulkner's increased maturity both as man and as artist. One can even think of the entire novel, deliberately located by Faulkner just a few months before that suicide of which *The Sound and the Fury* has already informed us, as a part of Quentin's drowning flashback—and of those desperate concluding words about the South ("*I don't hate it! I don't hate it!*"[20]) as embodying his final thoughts as he goes down

20. William Faulkner, *Absalom, Absalom!* (New York, 1936), 378.

for the last time. One *can* think this, although as I shall argue in my second lecture I'm not at all sure that one should.

There is, of course, irony in all this, since by the time *Absalom* was written and published, the original Yoknapatawpha pattern had long been shattered beyond repair, most obviously by Faulkner's having killed off Quentin in *The Sound and the Fury*, even though that did not prevent his continuing to use Quentin as a convenient narrative perspective.[21] If I am right about Faulkner's having conceived of that pattern in retrospective terms—and it seems significant that *Sartoris/Flags in the Dust* as well as the stories narrated by Quentin looks back at the past from the vantage point of the present—then it was in any case doomed to eventual destruction insofar as it made no allowance for the author's own existence in time, for the fact (or at any rate the likelihood) of his continuing to live and write on into the future, beyond the frozen moment, whenever it was originally intended to be, of Quentin's death. Backward and past-obsessed though it might seem and be, even Yoknapatawpha, even northern Mississippi, could not remain motionless and unchanging. This was something Faulkner came to understand very clearly in later years, when the concept of life as motion became central to his thought and his work, and that understanding was no doubt sharpened and confirmed by his own creative experience, by the way in which Yoknapatawpha itself had so rapidly and so radically burst the bonds of its initial time-bound and map-bound conception.

This is not, however, to suggest that it was for these reasons that Faulkner abandoned that conception—or, indeed, that he abandoned it on any clearly perceived or deliberately calculated grounds. To determine just what happened, and when, one would need, I suspect, to solve what is still the most intriguing of the many creative mysteries in Faulkner's career: How did he

21. The unidentified narrator of "The Old People" (*Harper's*, September 1940), for example, is the same person to whom Sam Fathers told the story of "A Justice."

come to write *The Sound and the Fury*? I would guess that the crucial moment occurred when he thought of Benjy as the unidentified narrator of an already written third-person short story about the Compson children on the night of their grandmother's death. Certainly the new departure, whenever it came and wherever it came from, was technical in nature, involving a realization of the potentialities inherent in point of view, in the multiplicity of points of view, and in the combination of such multiplicity with the manipulation, the resonating juxtaposition, of discrete structural units. Faulkner had already chosen his material, decided what it was he would write about. Now, as he recalled in 1933 in an unpublished introduction to *The Sound and the Fury*, he discovered for the first time the excitement of writing itself: "I said to myself, Now I can write. Now I can make myself a vase like that which the old Roman kept at his bedside and wore the rim slowly away with kissing it."[22]

If I am right, then, there were two great moments of discovery in Faulkner's career. The first, the moment when he perceived the whole rich prospect of his fictional county extended before him. The second, the moment when he perceived the infinite possibilities inherent in the diligent exercise and fearless extension of the fictional techniques pioneered by such writers as James and Conrad and Joyce. The triumph of Faulkner's late career, from *The Hamlet* onwards, was the perfect marriage that resulted from a return to his original subject matter with the technical wisdom gained from the experimentation of the late twenties and early thirties. But at the time that experimentation was all-absorbing, so that the publication of the first Yoknapatawpha map in the first edition of *Absalom, Absalom!* seemed less the culmination of a developing process than a rather arbitrary reassertion of a claim that had fallen somewhat into public disrepair, a way of insisting that all these new books and loca-

22. James B. Meriwether (ed.), "An Introduction for *The Sound and the Fury*," *Southern Review*, VIII (1972), 710.

tions and characters could indeed find a place within the original pattern—or, at the very least, a place on the map.

By then the tightness of that pattern had been irrevocably relaxed. It is true that Faulkner spoke sometime in the early 1930s of his eventual need to make his collected works consistent one with another. It is also true that towards the end of his life he made gestures towards achieving some kind of narrative consistency within the Snopes trilogy, only to abandon the attempt when he found that it would not be a matter of making the details of *The Mansion* fit those of *The Hamlet* and *The Town* but of revising *The Hamlet* and *The Town* in accordance with the matured vision of the later novel.[23] That prefatory note to *The Mansion* at once reflects the experience and justifies its outcome: "[T]he purpose of this note is simply to notify the reader that the author has already found more discrepancies and contradictions than he hopes the reader will—contradictions and discrepancies due to the fact that the author has learned, he believes, more about the human heart and its dilemma than he knew thirty-four years ago; and is sure that, having lived with them that long time, he knows the characters in this chronicle better than he did then."[24] If, as I said, Faulkner came to believe so strongly that life was motion, that was in part because it was a truth he had learned from his own creative experience. He began with a plan, conceived no doubt in the essentially two-dimensional terms of a landscape, a map. Then he forgot or laid aside the plan for a while, in what can perhaps be best called a burst of creative ecstasy; and then he suddenly found that he had a world on his hands. The original concept, he said in the *Paris Review* interview, opened up a gold mine of other people—or peoples: there is an unresolved textual crux at this point, but I assume he meant that the concept proved more

23. James B. Meriwether, in *Approaches to the Study of Twentieth-Century Literature* (East Lansing, Michigan, 1961), 43–44.
24. Faulkner, *The Mansion*, n.p.

richly generative than he had ever imagined. So, he continues, "I created a cosmos of my own."[25] A cosmos—a wholly unique and independent world—existing as such in time as well as in space and therefore subject to growth and change. An "ordered" world, as the Oxford English Dictionary's definition of "cosmos" insists, but not necessarily a systematic one, for the order in question is that which is synonymous with harmony and constitutes the opposite of chaos. It is the embodiment, that is to say, of those Faulknerian ideas about human existence which are so concisely restated in that same interview passage: "I can move these people around like God, not only in space but in time too. The fact that I have moved my characters around in time successfully, at least in my own estimation, proves to me my own theory that time is a fluid condition which has no existence except in the momentary avatars of individual people."[26]

In claiming such total power in relation to his created universe, Faulkner is really saying all that need be said on the question of inconsistencies as between one book and another. It would have been an abandonment of Faulkner's whole stance as an artist to have allowed the system to control the work, or to have denied the fact of growth in himself, as man and artist, or in the world which he had invented and which he never ceased creating. When Faulkner reintroduced into such late novels as *The Mansion* and *The Reivers* characters who had not otherwise appeared in his work since 1930 or thereabouts, that did not mean that he himself had lost sight of them in the meantime. Like all his other characters they had always been there, waiting in what Faulkner liked to call the attic, ready to make another public appearance—probably with a somewhat refurbished act—whenever called upon to do so. Faulkner's whole world seems to have remained perpetually alive and active in his

25. Meriwether and Millgate (eds.), *Lion in the Garden*, 255.
26. *Ibid.*

imagination, as something quite apart from his capacity, as a time-bound human being, to realize that world on paper. There is plenty of evidence to suggest that not only large patterns of narrative development but detailed scenes and incidents were fully conceived and worked out in Faulkner's mind years before he actually got around to writing them down. And his comments in interviews about characters in books written years before, and apparently not reread in the interim, show how vividly they remained present to him.

Yoknapatawpha is thus, to an extraordinary degree, an organically unified world, a cosmos, ordered and harmonious, growing progressively and ever more richly out of a single original conception. But it is also, and for the same reasons, an infinitely fluid world, in which the maturing creative imagination of the author is under no obligation to observe a rigid consistency in such matters as geography, chronology, or characterization. Thus we should not be surprised or disturbed that Faulkner seems to have shifted the location of Jefferson, that the time-scheme of the Snopes trilogy is something less than exact (it is a rare novelist, incidentally, who can get the chronology even of a single novel absolutely correct), that the recurrence of a named character does not necessarily mean that he will behave in precisely the same fashion as he did before, or even have exactly the same personal history.

These things would no doubt have become clearer had Faulkner lived to complete that Golden Book of Yoknapatawpha County of which he speaks at the very end of the *Paris Review* interview: "My last book will be the Doomsday Book, the Golden Book, of Yoknapatawpha County. Then I shall break the pencil and I'll have to stop."[27] As James B. Meriwether has pointed out, by "Golden Book" Faulkner apparently had in mind

27. *Ibid.*

the ancient genealogical register of the nobility of Venice,[28] and Professor Blotner describes a brief manuscript of 1933 as headed "The Golden Book of Jefferson & Yoknapatawpha County" and as containing a 700-word biography of John Sartoris.[29] The Compson appendix is evidently the best published example of the kind of thing Faulkner had in mind, and it clearly represents a desire on Faulkner's part to express more fully on paper his sense of godlike proprietorship over his world, to move backwards and forwards in time with ease and swiftness, to endow his characters in public, as it were, with those personal and family histories they had so long possessed in the privacy of the author's mind. Faulkner also uses the term Doomsday Book, almost as if he foresaw some final day of judgment which he would visit upon his own creation—godlike, or at least Prospero-like, since that threatened breaking of his pencil sounds suspiciously like an allusion to Prospero's burning of his books. But since Doomsday Book is apparently interchangeable here with Golden Book, he must have been thinking chiefly of the analogy with the economic survey of England undertaken in the eleventh century immediately following the Norman Conquest, though perhaps also of the long poem, *Domesday Book*, by Edgar Lee Masters, whose work he certainly knew.

Masters's poem recounts, from many different points of view, the story of a coroner's investigation into the death of a young woman, "A word now on the Domesday book of old," writes Masters, with his bland blank verse, and his dubious etymology:

Remember not a book of doom, but a book
Of houses; domus, house, so domus book.
And this book of the death of Elenor Murray
Is not a book of doom, though showing too
How fate was woven round her, and the souls

28. James B. Meriwether, "The Novel Faulkner Never Wrote: His *Golden Book* or *Doomsday Book*," *American Literature*, XLII (1970), 93–96.
29. Blotner, *Faulkner*, 791.

> That touched her soul; but it is a house book too
> Of riches, poverty, and weakness, strength
> Of this our country.[30]

The poem, writes Masters, is thus designed both as "a census spiritual / Taken of our America" and as a demonstration of "The closeness of one life, however humble / With every life upon this globe."[31]

Faulkner certainly seems to have projected his own Doomsday book as a book of houses, of families; and Masters's sense of human interdependence, of the possibility of approaching the universal through the particular, is of course embodied in Faulkner's own work in ways far richer than Masters could ever have conceived. When Faulkner spoke in the *Paris Review* interview of sublimating the actual to apocryphal, he meant not making the true untrue but making the real symbolic, taking the stuff of everyday experience and refining it to the condition of legends or of what he liked to think of as fables, universally apprehensible embodiments of the eternal verities.

In a sense, therefore, the whole body of his fiction can be seen as a Doomsday Book, a vast compendium of narrated tales and lives, of legends and speaking fables. Asked in Japan about the creation of Yoknapatawpha, Faulkner first gave his usual reply—that it was simple, convenient, and economical to work with just one area—and then asked: "Or it may have been the same reason that is responsible for the long clumsy sentences and paragraphs. I was still trying to reduce my one individual experience of the world into one compact thing which could be picked up and held in the hands at one time."[32] Faulkner's ambition, early and late, was thus for a microcosmos, a distillation of the human world and its whole experience in time, but one which should be quite specifically an artifact, one compact

30. Edgar Lee Masters, *Domesday Book* (New York, 1920), 3–4.
31. *Ibid.*, 3, 21.
32. Meriwether and Millgate (eds.), *Lion in the Garden*, 133.

41

thing, capable of being looked at from all sides, contemplated whole and entire like a Grecian urn or that vase whose rim the old Roman wore slowly away with kissing—like that intact world he so much admired in Balzac, unlike the ultimately incoherent world he had found in Anderson who, he once said, seemed not to have had a "concept of a cosmos in miniature."[33] He was also, I believe, quite consciously seeking to create a world that would in its conceptual integrity and distinctively regional character be implicitly pastoral, in the sense in which John Lynen uses that term in his fine study of Robert Frost[34]—a world in which basic human values and passions emerge with unusual directness and simplicity and which hence provides a standard by which those of us who live in more modern and complex societies can contemplate and evaluate our own conduct and assumptions.

Faulkner never realized on paper all that he had conceived in his imagination, and because he remained to the end of his career determined to explore new narrative techniques, nice questions of Yoknapatawphan consistency were always likely to take second place. For the reader, however, there is an unmistakable coherence, at once imaginative and tangible, about the Faulknerian world. The novels and stories illuminate, modify, and support each other to a degree with which we have scarcely as yet begun to come to terms. And it is clear that for Faulkner himself Yoknapatawpha always retained as it grew and changed in his imagination an absolute integrity and reality. Asked in 1955 about his books being read and discussed all over the world, Faulkner replied that he liked it: "I like the idea of the world I created being a kind of keystone in the universe. Feel that if I ever took it away the universe around that keystone would crumble away. . . . If they believed in my world in America the way they do abroad, I could probably run one of

33. Gwynn and Blotner (eds.), *Faulkner in the University*, 232.
34. John F. Lynen, *The Pastoral Art of Robert Frost* (New Haven, 1960).

my characters for President . . . maybe Flem Snopes."[35] Faulkner as usual, was speaking only half-humorously. From our present perspective we can already see that his keystone image was
absolutely to the point, so integral has his work become to the
whole texture of our civilization. And it is not for a Canadian to
suggest whether or not he was any less perceptive in nominating
Flem Snopes as the likeliest of his characters to succeed at the
highest levels of American politics.

---

35. Meriwether and Millgate (eds.), *Lion in the Garden*, 233; the penultimate word
represents my emendation of the original's "Lem."

Flags in the Dust and Sartoris

MERLE WALLACE KEISER

We are gathered in this place this week to celebrate fifty years of Yoknapatawpha County, fifty years beginning on January 31, 1929, with the publication of *Sartoris*, a novel cut from a sprawling typescript William Faulkner entitled *Flags in the Dust*. The cutting of the *Flags* typescript to form the introductory novel of the Yoknapatawpha saga is a fascinating story in bibliography, one which cannot be told however without minor incursions into the "lumber room" of a major American literary artist as well as into biographical and critical materials recently become available.

Let me recommend particularly two bibliographical dissertations: (1) "The Making of *Sartoris*: A Description and Discussion of the Manuscript and Composite Typescript of William Faulkner's Third Novel," 1969, Cornell University, by Stephen Neal Dennis; and (2) "Faulkner's *Flags in the Dust* and *Sartoris*: A Comparative Study of the Typescript and the Originally Published Novel," 1974, University of Texas, by Melvin Reed Roberts. In the 1969 study, Dennis describes the manuscripts and the composite typescript, and postulates a new setting copy of *Sartoris* which has not survived. He says that there are six major stages in Faulkner's work before the publication of *Sartoris*, including ten drafts within the second stage. He suggests that the published book may be a seventh stage, all of these making fifteen levels of revision. With the Dennis dissertation in hand, I also studied the manuscripts and typescripts of the *Flags* materials, as well as the unpublished "Elmer" papers, for several days on two separate trips to the Alderman Library of the University of Virginia. I remember vividly a librarian there who offered me a large magnifying glass when I had reached the point of tears in trying to read William Faulkner's beautiful, minute, and essentially unreadable script, as I followed the painstaking steps Dennis describes.

The Dennis dissertation is technical and bibliographical, reconstructing from the manuscript and the various typescripts Faulkner's probable actions in the process of producing *Sartoris* from conception to publication. He deduces the six major drafts from such evidence as the following: textual overlapping at the bottom of one page and at the top of another; pagination, where multiple page numbers give mute evidence of page and section shifts and typed, inked, or penciled numbers suggest the draft to which such papers belong; the paper itself, where watermarks, or lack of them, and careful measurement of sheets make possible identification of sequences from typescript drafts. And Dennis includes a useful summary of the various drafts of *Sartoris*:

1. The manuscript, including pages 01–05 and 002–003 which seem to be very early manuscript drafts.
2. The first typescript, which Faulkner began to type before he had completed his manuscript. There are 447 pages from this in the composite typescript.
3. The second typescript. Faulkner probably prepared this after he had completed the manuscript and the first typescript. There are only 99 pages from this draft in the composite typescript. This, rather than the first typescript, may have been the first draft submitted to a publisher.
4. The third typescript. This is essentially a revised second typescript, expanded at some points and contracted at a few others, and completely numbered. There are 146 pages from this third typescript

45

in the composite fourth typescript. This typescript, and the second typescript, may have been submitted to and rejected by several publishers.

5. The fourth typescript. This is the composite typescript now at the University of Virginia, a combination of pages from the first type-script and the third typescript. It is impossible to see how this could have been submitted to publishers. It is incomplete, and there is a great deal of overlapping material in it.

6. The fifth typescript. This would have been the novel's setting copy, which has apparently not survived; it is the typescript which was submitted to Harcourt, Brace for Faulkner by Ben Wasson and which Wasson cut, under Faulkner's direction, in order to reduce the novel to a length acceptable to Harcourt, Brace. Faulkner had, however, expanded the novel very slightly in a good many places in preparing this setting copy from the composite typescript. It may have been seen by publishers other than Harcourt, Brace.[1]

In viewing his findings, Dennis muses: "I cannot say why Faulkner produced the composite fourth typescript instead of retaining the presumably complete third typescript draft of *Sartoris*. So far as I have been able to determine, for the composite typescript Faulkner took from the third typescript rather than the first . . . those portions of the novel which differed greatly between the first and third."[2]

Apparently 447 pages from the first typescript, the earliest typed draft of his work, form the major segment of the composite fourth typescript, which has now been published as *Flags in the Dust*. The most interesting aspect of this bibliographical puzzle concerns the differences that exist among the manuscript, which comprises the earliest work on *Sartoris* to survive; the composite fourth typescript, now *Flags in the Dust*, which is the last work to survive; and the published text of the novel

1. Stephen Neal Dennis, "The Making of Sartoris: A Description and Discussion of the Manuscript and Composite Typescript of William Faulkner's Third Novel" (Ph.D. dissertation, Cornell University, 1969), 70–71.
2. *Ibid.*, 113.

Sartoris. Who made the creative changes; who, the deletions; and who, the mechanical corrections?

Dennis posits a fresh typescript, which Faulkner himself prepared from the composite typescript he had put together for that specific purpose, and in which he incorporated creative alterations in accordance with his custom when he retyped his work. At this point in the process, Faulkner could have, and would have, made the changes which have puzzled scholars and critics. A comparison of the printed text of *Sartoris* with the composite typescript seems to substantiate the argument that a new draft, the lost fifth typescript, is a necessity of the complex bibliographical history of the novel *Sartoris*. Dennis argues further that "whoever typed the setting copy must have had access to Faulkner's manuscript for the novel, since at one point in the composite typescript, between pages 156 and 157, three pages are missing. Text pages 109–11 of *Sartoris* are very close to the material on manuscript pages 52-d and 52-e, the manuscript pages that correspond to the three missing typescript pages. Clearly the pages in the setting copy must have been typed directly from Faulkner's manuscript, and almost certainly by Faulkner."[3]

The publication in 1973 of *Flags in the Dust*, edited and introduced by Douglas Day,[4] has opened to fresh critical survey William Faulkner's first novel laid in his native countryside. And in 1974 Melvin Reed Roberts, working with the typescript of *Flags in the Dust* and the published version of *Sartoris*, followed the work of Dennis with a bibliographical study covering a critical evaluation of the significant differences between the typescript of *Flags* and the published novel *Sartoris* and including a convenient two-column listing of actual omissions and additions.

3. *Ibid.*, 96.
4. William Faulkner, *Flags in the Dust*, ed. Douglas Day (New York: Random House, 1973).

Anyone who would appreciate the rich elements of either novel, the 1929 *Sartoris* or the 1973 *Flags in the Dust*, should review, at least in a cursory manner, the unique bibliographical history which affected the form of the book published in 1929 as *Sartoris*. All through this period of creative vision and rigorous revision, Faulkner evidently suffered from discouragement and even dejection. An excerpt from Joseph Blotner's report of a letter Faulkner wrote his Aunt Bama reflects his hard work and discouragement at the time: "Every day or so I burn some of it and I think I shall put it away for a while and forget it."[5] Fortunately, he did not burn all of the *Flags*, or *Sartoris*, papers, which today lie in their blue boxes on the shelves of the Alderman Library of the University of Virginia, providing for scholars a tantalizing glimpse into the workshop of William Faulkner.

In his introduction to the 1973 edition of *Flags in the Dust*, Douglas Day gives an abbreviated account of the frustrating attempt to sell the novel, which Faulkner had completed in 1927; and in his biography of Faulkner, Joseph Blotner gives an extended account. Horace Liveright, who had published *Soldiers' Pay* and *Mosquitoes*, refused the book, declaring that it was diffuse and had no clear plot, and recommended that no revision be attempted. That Faulkner ignored this advice, however, is evident from the existing manuscript and typescripts.

It was doubtless the fifth draft of the novel, almost certainly typed and polished from the fourth composite typescript, which Faulkner sent to his good friend and literary agent, Ben Wasson of Greenville, Mississippi, at that time with the American Play Company, a literary agency in New York. Evidently Wasson received a large number of rejections before Harcourt, Brace accepted the novel under a contract dated September 20, 1928, stipulating that a cut version of 110,000 words, renamed *Sartoris*, be submitted within sixteen days.[6] Blotner states that Alfred

5. Joseph Blotner, *Faulkner: A Biography* (New York: Random House, 1974), I, 562.
6. *Flags in the Dust*, viii.

Harcourt asked Wasson to cut the novel, and Harcourt Brace paid him to do so; and that Wasson asked Faulkner to come to New York to assist with the revisions. He sent the $300 advanced on royalties, suggesting that Faulkner use the money for the trip. "He could bring along whatever he was doing and maybe they could place that too while he was there."[7]

Critics and literary historians agree that Faulkner went to New York, where he worked on his new novel, *The Sound and the Fury*, in Wasson's room in Greenwich Village, while Wasson cut the typescript of *Flags in the Dust* into a novel to be called henceforth *Sartoris*. It is not clear, however, and probably never can be clear, what part each of these friends played in the actual revisions. In a telephone conversation with me, confirmed later by letter, Ben Wasson stated that it is hard for him to remember exactly what each of two young men in New York nearly fifty years ago had cut or added to the *Flags* materials. Wasson noted that he himself never has seen the manuscript of *Flags in the Dust*. He stated quite positively that he had worked entirely from a typescript, since lost. In his letter dated July 12, 1976, Wasson made some other very interesting comments:

First of all let me categorically deny any suggestion that I did, even the least, writing for *Sartoris*. Yes, admitted, I did edit *Flags* and WF gave me a completely free hand to do so. It's been a long time since I did this, and [it is] difficult to recall after so long a time exactly everything that happened.

In the order of your questions:

1. I used a typescript. . . .

2. The setting copy . . . [and] galley proofs must have been retained by Harcourt, Brace, publisher.

3. There was considerable discussion about the title change, and whether this was done by Harcourt, WF, [or] I [*sic*], I don't remember, but at any rate all of us concurred in the final selection.

4. Frankly, I don't remember whether I or WF wrote the "bridge

7. Blotner, *Faulkner*, I, 580–81.

passages," but I believe I wrote some of them and WF the remainder.

5. WF did not do any of the revision.

6. All of the cutting occurred in my room—and it certainly wasn't an apartment!

7. I could tell you a great deal more about what went on during the cutting, but to me the main thing was that WF looked over the manuscript when I had completed my job and said that he felt I had done, overall, a good job and that he realized it had been a difficult one indeed.

Hope this helps you.[8]

The intriguing words "I could tell you a great deal more" made inevitable another telephone call, which this time elicited an invitation to visit him. Over sherry in his home in Greenville, Mississippi, later on a drive to see the graceful old Delta town, and finally at dinner in a delightful Chinese restaurant, Ben Wasson discussed the puzzle of the cutting of *Sartoris*. He added little more to the facts included in his letter, though he elaborated upon some details. By "bridge passages," for example, he meant slight transitional material, a word, a phrase, a sentence or two perhaps, to bridge the gaps left by the cutting. He emphatically denied that he had done any creative writing for *Sartoris*. He did say, however, that his guiding principle in the deletions had been elimination of description when the action and dialogue were clear without such descriptive passages.[9]

---

8. Ben Wasson to Merle Keiser, unpublished letter, July 12, 1976.

9. In a morning spent in Greenville, Mississippi's public library, I read Wasson's novel, *The Devil Beats His Wife*, published by Harcourt, Brace during the same year that they published *Sartoris*, and reviewed, according to Blotner in his *Biography* (I, 611) by Donald Davidson as "a really promising first performance," in the Nashville *Tennessean*, the Knoxville *Journal*, and the Memphis *Commercial Appeal*. *The Devil Beats His Wife* is a charming novel with a southern plantation heroine named, interestingly, "Narcisse." An indiscretion with a "Yankee" visitor and the repercussions of that experience in the lives of Narcisse, her family, and a faithful Negro "mammy," form the nucleus of a plot filled with action and dialogue. The characterization of the Negro woman rivals some of Faulkner's work. The cat's funeral might well represent for Wasson such an image as Caddy's "muddy drawers" became for Faulkner. Wasson's novel stands

Ben Wasson is a charming, gracious, and very modest "southern gentleman." His words have the ring of truth.

Of the actual cutting process, Blotner says that Faulkner vehemently refused to "have anything to do with the matter," and said to Wasson at the time: "A cabbage has grown, matured. You look at that cabbage; it is not symmetrical; you say, I will trim this cabbage off and make it art; I will make it resemble a peacock or a pagoda or 3 doughnuts. Very good, I say; you do that, then the cabbage will be dead." After the cutting, according to Faulkner, Wasson commented: "The trouble is . . . that you had about 6 books in here. You were trying to write them all at once." Faulkner continued, "He showed me what he meant, what he had done, and I realized for the first time that I had done better than I knew."[10] Expressing a debt to both Dennis and Day, Blotner reports:

The cutting was extensive. Ben deleted a long passage of Narcissa's reflections about Bayard as a boy. . . . He did the same thing with other passages in which Narcissa conveyed background material. Several scenes involving Byron Snopes, Virgil Beard, and Mrs. Beard were cut from the text. Long passages also went [,] in which he had described Byron Snopes's twin torments: his anonymous lust for Narcissa and Virgil's blackmail. His final flight from Jefferson to Frenchman's Bend disappeared, as did the brief appearances of I. O. Snopes and his son Clarence. Horace's role was reduced: his one-time desire to become an Episcopal minister, his sense of doom, his affair with Belle, a brief affair with her sister Joan, his prior involvements, his incestuous feelings toward Narcissa—all these were removed or drastically cut.[11]

Of course, under Dennis's theory concerning a missing "fifth transcript," or setting copy, which Faulkner typed himself, some

---

as published evidence that he was capable of writing "bridge passages" and preferred action to description.

10. Blotner, *Faulkner* I, 583–84.

11. *Ibid.*, 584.

of these deletions Blotner mentions—as well as all the major additions and shifts of existing scenes observable in the collation of Melvin Reed Roberts[12] of the composite typescript and the originally published novel—could have been made by the author. Apparently accepting the theory of the missing "fifth transcript," Douglas Day observes further: "The final complete typescript, which must have served as setting copy for the Harcourt, Brace edition of *Sartoris* (and which must have been the draft in which Wasson made his cuts), has not survived. Nor have any galley proofs. All we had to work from, then, was the composite typescript, by any scholar's standards a suspect source. There was no way, finally, to tell which of the many differences between *Flags in the Dust* and *Sartoris* were the result of Faulkner's emendations in the hypothetical setting copy and the galley proofs, and which belonged to Wasson."[13]

As for possible galley proof changes, Edward Hodge of Harcourt, Brace informed Dennis that "to his knowledge there are no manufacturing records at Harcourt, Brace from 1929 which might indicate whether changes were made in the galley proofs for *Sartoris*." Noting that Carvel Collins "believes that Faulkner did not make changes in the novel's galley proofs because he did not have enough money in 1928 and 1929 to pay for such author's changes," Dennis concludes that "until new evidence proves otherwise, it must be assumed that Faulkner did not revise the galleys for *Sartoris*."[14] The rigorous efforts that Faulkner expended on the *Sartoris* revisions which are still available for inspection confirm what Meriwether observes of his work in general: "It is apparent [that the writing] was characterized by the most rigid discipline, a discipline made equally evident at every stage in the writing, from revision involving the rearrangement

12. Melvin Reed Roberts, "Faulkner's *Flags in the Dust* and *Sartoris*: A Comparative Study of the Typescript and the Originally Published Novel" (Ph.D. dissertation, University of Texas, 1974).
13. Faulkner, *Flags in the Dust*, Douglas Day, ed., ix–x.
14. Dennis, "The Making of *Sartoris*," 91.

of whole chapters in a novel to the almost endless process of minor stylistic polishing."[15]

Certainly Ben Wasson did the cutting of *Sartoris* from Faulkner's typescript. Doubtless Wasson and Harcourt, Brace made some mechanical corrections. Dennis notes that someone even added, on text page 374, a comma missing between "men" and "who" on the corresponding material on the composite typescript page 576, thus changing the meaning of Miss Jenny's thought concerning the "joke They [sic] had played on him [old Bayard]—forbidding him opportunities for swashbuckling and then denying him the privilege of being buried by men who would have invented vainglory for him."[16]

Although it never may be ascertained who did what in the final revision of the *Sartoris* papers, my own judgment, based on the evidence available at this time, is that William Faulkner himself made the major additions, and probably did the shifting of scenes and some of the cutting as well, when he typed a clean copy from his composite typescript to send to Ben Wasson for submission to publishers in New York. Perhaps Carvel Collins, in his long anticipated book of biography and criticism, will explore this intriguing problem in bibliography and human relations.

Whether *Flags in the Dust*, published in 1973, or *Sartoris*, published in 1929, is the "better" novel is not in question here. The additions and deletions made by Faulkner and Wasson are of interest because they affect the structure, narrative technique, and style of the 1929 matrix novel of the Yoknapatawpha saga. Anyone interested in the actual changes can set himself the delightful task of reading the two novels together and marking the differences, or he can follow the painstaking work of Dennis and Roberts and study the significance of the changes.

15. James B. Meriwether, *The Literary Career of William Faulkner: A Bibliographical Study* (Columbia: University of South Carolina Press, 1971), 61.
16. Dennis, "The Making of *Sartoris*," 101–102.

Because of the press of time and space, I have chosen one example to illustrate the kinds of changes which the cutting hands and minds made to form *Sartoris* from the typescript. Rather arbitrarily I have selected the Snopeses of *Sartoris* and *Flags in the Dust* for comparison.

An examination of the Snopes stories of the Yoknapatawpha novels and short stories and of the criticism concerning Snopeses leads to the conclusion that the maker and mover of Snopeses, as he has said, indeed did think "of the whole story at once like a bolt of lightning lights up a landscape."[17] But before the bolt struck, there was a long quiescent period, some of it spent in Phil Stone's office, just off the square in Oxford. "There in Stone's law office the two men would talk about the actual doings of people like the Snopeses. And when the fancy struck them, they would make up wild, outrageous stories of things which no Snopes-counterpart may have done, but things of which they thought them perfectly capable."[18] When the Snopes trilogy books were published many years later, Faulkner dedicated them to Phil Stone, who "did half the laughing for thirty years."[19]

According to John B. Cullen, a native of Oxford: "All the stories about the Snopeses are great exaggerations of actual persons and events. . . . Faulkner has taken every crime and all the cheating and every instance of brutality he has remembered and told them all in his stories and novels, and time after time he has attributed these crimes and inhumanities to the Snopeses. . . . He has pieced together and expanded all the worst traits of the worst people he has known."[20] And then Cullen names some of the people and tells their actual anecdotes.

The Snopeses are a new breed of southerners, a part of the

17. Joseph Blotner (ed.), *Faulkner in the University: Class Conferences at the University of Virginia, 1957–1958* (New York: Random House, 1959), 90.

18. Blotner, *Faulkner*, I, 537.

19. William Faulkner, *The Town* (New York: Random House, 1957, Vintage ed. 1961).

20. John B. Cullen, with Floyd C. Watkins, *Old Times in the Faulkner Country* (Chapel Hill: University of North Carolina Press, 1961), 99–100.

"red-necks," or tenant farmers, who appeared seemingly from nowhere after the Civil War. In Faulkner's stories, they are a "tribe of people which would come into an otherwise peaceful little Southern town like ants or like mold on cheese." Faulkner himself admitted they were exaggerated: "They were simply over-emphasized, burlesqued if you like, which is what Mr. Dickens spent a lot of his time doing, for a valid . . . reason, which was to tell a story in an amusing, dramatic, tragic, or comical way."[21]

In 1927 Faulkner was working on the *Flags* materials and alternately on a manuscript which he tentatively entitled "Father Abraham." "Faulkner's title and intention [were] ironic [for] he was thinking . . . [of] the patriarch who migrated from Ur of the Chaldees, leading his people into the land of Canaan, where they prospered greatly. Flem Snopes was the local Abraham, and the clan he led displayed his traits: cunning, rapacity, and utter amorality, plus the seething vigor of a swarm of vermin."[22] After more than 14,000 words,[23] Faulkner abandoned the "Father Abraham" manuscript, which in later years became, however, a "lumber room" of great value, and which today reposes in the Arents collection at the New York Public Library.

Faulkner then devoted his full energies to the materials that would one day become *Sartoris*, in an effort, as he would recall later, "to recreate between the covers of a book the world [he] . . . was already preparing to lose and regret."[24] As *Sartoris*, in a sense, is an overview of the Yoknapatawpha world, he immediately withdrew from his lumber room at least an overview of Snopeses as denizens of the fictional community:

[The Snopeses were] a seemingly inexhaustible family which for the last ten years had been moving to town in driblets from a small

21. *Faulkner in the University*, 193, 61.
22. Blotner, *Faulkner*, I, 527.
23. *Ibid.*, 528.
24. *Ibid.*, 531.

settlement known as Frenchman's Bend. Flem, the first Snopes, had appeared unheralded one day behind the counter of a small restaurant on a side street, patronized by country folk. With this foothold and like Abraham of old, he brought his blood and legal kin household by household, individual by individual, into town, and established them where they could gain money. Flem himself was presently manager of the city light and water plant, and for the following few years he was a sort of handy man to the municipal government; and three years ago [in 1916], to old Bayard's profane astonishment and unconcealed annoyance, he became vice president of the Sartoris bank, where already a relation of his was a bookkeeper.

He still retained the restaurant, and the canvas tent in the rear of it, in which he and his wife and baby had passed the first few months of their residence in town; and it served as an alighting-place for incoming Snopeses, from which they spread to small third-rate businesses of various kinds—grocery stores, barber shops (there was one, an invalid of some sort, who operated a second-hand peanut roaster)— where they multiplied and flourished.[25]

Only two other Snopeses are named in *Sartoris*, and only one is dramatically realized. I. O. Snopes and his son Clarence became casualties of the cutting of *Flags* to form *Sartoris*, although a small part played by the horse trader who owns the wild stallion Bayard rides is easily identified as that of I. O. because of his activities in the short story "Mule in the Yard." I. O., then, is a rapacious, amoral Snopes in the novel *Sartoris*. Another Snopes, Montgomery Ward, turned down for military service because of a heart condition when he had volunteered just before the draft, had accompanied Horace to Europe, where he held a position in the YMCA. The "story got out" after his departure that on the day he had offered for military service, he had "traveled all the way to Memphis . . . with a plug of chewing tobacco beneath his left armpit" (S, 173). Horace admits to having been disappointed in Montgomery Ward Snopes,

25. William Faulkner, *Sartoris* (New York: Random House, 1929, 1946), 172–73. Subsequent references to this edition will appear in the text.

and dismisses individuals like that as "parasites" (S, 174). Of Snopeses in general, Aunt Sally Wyatt comments, "General Johnston or General Forrest wouldn't have took a Snopes in his army at all" (S, 174).

Byron Snopes, ironically named for the great Romantic poet and lover, is the only Snopes of any consequence in *Sartoris*. Critical opinion on this Snopes is meager, and what there is varies widely. H. Edward Richardson dismissed Byron as "the skulking Snopes" who "writes anonymous love letters to Narcissa through an amanuensis, young Virgil Beard."[26] Hyatt H. Waggoner spoke of Byron as "perfect," but different from the "solidly created" other minor characters. "His fictional greatness," Waggoner continues, "we are not likely to estimate accurately unless we recall how 'villainous' he is, and how difficult, if not impossible, we find it today to believe in any 'villain' in fiction—yet how convincing this one is."[27] Walter K. Everett contended that Byron is "drawn so vividly and realistically, he transcends the type character classification"; he is "named for a quite sanguinary literary figure"; he is "the only character in *Sartoris* who bleeds"; and "his digression has strengthened the primary action of the novel."[28]

But Melvin Reed Roberts made some critical judgments open to questioning. He contended that in *Flags* "Faulkner originally provided impressive interior exposure to soften, if not entirely remove, the villainous mask." He said that this focusing "on the extent of his [Byron's] obsession . . . [results in] an infinitely more compassionate treatment than that eventually provided in *Sartoris*." Then Roberts commented that "the grotesque half-man, . . . reduced to a strictly functional role in

26. H. Edward Richardson, *William Faulkner: The Journey to Self-Discovery* (Columbia: University of Missouri Press, 1969), 170–71.
27. Hyatt H. Waggoner, *William Faulkner: From Jefferson to the World*, (Lexington: University of Kentucky Press, 1966), 27.
28. Walter K. Everett, *Faulkner's Art and Characters* (Woodbury, N.Y.: Barron's, 1969), 92.

Sartoris, is so impressively fleshed out in the typescript."[29] On these points Roberts mentioned, the characterization, the style, and the cutting of *Sartoris* are inextricably interwoven. As a matter of fact, nowhere else has the cutting hand been more professional than in the characterization of Byron Snopes and in the style of the passages involved. Whoever did the cutting here provided *showing* instead of *telling* in character depiction. The changes reveal a man ruled by an obsession and in the toils of despair. Not all interior exposure has been removed, however.

Byron Snopes's frustration, or impotent rage, when he hears of the engagement of Narcissa provides a convenient comparison. In *Flags*, at this point in the story, there is the almost unbearable inner torment, and the jealousy is stated:

His mind coiled and coiled upon itself, tormenting him with fleeing obscene images in which she moved with another. He had thought it dreadful when he was not certain that there was another; but now to know it, to find knowledge of it on every tongue . . . and young Sartoris, at that: a man whom he had hated instinctively with all his sense of inferiority and all the venom of his worm-like nature. Married, married. Adultery, concealed if suspected, he could have borne; but this, boldly, in the world's face, flouting him with his own impotence. . . . He dug a cheap, soiled handkerchief from his hip pocket and wiped the saliva from his jaws.[30]

And so, in *Flags*, the morning wears away, with "more Coca-Colas" and more work at his desk. "The images still postured in his mind, but they were now so familiar as to be without personal significance. Or rather, his dulled senses no longer responded so quickly; and one part of him labored steadily on with steady neat care while the other jaded part reviewed the coiling shapes with a sort of dull astonishment that they no longer filled

---

29. Roberts, "Faulkner's *Flags in the Dust*," 45, 47.
30. Faulkner, *Flags in the Dust*, 249. Subsequent references to *Flags* will appear in the text.

his blood with fire maenads" (*F*, 250). At this point his "dulled nerves reacted" to Virgil Beard's entering the bank.

The passage in *Sartoris*, on the other hand, has been drastically pruned:

All the forenoon he bent over his ledgers, watching his hand pen the neat figures into the ruled columns with a sort of astonishment. After his sleepless night he labored in a kind of stupor, his mind too spent even to contemplate the coiling images of his lust, thwarted now for all time [by Narcissa's engagement], save with a dull astonishment that the images no longer filled his blood with fury and despair, so that it was some time before his dulled nerves reacted to a fresh threat and caused him to raise his head. Virgil Beard was just entering the door (*S*, 264).

The reader can see the half-crazed man vent his rage, in a very human manner, by "whuppin'" his young accomplice. Where *Flags* has the "whuppin'" after two or more pages of description of Snopes's inner state and his morning routine in the bank, *Sartoris* accomplishes it with the one paragraph. One wipe of "his drooling mouth with his handkerchief" (*S*, 264) reveals more madness and degradation than all the "coiling images" of his interior exposure. In *Flags*, the narrator states "the worm-like nature" of Byron; in *Sartoris* he displays it. Statement has largely turned to action in the cutting of this section of the typescript.

The cutting hand made some fortunate changes also in the passage recounting the visit of Miss Jenny and Narcissa to the bank. The *Flags* passage reads: "She remarked beneath the brim of her hat his forearms, from which the sleeves had been turned back, and the fine, reddish hair which clothed them down to the second joints of his fingers; and while Miss Jenny ceased momentarily to nurse her sense of helpless outrage, she remarked with a faint distinct distaste and a little curiosity, since it was not particularly warm today, the fact that his arms and hands were beaded with perspiration" (*F*, 93). The companion passage, in *Sartoris*, trimmed of Narcissa's hat, Miss Jenny's outrage, and the redundancy of the shirt sleeves, reads as follows: "She remarked the reddish hair which clothed his arms down to the second joints of his fingers, and remarked with a faint yet distinct distaste, and a little curiosity since it was not particularly warm, the fact that his hands and arms were beaded with perspiration" (*S*, 105). Actually, the extraneous ideas in the *Flags* quotation may represent Faulkner's attempt to reproduce consciousness, with its impingements of several lesser ideas upon the main thought. The important result of the cutting of this part of the Byron Snopes section, however, is the removal of the bits of pure description of Byron and the replacing of them with the action of this and other passages. For example, Narcissa's remarking the reddish hair stays; whereas "a thin youngish man with hairy hands" disappears.

In *Flags*, the bookkeeper, Byron Snopes, is "a hillman of indeterminate age, a silent man who performed his duties with tedious slow care and who watched Bayard constantly and covertly all the while he was in view" (*F*, 71), and "a thin, youngish man with hairy hands and covert close eyes that looked always as though he were just blinking them, though you never saw them closed" (*F*, 71). He moves "with his surreptitious tread" (*F*, 93), and he speaks "in an inflectionless voice" and "in a slow, nasal voice without inflection" (*F*, 71).

In *Sartoris*, the bookkeeper speaks "in a voice utterly without inflection" (*S*, 2); most of the rest of the pure description has disappeared. "His surreptitious tread" becomes: He "appeared suddenly and without noise beside them." A reader must decide whether or not this is a "surreptitious tread." In other words, the writing has become more factual, less judgmental. As to whether Byron is "fleshed out" in *Flags* and reduced to a functional portrait in *Sartoris*, as Roberts contends, is a matter of taste.

As to whether or not there is compassion in the portrait perhaps is also a matter of taste, or temperament of the critic. Byron in Narcissa's room seems somehow a poignant picture of a man deserving of pity, or compassion: "Her presence was all about him, and for a time his heart thudded and thudded in his throat and fury and lust and despair shook him. He pulled himself together; he must get out quickly, and he groped his way across to the bed and lay face down on it, his head buried in the pillows, writhing and making smothered, animal-like moanings" (S, 267). Perhaps this man with the "mad, shaking voice," the "drooling mouth," and the thwarted lust is simply disgusting. Obviously, he operates in abstract, mechanical time, as witnessed by his constant preoccupation with the clock. In any case, he is a citizen of Jefferson, one contributing to the hell on earth that community makes for itself. Indeed Byron Snopes is a realized villain in *Sartoris*, one the cutting hands have made more dependent on "showing" than on "telling," on action rather than description.

Perhaps some speculation is not completely out of place here concerning Faulkner's first title for the book that became *Sartoris* during the publishing process. On May 7, 1957, the following exchange took place at the University of Virginia:

Q. Mr. Faulkner, may I ask you if . . . there's something here in Mississippi folklore that I miss, not having grown up in Mississippi. Cora says, "His face looked like one of these here Christmas masts. . . ." What is a Christmas *mast*?

A. Oh, the toy mask, the comic faces that children buy . . . for Halloween and Christmas time.

Q. And *mast* is really for *mask*?

A. Mast, yes.

Q. Just like *dust* for *dusk*?

A. Yes. That's right. [31]

---

31. Blotner (ed.), *Faulkner in the University*, 126–27.

Calvin S. Brown, in his very useful *Glossary of Faulkner's South*, confirms this folk usage of "dust" for "dusk" or twilight in his discussion of "dust-dark" as "a folk etymology derived from *dusk-dark*."[32]

If *Flags in the Dust*, then, is really *Flags in the "Dusk*," or "Flags in the Twilight," then Faulkner's choice of title adds another piece to the mosaic of meaning. This reading, of course, offers two widely different meanings for the word "dust"; and as both *Sartoris* and *Flags in the Dust* are dusty novels indeed in the usual sense of the word, it lends a typical Faulknerian ambiguity to the original work. And "Flags in the *Dusk*" becomes a commentary on the moribund society of Jefferson and on the twilight of civilization itself. Read in this manner, the "flags" become affirmations in the society, the banners that fly proudly in those representative acts and persons maintaining a sense of community and continuity that will, in the Bergsonian sense, "endure." The quotation in the novel then becomes sensible: "'I danced a valse with him in Baltimore in '58,' and her voice was still as banners in the dust [dusk]" (*S*, 19). Perhaps the banners are not in the dust after all, as critics have maintained, but instead, just before taps are "proud and still" and high in the hushed twilight Faulkner loved.

Sartoris is William Faulkner's Inferno, Paradise Lost, Old Testament hell, his classical Hades, or Tartarus. Paradoxically, it presents a vision of life as a sense of community. It sets its "fair field" teeming with folk in the village of Jefferson and the surrounding countryside. The rivers which bound the fictional county may represent the Styx and the Acheron. Cerberus, the dog who guards the underworld of myth, is specifically named in connection with the campus security officer when Bayard is at the University of Mississippi, some miles away from Jefferson. Even Miss Jenny, for example, contributes to the overriding hell

32. Calvin S. Brown, *A Glossary of Faulkner's South* (New Haven: Yale University Press, 1976).

and devil imagery of the novel. She speaks of Bayard's "helling around the country," and of her brother, the "Carolina" Bayard, as one who "raised the devil like a gentleman, not like . . . Mississippi country people" (S, 230). To Narcissa she declares that Bayard is "storing up devilment" (S, 200) which will "burst loose all at once . . . and then there'll be hell to pay." At another time she speaks of having "too much to do to worry with the long devil" (S, 205). At Thanksgiving "Miss Jenny, behind her barricade of cups and urns and jugs and things, continued to breathe fire and brimstone" (S, 291). And even the Thanksgiving dessert carries eschatological connotations, making the pudding quite appropriate for feasting in Tartarus or in *Sartoris*: "Simon brought in . . . a small, deadly plum pudding, and a cake baked cunningly with whisky and nuts and fruits and ravishing as odors of heaven and treacherous and fatal as sin" (S, 296). Perhaps *Sartoris* is the house of the dead in hell itself, the home of Hades, or Pluto, or the devil. In this connection, *The Dictionary of Classical Antiquities* is helpful: "In works of art . . . [Hades] is represented . . . with gloomy features [,] . . . the key of the infernal world in his hand and the dog Cerberus at his side. Sometimes he appears as a god of agriculture. . . . The plants sacred to him were the cypress and the narcissus. . . . Connected with . . . [the belief that the dead preserved their consciousness and power of speech] is the notion that they have power of influencing men's life on earth in various ways."[33]

And Sir James G. Frazer's *Golden Bough*, which Faulkner read in New Orleans in the library of Sherwood Anderson,[34] furnishes another interesting clue:

The youthful Persephone, so runs the tale, was gathering roses and lilies, crocusses, and violets, hyacinths and *narcissi* [italics added]

33. Oskar Seyffert, *A Dictionary of Classical Antiquities: Mythology, Religion, Literature, Art*, rev. and ed. Henry Nettleship and J. E. Sandys (New York: Meridian Books, 1956), 263–66.

34. Blotner, *Faulkner*, I, 396.

in a lush meadow, when earth gaped and Pluto [Hades], lord of the Dead, issuing from the abyss carried her off on his golden car to be his bride and queen in the gloomy subterranean world. . . .

[Homer] tells us that it was Earth who . . . lured Persephone to her doom by causing the narcissus to grow which tempted the young goddess to stray far beyond the reach of help. . . .

We do no indignity to the myth of Demeter and Persephone—one of the few myths in which the sunshine and clarity of the Greek genius are crossed by the shadow and mystery of death—when we trace its origin to some of the most familiar, yet eternally affecting aspects of nature, to the melancholy gloom and decay of autumn and to the freshness, the brightness, and the verdure of spring.[35]

That there is no one-to-one correspondence in the symbolism of *Sartoris* to any mythological tales will bear reiteration. However, one cannot escape the notion that in the stately passing of the seasons are connotations evoking earth goddesses and fertility rites. A misty stream forms and dissolves above the bright land of the novel, in which a reader may form his own pictures from the classical, biblical, Shakespearian, romantic, and modern allusions and symbols. In this mythic stream the reader glimpses the lost Eden, the story of Cain and Abel, Abraham of old who brought Lot into land belonging to others, and even the birth of Christ. To be sure, the Faulknerian ironies and ambiguities suggest that the lost Eden, like the "lost cause," is a romanticism, but may not be completely lost. For the past, swollen with the experiences of the generations and romanticized into legends of things that really never were, still gnaws into the present and rearranges the future.

That William Faulkner was obsessed with the effect of the past on the present is a commonplace of the criticism. But that in *Sartoris* he laid out a community weakened by its tradition, delineated some forces contributing to its moribund condition,

---

35. Sir James George Frazer, *The Golden Bough: A Study in Magic and Religion* (New York: Macmillan, 1958), 456–62.

affirmed some values pointing toward a better life for man, and suggested the necessity for accommodation to change, is relatively neglected. Old Bayard presents an example of a character weakened by nostalgia and romanticism and yet struggling to accommodate change. Although he looks backward with pride, he recognizes the inevitability of change. His clashing, crashing, thumping, "trompling," and roaring may symbolize the clash of nineteenth- and twentieth-century values, for old Bayard wanders "between two worlds, one dead, / The other powerless to be born."[36] The "chandelier of crystal prisms and shades" in the hall of the plantation house, "fitted originally for candles" (S, 7), by 1918 has been wired for electricity. The pump behind the barn, supplying the power for the place, creaks and groans throughout the novel. A tractor presently handles the heavy work on the Sartoris section of the plantation. Sharecroppers have divided the rest of the Sartoris holdings. Snopeses have encroached not only upon the town but also upon the bank. Who but old Bayard could have presided over these compromises of the old with the new?

Old Bayard's fatal flaw, symbolized by his heart condition, consists of nostalgia, or romanticism, and of violence. Although he speculates on "the unturned corners of man's destiny," and even makes some accommodation to change even to the point of riding in young Bayard's automobile, he looks backward with a little of his father's "vanity and poppycock" (S, 92). He is willing, like Moses of old, to take a stick and commit an act of violence. Kind, benevolent, responsible, even paternal despite his testiness, he expects nevertheless, with his symbolic stick of stove wood, not only to return Caspey to "good nigger" status, but in general to keep the Negro "in his place." He is willing to have the poor in the poor house and the near paupers deprived of

36. Matthew Arnold, "Stanzas from the Grande Chartreuse," *Arnold: Poetical Works*, ed. C. B. Tinker and H. F. Lowry (New York: Oxford University Press, 1950), 302.

automobiles. In his bank, he presides over the decline of the county's aristocrats with every sharecropping loan he makes. Like the patriarch Moses, Colonel Bayard Sartoris can carry his people toward the promised land of the twentieth century; but because of the romantic flaw in him, he will not himself partake of the fruits of progress toward the brotherhood of man. He is one of the old people who must die, as Faulkner said, before full accommodation to change can be made.

No system, Faulkner is saying, can survive if that system is based on injustice, greed, and violence. Exploitation of the sharecroppers, whether black or white, begets even worse conditions than those existing under slavery. Perhaps old Bayard understands that the system itself is doomed, that aristocrats are as outmoded as anchovies in wartime, and that he himself is living in the twilight of civilization as he has known it. There are some ennobling effects, to be sure, in the Code of a Gentleman under which Colonel Bayard Sartoris has grown to old age, but there is death in it also. Riding a dream, the old settlers had come into the country, pushed back the Indians, and with slave labor pushed back the wilderness also. These glorified, exalted, idealized ancestors, "elegant and flamboyant," have become, like the Toledo's sheath in the Sartoris attic, "soiled" (S, 91) with greed, exploitation, and violence.

In the South, perhaps as nowhere else on earth, history has turned to legend. Every southerner of Faulkner's generation had to come to grips not only with heroes larger than life but with a code of behavior inculcated from infancy. It was the grandfathers and uncles of Faulkner's generation who fought in the battles which never were and the grandmothers and the aunts who never surrendered, but who passed along stories which in time became legends and myths of a South that never was, where music played softly and the dusk was "peopled with ghosts of glamorous and old disastrous things" (S, 380). Just as Miss Jenny's tales of the Civil War have mellowed with retelling until what had been "two heedless and reckless boys wild with their own youth" became "two angels valiantly fallen and strayed" (S, 9), so young Bayard polishes his own stories of the First World War. In the last of the several accounts of his brother's death, in his reliving the situation as one "might run over a printed, oft-read tale," he has added a romantic "gay flapping of an orange pennon from the nose of John's Camel."

Looked at from the point of view of young Bayard, the novel is a search for personal identity in the face of overwhelming forces of heredity and environment, with these complicated by twinship, sibling rivalry, and most of all, by war. To understand young Bayard, as well as the rest of the Yoknapatawpha world, the reader must realize that Faulkner defined "environment" as "not just the field, the house, the town you live in, but all the memory, all the tradition . . . just like the air you breathe."[37] On another occasion, he repeated his definition and refined it somewhat: "By environment . . . I mean his tradition, the air he breathes, his heredity, everything which surrounds him. And his past is certainly a very immediate part of anyone's present."[38]

The events of the present of the novel *Sartoris* cover a little more than a year, from late spring of 1919, after the wisteria has bloomed and fallen, through late June of 1920, after young Bayard and Simon Strother have joined the rest of the Sartoris men in the Jefferson cemetery. Only the two women, Aunt Jenny and Narcissa, are left to cherish the baby, Benbow, the last of the Sartoris line. The larger action of the novel, however, spans the period from the Civil War through World War I, much of it occurring as flashbacks, romanticized tales, and other musings, as reflected through the consciousnesses of the characters and aided by the chronicling voice. "The bright land," the "kind land" are in the mind of the romantic old Bayard, and "the

37. James B. Meriwether and Michael Millgate (eds.), *Lion in the Garden: Interviews with William Faulkner, 1926–1962* (New York: Random House, 1968), 210–11.
38. *Ibid.*, 203–204.

meaning of peace" in that of the romantic Horace Benbow. Actually, however, the land is amoral, and all of nature itself is amoral. Just as the bull bats, "swooping against the serene sky, silent as drops of water on a windowpane; swift and noiseless and intent as though their wings were feathered with twilight and with silence" (S, 144), eat the gnats that spin and whirl above the water, the people of Jefferson prey upon one another: Sartorises, Benbows, Mitchells, and Snopeses.

The facts of the plot are remarkably simple. In this book about time and tradition and the impact of violence, technology, and change on individuals and community, five young men return in 1919 from the war in Europe to their small southern town. Young Bayard Sartoris, scion of planter aristocrats, slips into Jefferson on the railroad his great-grandfather had built. Shortly after young Bayard's arrival, Caspey Strothers returns from his experiences in Europe, with notions which, unless altered shortly, are certain to cut short his career in Mississippi. For war has changed his ideas, and he "don't take nothin' fum no white folks no mo'" (S, 62). A few weeks later Horace Benbow comes home to Jefferson and to his loving sister Narcissa. Montgomery Ward Snopes returns from his job with the YMCA in Europe, carrying, as Faulkner will reveal in a later work, the pornographic French postcards. And Virginius MacCallum, Jr., called "Buddy," one of the six sons of the patriarch of the hill country, comes home with a medal but is himself almost untouched by his war experiences, having been protected perhaps by his innocence, ignorance, and simple dignity. What these veterans of a horrible and incomprehensible modern war think and say and do, along with their impact upon and adjustment to the rest of the community, as well as their relationships to the land and to the past—all of these woven together and interspersed with comic interludes of daily life, constitute the narrative pattern of the novel.

William Faulkner obviously was attempting in *Sartoris*, or

Flags in the Dust, to arrest the motion of one small town in order to look at the antics and institutions of its inhabitants. Like Keats in his "Urn" poem, Faulkner concerns himself with the relationship between art and reality and between life and death. Although Faulkner is concerned, as a structural element, with the frieze decorating the Grecian urn, the arrested motion at which he aims is that which appears, not on the urn itself, but in the mind of Keats. For William Faulkner sought to arrest the entire "little town" evoked by the "sylvan historian." Jefferson is the little town, and Faulkner the sylvan historian, the poet who expresses his "flowery tale," his "leaf-fringed legend" haunted with, if not deities, at least with ghosts and mortals. He arrests the "breathing human passion," the hearts "high-sorrowful and cloyed," the "burning" foreheads, and the "parching" tongues. He snatches truth and beauty, as well as good and evil, from the "duration" or "flux" of "slow Time." In the little town and its folk, he provides the major structural element of the novel, thus unifying structure, theme, and imagery.

The circle, the line, and the web represent the form of the novel. The cycle of nature, the flowing of concrete time, the artificiality and stasis of abstract time, and the interrelatedness of human activity are the difficult subjects which contribute to the difficult structure and style. The fictional Mississippi county is a social model, though certainly not a Utopian one. In his stories of "the human heart in conflict with itself and with its environment," William Faulkner has made his Yoknapatawpha a model of what *is*, a microcosm in which one can look at the human situation arrested in art. The county and its people, with the Faulknerian ironies and ambiguities playing over them, present a theory of education, at least through implication, capable of transforming that society into a coherent and slowly progressing social order.

But William Faulkner was a poet, not a sociologist or a critic of culture, and it is in the poetical terms of metaphor, symbolism, imagery, allusion, paradox, ambiguity, and irony that *Sartoris* becomes a theory of a coherent society and slowly progressing social order as it develops its major theme: that there is a tension between the ennobling and crippling power of tradition and environment on individuals and community, with war upsetting traditional patterns and accelerating technological and social change.

With very few dissenting voices, *Sartoris* is usually grouped with the "apprentice" work of William Faulkner. But *Sartoris* is no apprentice novel. It is mature work, perhaps in some ways one of the great books of the Faulkner canon. Although it is diffuse and difficult, as critics have noted, it provides a pleasurable, an exciting, and at the same time a terrifying experience for a discriminating reader. One of the easiest of Faulkner's books to read and one of the most difficult to understand, the novel can serve appropriately, not only as an entrance into the Yoknapatawpha world, as Faulkner himself suggested, but in the *Flags* form as a fitting departure point also. For *Sartoris* and *Flags in the Dust* treat of first and last things: of birth, life, fertility, time, death, heaven, and hell. And as in the best of T. S. Eliot's work, the mythological and other references open up and enlarge the meaning. The reader himself must integrate the several levels of the plot, structure, imagery, themes, and allusions into an emotional and intellectual experience.

"Strange Times" in Yoknapatawpha

JOHN PILKINGTON

Although scholarly critics and nonprofessional readers alike have agreed that "An Odor of Verbena" is the outstanding chapter in Faulkner's *The Unvanquished,* the preceding story, "Skirmish at Sartoris," has merits that make it deserving of greater recognition than it has yet received. Artistically, "Skirmish at Sartoris," the story of Drusilla Hawk's marriage and the killing of the two carpetbaggers, is a splendid example of Faulkner's narrative technique of counterpoint. Thematically, the story effectively dramatizes the novelist's mixed emotions about the Civil War and Reconstruction. And functionally, it would have provided an appropriate ending for the book even if Faulkner had not written "An Odor of Verbena." Without taking anything from the final story, one can also observe that "Skirmish at Sartoris" offers a fitting introduction to the white-Negro relationships discussed in *Go Down, Moses.*

Faulkner found the story difficult to write. Initially, "Skirmish at Sartoris" was one of six stories written to make some ready cash, tailored for readers of the *Saturday Evening Post,* and possibly regarded by Faulkner with a degree of contempt. In the spring of 1934, he pushed aside *Absalom, Absalom!,* which he was then writing, to compose "Ambuscade," "Retreat," and "Raid." At this point he seems to have lost his inspiration. Early in the summer of 1934, he wrote his agent: "I have been stewing for about three weeks now on the *Post* stories. I have

71

been trying to cook up three more with a single thread of continuity, like the other three, with the scene during Reconstruction time. I cannot get started."[1] He never really solved this problem of continuity. When the completed series of stories was much later assembled in *The Unvanquished*, the disparities in tone, atmosphere, and content between the first three stories and those which followed remained apparent.

While continuing to "stew" over the continuity of the episodes, Faulkner accepted an offer to work in Hollywood during July. When he returned to Oxford at the end of the month, he was still undecided about whether to continue the series for the *Saturday Evening Post* or to resume work on *Absalom, Absalom!* In September, however, he mailed the editors "The Unvanquished" (now called "Riposte in Tertio") and "Vendée," and by mid-October he had finished "Drusilla," the story now called "Skirmish at Sartoris." Meanwhile, the editors of the *Saturday Evening Post* had published the first three stories,[2] but for some reason they held the fourth and fifth stories for more than two years. By that time Faulkner had sold "Skirmish at Sartoris" to *Scribner's Magazine*, which published it in April, 1935.[3]

Faulkner designed these short stories to exhibit a kind of progression (though not necessarily the kind of progression required for a novel). They dealt, moreover, with a subject that had occupied him from almost the beginning of the Yoknapatawpha stories—the Civil War and Reconstruction. Yet, in a letter to Morton Goldman, his literary agent, Faulkner seems to have written disparagingly of them. He declared that so long as he was forced to write "trash," he did not care who bought it so long

1. Joseph Blotner (ed.), *Selected Letters of William Faulkner* (New York: Random House, 1977), 80–81.

2. William Faulkner, "Ambuscade," *Saturday Evening Post*, CVII (September 29, 1934), 12–13, 80–81; William Faulkner, "Retreat," *Saturday Evening Post*, CVII (October 13, 1934), 16–17, 82, 84–85, 87; William Faulkner, "Raid," *Saturday Evening Post*, CVII (November 3, 1934), 18–19, 72–73, 75, 77–78.

3. William Faulkner, "Skirmish at Sartoris: A Story," *Scribner's Magazine*, XCVII (April, 1935), 193–200.

as the price was high. When he sacrificed a high price to a lower one, it would be, as he said, to "write something better than a pulp series like this."[4] The comment is tantalizingly brief. Exactly what features of the stories he considered trash and pulp, he did not specify. Unfortunately, the remark has followed the stories from the *Saturday Evening Post* and *Scribner's Magazine* into *The Unvanquished* and lent support to the belief that the book is not a piece with Faulkner's other art and thought.

At this point, the literary history of *The Unvanquished* becomes a complicated tangle of events and motives, though certain facts can be readily established. Faulkner spent a large part of 1935 working on *Absalom, Absalom!* and writing short stories for such magazines as the *Saturday Evening Post* and *Scribner's*. In January, 1936, he finished the novel; and except for brief intervals, he worked in Hollywood throughout the remainder of the year. *Absalom, Absalom!* was published on October 26, 1936. At that time, Faulkner had no immediate plans for writing another novel. But on December 28, shortly after the fourth and fifth of his Civil War series had appeared in the *Saturday Evening Post*, Faulkner wrote Bennett Cerf at Random House to ask what he thought about publishing the stories as a book.[5] Without obtaining a commitment from Cerf, Faulkner returned to Hollywood, where throughout the first half of 1937 he contributed substantially to the film version of *Drums along the Mohawk*.

Eventually, probably before the middle of June, 1937, Bennett Cerf decided to publish Faulkner's Civil War book. His decision to publish it may have been prompted in part by his desire to cement Faulkner's connection with Random House after the departure of the novelist's friend and former editor-publisher Hal Smith from the firm. Moreover, after the astonishing success first of Stark Young's *So Red the Rose* in book form from

4. Blotner (ed.), *Selected Letters*, 84.
5. *Ibid.*, 97–98.

Charles Scribner's Sons and then as a motion picture and, second, of Margaret Mitchell's *Gone with the Wind* from the Macmillan Company, Bennett Cerf may have been convinced that the Civil War was a very saleable item in the marketplace. That these six stories, possibly enlarged by a seventh, would make much easier reading for Faulkner's public than most of his other works, especially the recently published *Absalom, Absalom!*, may also have been a factor in Cerf's decision.

While in Hollywood, Faulkner made revisions and additions to the already published six stories. Near the end of July, 1937, Faulkner, still in Hollywood, wrote his agent that because Random House needed an additional story to fill out the volume, he had just finished "An Odor of Verbena."[6] In the same letter, Faulkner remarked that he would leave Hollywood about the middle of August for Oxford but expected to be in New York early in October. By the time he reached New York, *The Unvanquished* was well along on its way to publication, and not a great deal of time remained for any final revisions. The volume appeared on February 15, 1938.[7]

The textual history of *The Unvanquished* reminds one of Faulkner's revision of the first manuscript version of *Sanctuary*. In revising that novel, Faulkner said he transformed a "basely conceived" manuscript ("a cheap idea," he wrote, "because it was deliberately conceived to make money") into a work of art which he felt would not "shame" his finer novels.[8] As has been said, his Civil War stories had also been designed to make money, and upon at least one occasion Faulkner had referred to them as "trash" and "pulp." He now had the opportunity to reshape or

6. *Ibid.*, 100.

7. William Faulkner, *The Unvanquished* (New York: Random House, 1938); the text of the first edition, including the pagination, has been reproduced photographically by Random House and by Vintage Books, a division of Random House. Hereafter this work will be cited in the text as *U*.

8. William Faulkner, Introduction to *Sanctuary* (New York: Modern Library, Random House, 1932).

rewrite them into a work of art; and very probably he began his revisions with that intention. In the first three stories—"Ambuscade," "Retreat," and "Raid"—he made a multitude of small changes of the kind that an experienced writer would make in his rough draft to add color, definiteness, and interest to his manuscript. In a few places, he added incidents or lengthened descriptions to add substance to the plot. More importantly, he filled out the character of Colonel Sartoris, added significance to the roles of Ringo and Loosh, and greatly enhanced the part of the narrator Bayard Sartoris. A comparison between the revisions in these first three stories and those he made in the ones which followed, however, shows very clearly that either Faulkner's interest in revising flagged or that he felt that his original drafts, that is, the magazine versions, became progressively better. By the time he reached "Skirmish at Sartoris," the number and extent of his revisions and additions decreased notably.

The foregoing comment is not intended to imply that Faulkner made no revisions in "Skirmish at Sartoris." In the first paragraph, for example, he made several changes: "Father and Drusilla standing on the ground . . . and opposite them the ladies on the porch and the two sets of them, the men and the ladies, facing one another like they were both waiting for the sound to charge" becomes "Father and Drusilla on the ground . . . and opposite them the women—Aunt Louisa, Mrs. Habersham and all the others—on the porch and the two sets of them, the men and the women, facing one another, like they were both waiting for a bugle to sound the charge." At the end of this paragraph, Faulkner again changed ladies to women so that the well-known sentence which originally was published in *Scribner's Magazine* as "the ladies had never surrendered" becomes in *The Unvanquished* "the women had never surrendered." This type of revision, nevertheless, very abundant in "Ambuscade," "Retreat," and "Raid," occurs only infrequently in "Skirmish at Sartoris."

Other revisions in the story are less successful, and there are passages which Faulkner should have revised and did not. In the *Scribner's Magazine* version, Faulkner writes that "Granny wasn't there to read" the letter, received just before Christmas, 1864, telling the whereabouts of Drusilla. In the book version, Faulkner adds an explanatory phrase; the passage reads: "So then the next letter came. Only Granny wasn't there to read it because she was dead then" (*U*, 218). But earlier, in the fourth story, "Riposte in Tertio," Faulkner had already written: "It was Christmas [1864]; we had just heard from Aunt Louisa at Hawkhurst and found out where Drusilla was" (*U*, 169–170). In other words, in the earlier story, Granny was not only alive but also read the letter. Again, in revising the exposition which Faulkner had felt necessary to include in the *Scribner's Magazine* version, he changed the time of the visit of Granny, Ringo, and Bayard to Hawkhurst from "two years ago" to "eighteen months ago" (*U*, 217). But later in the same story, he allowed to stand unchanged the remark "when we were in Hawkhurst two years ago" (*U*, 230). Still other time discrepancies depict Colonel Sartoris fighting in Carolina before any fighting took place there.[9]

Today's readers, alert to factual errors and internal inconsistencies, wonder why Faulkner did not make some of these corrections. Even more, one wonders why the copy readers or editors at Random House did not insist that the most glaring inconsistencies be corrected before the book was published. The problem is not confined to "Skirmish at Sartoris" or to the other stories in *The Unvanquished*. Discrepancies of various sorts, including time, are involved in an impressive number of Faulkner's works. Many of these inconsistencies seem to arise from his fondness for providing exact dates, times, numbers, and concrete references in his fiction. Perhaps the best explanation for his reluctance to make corrections or his willingness to ignore

---

9. In his dissertation, "The Place of *The Unvanquished* in William Faulkner's Yoknapatawpha Series" (Princeton, 1958), James B. Meriwether has pointed out a number of inconsistencies in the novel.

the conflicts may be that he felt they did not interfere with the spirit of the work and would not bother most readers; but for the reader who wishes his fiction tidy in every respect, these matters can be frustrating.

At least one alteration Faulkner made in the facts of history can be justified artistically. From Bayard's comment "it was spring and the war was over" (U, 221), the reader learns that the story takes place sometime in the spring of 1865. Lee had surrendered to Grant at Appomattox Court House on April 9; Johnston had surrendered to Sherman at Durham's Station on April 26; Taylor's force, which included a considerable number of Mississippians like Stark Young's father, surrendered at Citronelle, Alabama, on May 4. The trans-Mississippi Confederate forces under Kirby Smith did not surrender until May 26. Thus, Faulkner's story must take place almost as soon as the men could have arrived home. Colonel Sartoris and Drusilla, in fact, had reached Jefferson in February, at which time Louvinia, greeting Bayard and Ringo just back from killing Grumby, exclaims: "Hit done finished! All but the surrendering. And now Marse John done home" (U, 212). The "strange times," so designated by Bayard twice in the story (U, 223, 227), are about to begin.

During the last years of the war, local and state government, particularly in areas like Jefferson or Oxford, intermittently occupied first by Confederate and then by Union troops, had almost completely broken down. Bayard remembers that "there were no men there at all anymore" and that "we lived in a world of burned towns and houses and ruined plantations and fields inhabited only by women" (U, 216). Colonel Sartoris and the soldiers of his troop were trying to build back Jefferson, the courthouse, the stores, and the houses; but they were also trying to restore civil government. One of the two main incidents of "Skirmish at Sartoris" focuses on the election of the town marshal and the issue at stake relates to Negro voting. The carpetbaggers threaten to take over the town government and rule through their control of Negro votes. No such issue was present in Oxford or elsewhere in Mississippi in 1865. In fact, the Radical Military Reconstruction Acts passed by Congress which enabled blacks to vote did not take effect in Mississippi until the autumn election of 1867, more than two years after Faulkner's story takes place, and the Fourteenth Amendment did not become a part of the Constitution until July, 1868. Although there is a possibility that Faulkner was not aware of the historical discrepancy of this part of the story, it is much more likely that he deliberately telescoped these years to make the action take place almost immediately after the events of "Vendée" and thus include the incident in Bayard's boyhood.

An even more compelling reason for telescoping the events of history may be found in the other important incident of the story—Drusilla's marriage. During the visit of Bayard, Granny, and Ringo to the Hawks in the story "Raid," Drusilla said to Bayard: "When you go back home and see Uncle John, ask him to let me come there and ride with his troop" (U, 115). Shortly afterwards, she disappeared from her home, and for more than a year, as Aunt Louisa writes in "Skirmish at Sartoris," Drusilla, "in the garments not alone of a man but of a common private soldier" had been a member of Colonel Sartoris's troop, "bivouacking at night surrounded by sleeping men and not even bothering to put up the tent for her and . . . [the Colonel] except when the weather was bad" (U, 220). And after their return from the fighting, the sleeping arrangements in the cabin place the Colonel and Bayard on a pallet on the floor and Drusilla in the bed behind only a quilt curtain. If the Drusilla marriage episode was to have any point, Faulkner could not have allowed this situation to continue until the fall of 1867 when Negro voting became a historical possibility. Even less, of course, could he have permitted it to continue until 1872, the date which old man Falls in Sartoris assigns to the killing of the carpetbaggers,

78

or still less to 1874, the year Joanna Burden in *Light in August* implies that the event occurred. Thus, if "Skirmish at Sartoris" was to be successful artistically, Faulkner had to take certain liberties with historical facts and with his own earlier fiction.

For the ladies of Yoknapatawpha, Aunt Louisa, Mrs. Compson, Mrs. Habersham, and the others, the issue at stake in their skirmish is the restoration of the social and moral standards which they feel have broken down during the war and its aftermath. In their eyes, any woman who had done what Drusilla had done would certainly be compromised. For them, as Aunt Louisa wrote, Drusilla had flouted and outraged "all Southern principles of purity and womanhood that our husbands had died for" (U, 222); and when Mrs. Habersham showed the other ladies of Jefferson the quilt and the pallet in the cabin and pointed out the places where the Colonel, Bayard, and Drusilla slept, they were convinced. They could imagine no other reason why Drusilla would "conceal herself down there in the woods all day long, lifting heavy weights like logs" (U, 224) and otherwise acting like a man. The Colonel must have already taken advantage of her. At this point, the story, which from the beginning has had a humorous coloring, becomes definitely comic. Bayard observes that the sight of the trunks filled with her old dresses defeats Drusilla. "That's what beat Drusilla: the trunks" (U, 230), and, as he says, "like as soon as she let them put the dress on her she was whipped; like in the dress she could neither fight back nor run away" (U, 231). The contest reaches a climax when Aunt Louisa formally addresses Colonel Sartoris: "Colonel Sartoris, . . . I am a woman; I must request what the husband whom I have lost and the man son which I have not would demand, perhaps at the point of a pistol. . . . Will you marry my daughter?" (U, 233). Ironically, in making the request, she has herself assumed the role of a man.

Faulkner's artistic triumph in the handling of the incident

reaches its peak in the integration of Drusilla's wedding with the election dispute. In dealing with the marriage, Faulkner sustains the comic note, underscored by Aunt Louisa's outcry when she hears that the carpetbaggers have been shot: "Do you mean to tell me that Drusilla and that man are not married yet?" (*U*, 236). Aunt Louisa is even more outraged when Drusilla rather lamely admits that she "forgot." The comedy intensifies, if possible, when Aunt Louisa looks at the men in the saddles and asks Drusilla: "And who are these, pray? Your wedding train of forgetters? Your groomsmen of murder and robbery?" (*U*, 240). Acting wholly in character, she snatches the ballot box from Drusilla and flings it across the yard.

The voting, which finally takes place after the ladies have retreated back into the house and the ballot box is retrieved, marks the climax of the other skirmish at Sartoris. This portion of the incident had been a part of Faulkner's stock of Yoknapatawpha tales ever since 1927 when he wrote *Sartoris*. In 1931, when writing *Light in August*, he told the story for the second time, and three years later, in 1934, he wrote the magazine version later published in *Scribner's Magazine*. Although an argument can be made that one story should not be used as commentary upon another, Faulkner's fondness for this incident and his repeated efforts to tell it may justify an exception. In any event, a brief consideration of the three versions may reveal something about Faulkner's attitude toward the issues involved.

In *Sartoris* (the account is virtually identical in *Flags in the Dust*), old man Falls tells the story to Bayard. According to Falls, the Colonel "stood in the do' of that sto' the day them two cyarpetbaggers brung them niggers in to vote 'em that day in '72. Stood thar in his Prince Albert coat and beaver hat, with his arms folded, when ever'body else had left, and watched them two Missouri fellers herdin' them niggers up the road to'ds the sto'; stood right in the middle of the do' while them two cyarpetbaggers begun backin' off with their hands in their pockets

80

until they was cl'ar of the niggers, and cussed him."[10] When the
carpetbaggers had backed down the road, the Colonel took the
ballot box from behind the door and put it between his feet. He
invited the Negroes to come up and vote; and when they broke
and scattered, according to old man Falls, the Colonel "let off
that 'ere dang der'nger over their heads a couple of times; then
he loaded hit agin and marched down the road to Miz Winterbottom's, whar them two fellers boa'ded" (S, 235). With Mrs.
Winterbottom's permission, the Colonel climbs the stairs and
walks into the room where the carpetbaggers are sitting behind
a table with their pistols lying upon it. Outside, old man Falls
and others hear three shots. They rush into the house, see the
Colonel coming down the stairs, and hear him apologize to Mrs.
Winterbottom "fer havin' been put to the necessity of extermi-
natin' vermin on yo' premises" (S, 236).

Of the three accounts of the incident, old man Falls's version
may be the least reliable, though one cannot be certain. At age
ninety-four, he has been telling the story for the past fifty years,
and in the repetition and the old man's veneration of the Colonel, considerable embroidery may have taken place. The single
confrontation related in the other two accounts has been dou-
bled, the hotel has become a store, the Colonel has hastened
the flight of the Negroes by firing shots over their heads, and
the shoot-out takes place in Mrs. Winterbottom's boardinghouse. Neither Drusilla nor Bayard is mentioned as being
present.

The most significant addition to the story in *Light in August*
relates to the background of the carpetbaggers. In that novel,
Faulkner identifies the two men whom the Colonel shot as
Joanna Burden's grandfather and half-brother, both named Calvin Burden, and provides a lengthy account of her family, certain aspects of which bear upon "Skirmish at Sartoris." Joanna

10. William Faulkner, *Sartoris* (New York: Harcourt, Brace and Company, 1929),
193–94. Hereafter this work will be cited in the text as *S*.

narrates the story to Joe Christmas. According to her, the first Calvin Burden was one of ten children in the family of a New England Unitarian minister. As a boy, he ran away from home, became a Catholic, and ultimately settled in St. Louis, where he renounced Catholicism because, he said, "he would not belong to a church full of frog-eating slaveholders."[11] His hatred of southern slaveholders and slavery soon became an obsession with him. When his son, Nathaniel, was five, Calvin killed a man in an argument over slavery and had to leave St. Louis to live in a small settlement to the west. There he drank whiskey, talked politics, and in his harsh, loud voice continued to curse slaveholders and slavery. Always he carried a large pistol, and no one dared to cross him. His character emerges as that of a tough, hard-drinking, violent, intolerant, religious fundamentalist filled with hate towards the southern slaveholders.

Joanna also relates that Calvin's son, Nathaniel, shared many of his father's traits. Like Calvin, Nathaniel ran away from home at an early age. In Mexico, he killed a man over a horse, lived with a Mexican woman until their child, also named Calvin, was twelve, and then, in 1866, returned to Missouri to get married. After the wedding, the Burdens remained in Missouri for about a month; and then one day, according to Joanna, Nathaniel and her grandfather Calvin went to Washington and "got a commission from the government to come down here, to help with the freed Negroes" (L, 220). Joanna's narrative is silent about their activities in the next eight years; but when her half-brother Calvin, then as big as his grandfather, had "just turned twenty" (L, 217), that would be in 1874, he and his grandfather were shot by Colonel Sartoris over a question of Negro voting.

In *Light in August*, Joanna Burden's account of the killing of her grandfather and half-brother, an event which took place fourteen years before she was born, differs notably from that

11. William Faulkner, *Light in August* (New York: Modern Library, Random House, 1950), 211. Hereafter this work will be cited in the text as *L*.

given by old man Falls in *Sartoris*. As has been seen, Joanna places the incident in 1874, whereas old man Falls says it took place in 1872. Although Joanna has said that her grandfather habitually carried a pistol and that her half-brother, aged twenty, was as large a man as the grandfather, in telling about the shooting she refers to them merely as an old onearmed man and a boy. Old man Falls had said that the Burdens had their pistols on the table in front of them when Colonel Sartoris entered the room and that one of the Burdens fired a shot. Joanna says nothing about the Burdens either having a pistol or, much less, firing a shot. In fact, her account contains nothing about the details of the shooting except the comment that the issue was Negro voting. Her version of the killing is confined to a single sentence: "I suppose that Colonel Sartoris was a town hero because he killed with two shots from the same pistol an old onearmed man and a boy who had never even cast his first vote" (L, 218).

Each of them, old man Falls and Joanna, tells the story from his side, and each passes judgment upon the affair. Old man Falls depicts the Colonel as a courageous, if arrogant, leader of men whose deeds have almost become a legend. Alone he has faced the Burdens, the other carpetbaggers, and the Negroes and made them back down. Singlehandedly, he faces the two Burdens whose pistols are lying in readiness on the table before them. Old man Falls is filled with pride as he recounts the Colonel's actions, and his admiration reaches its peak in his final remark: "I sort of envied them two Nawthuners, be damned ef I didn't. A feller kin take a wife and live with her fer a long time, but after all they ain't no kin. But the feller that brings you into the world or sends you outen hit . . ." (S, 236). He never finishes the sentence but the implication is clear.

Although she never concedes that the Colonel showed any courage or heroism in killing the onearmed man and the boy, Joanna Burden, as she relates the story to Joe Christmas more than fifty years later, seems uncertain about the rights and wrongs of the affair. "They hated us here," she explains. "We were Yankees. Foreigners. Worse than foreigners: enemies. Carpetbaggers. And it—the War—still too close for even the ones that got whipped to be very sensible. Stirring up the Negroes to murder and rape, they called it. Threatening white supremacy. . . . Maybe they were right. I dont know" (L, 218). What Joe Christmas, however, cannot understand is why Joanna's father did not avenge the death of his father and son by killing the Colonel. Indeed, Nathaniel faces the same question that Bayard faces in "An Odor of Verbena." In reply, Joanna's remarks seem almost a comment upon the end of Reconstruction. She says, "It was all over then. The killing in uniform and with flags, and the killing without uniforms and flags. And none of it doing or did any good. None of it" (L, 223). Her final comment suggests the position taken by Cass Edmonds in *Go Down, Moses*. Joanna says: "And we were foreigners, strangers, that thought differently from the people whose country we had come into without being asked or wanted. And he [that is, Nathaniel, her father] was French, half of him. Enough French to respect anybody's love for the land where he and his people were born and to understand that a man would have to act as the land where he was born had trained him to act. I think that was it."[12]

While writing "Skirmish at Sartoris," Faulkner must have been aware of his earlier treatments of the carpetbagger killing in *Sartoris* and *Light in August*. Yet he did not hesitate to make important changes that may make the third telling represent Faulkner's final thinking about certain aspects of Reconstruc-

---

12. The two passages offer an interesting parallel in ideas. Earlier, Nathaniel had said: "The curse of the black race is God's curse. But the curse of the white race is the black man who will be forever God's chosen own because He once cursed H[h?]im" (*Light in August*, 222). In *Go Down, Moses* Cass Edmonds says: "And anyway, you [Isaac McCaslin] will be free.—No, not now nor ever, we from them nor they from us. So I repudiate too. I would deny even if I knew it were true. I would have to. Even you can see that I could do no else. I am what I am; I will be always what I was born and have always been." William Faulkner, *Go Down, Moses* (New York: Modern Library, Random House [1955]), 299–300.

tion. This final version of the thrice-told tale gains reliability from the fact that it is narrated by an eye-witness who though he may have been involved emotionally was certainly not in his dotage. There is little reason to suspect that Bayard substantially altered the facts in his recital of these strange times in Yoknapatawpha.

In Bayard's account, while the Colonel and other men are trying to build back the courthouse and other buildings on the square, he refuses to permit Drusilla, Bayard, or Ringo to go into Jefferson. One day, Ringo slips away to town and returns with a new scrip dollar, "drawn on the United States, Resident Treasurer, Yoknapatawpha County, Mississippi, and signed 'Cassius Q. Benbow, Acting Marshal' in a neat clerk's hand, with a big sprawling X under it" (U, 228–229). When Bayard expresses surprise and asks if Ringo really means Cassius Q. Benbow, Ringo repeats: "Co-rect . . . Uncle Cash that druv the Benbow carriage twell he run off with the Yankees two years ago. He back now and gonter be elected Marshal of Jefferson." In explanation, Ringo says that the two Burdens are trying to organize the Negroes into Republicans and that the Colonel and others are trying to prevent them. The voluble Ringo adds his own commentary: "Used to be when you seed a Yankee you knowed him because he never had nothing but a gun or a mule halter or a handful of hen feathers. Now you don't even know him and stid of the gun he got a clutch of this stuff in one hand and a clutch of nigger voting tickets in the yuther."

Faulkner has thus presented the issue much more specifically here in "Skirmish at Sartoris" than he had in the two earlier accounts. He has even identified the carpetbagger candidate for the election. Bayard remembers that the tension over the election mounted as the time for voting drew near. "Now everybody was talking about the election," recalls Bayard, "and how Father had told the two Burdens before all the men in town that the election would never be held with Cash Benbow or any other nigger in it and how the Burdens dared him to stop it" (*U*, 232). None of these details has a parallel in the accounts by old man Falls or Joanna Burden.

The shoot-out, likewise, differs in "Skirmish at Sartoris" from the earlier versions. In *The Unvanquished*, the Burdens have the Negroes camped in a cotton gin on the edge of town under guard. As Bayard enters the square on election day, he sees "the crowd of niggers kind of huddled beyond the hotel door with six or eight strange white men herding them, and then . . . the Jefferson men that I knew, that Father knew, running across the square toward the hotel with each one holding his hip like a man runs with a pistol in his pocket. And then I saw the men who were Father's troop lined up before the hotel door, blocking it off" (*U*, 236–37). As Bayard slides off his horse, he sees George Wyatt trying to hold Drusilla back, but she slips away. Then Wyatt grabs Bayard. They hear three shots, and Wyatt says, "The last two was that derringer" (*U*, 237). Drusilla comes out with the ballot box, and the Colonel follows brushing his hat on his sleeve. He says, "I let them fire first" (*U*, 238).

Bayard's version of the shoot-out is much simpler than the double confrontation related by old man Falls. Likewise, the account in *Sartoris* contains little about the motives of the participants or the nature of the issue itself. Joanna Burden dwells upon the prejudice of the Jefferson community against "foreigners," its accusations that the Burdens were stirring up the Negroes to murder and rape, and white supremacy. Her sketches of the earlier lives of her grandfather and father reveal the depth of the Burdens' hate of southern men like Colonel Sartoris and the Burdens' willingness to resort to violence. Thus, her account throws some significant light upon the carpetbaggers. Bayard makes no reference to these matters; but implicitly, at least, he does present a case against the Burdens. They have bought Negro votes and are endeavoring to manipulate or control the Negroes' votes in order to elect as law enforcement officer in the community a former runaway slave who cannot even sign his own name. Lastly, Bayard's account agrees with old man Falls's statement that the Burdens fired a shot; Bayard, in fact, goes further by quoting George Wyatt as saying that the last two shots were from the Colonel's derringer, thereby confirming the Colonel's assertion that he let the Burdens shoot first. After recounting these events, Bayard makes no judgment upon the rightness or wrongness of his father's action; but he recalls that immediately after the shooting the Colonel says that he is going to the sheriff to make bond because "we are working for peace through law and order" (U, 239). Whether Faulkner's readers interpret this statement as ironical or factual may depend somewhat upon their attitude toward the early days of Reconstruction. Insofar as "Skirmish at Sartoris" is concerned, the Colonel's rather ambiguous remark leaves the final verdict open. Most likely, Faulkner deliberately intended to make no ultimate judgment. For the present, at least, Colonel Sartoris has won the skirmish, but in his victory the separation of the whites from the Negroes has advanced one step further. Paradoxically, had Colonel Sartoris lost and Cassius Q. Benbow been elected town marshal by Negro votes controlled by carpetbaggers, the same development would probably have taken place.

In uniting the two dissimilar stories of "Skirmish at Sartoris," Faulkner faced a problem similar to that he had encountered in *Light in August*. In that novel, one of his major artistic problems lay in the disparity between Lena Grove's somewhat comic saga and the grim, unhappy, tragic wanderings of Joe Christmas. In "Skirmish at Sartoris," Drusilla's marriage and the shoot-out between Colonel Sartoris and the Burdens seem equally separate, unrelated incidents. In narrating this story, Faulkner was completely successful in fusing the two actions, and the process by which he achieved his success underscores his genius as a writer.

As has been suggested earlier, Faulkner must have under-

87

stood at once that to unite these two incidents he must first make the voting dispute take place before it could have occurred historically. Faulkner must also have understood that the marriage incident, though comic, must have a serious, credible undertone or base. Despite the humorous aspect of the zeal of the Jefferson ladies to make Drusilla an "honest woman" and Bayard's remarks about the thoughts of women over the follies of men, Drusilla's marriage is more than a mere tempest in a teapot. To those who protest Drusilla's innocence and view her marriage as a trivial matter compared to the voting issue, these outraged ladies could reply that after the war or, for that matter, anytime, the enforcement of moral standards in the community should not take second place to the election of town officials. On the other hand, the readiness of these women to throw away the ballot box to hasten a marriage ceremony may be seen as Faulkner's criticism of the lack of interest of southern women in the political problems of the community. Faulkner may also have intended to use the women's insistence upon Drusilla's marriage as an illustration of the growing inflexibility of southern society and to state this truth in lighter vein. In a much more serious manner, the voting incident makes the same point.

In any event, to make Drusilla's marriage and the election take place on the same day was a stroke of genius. Bayard makes this conjunction plausible by saying that the women may not have known that the day appointed was election day, and that if they did know, they did not care. The arrival of Bayard and Drusilla in her wedding gown on the square at the moment of crisis has been plausibly motivated; and after the shooting, the removal of the ballot box to the Sartoris place seems well within the bounds of credibility. That the wedding and the voting should be joined a second time cements the two threads of the plot. Finally, when Louisa throws away the ballot box, the comic episode has been fully interwoven with the tragic dispute between the ex-Confederates and the carpetbaggers; and although

Drusilla's marriage is not solemnized in "Skirmish at Sartoris," when the curtain rises on the next and final episode in *The Unvanquished*, Drusilla has been married.

Faulkner rightly saw that for the South, the war and its immediate aftermath must be understood as the single point from which progress or movement in this region must be measured. The killing of carpetbaggers will eventually cease, but the problems of men and women, white and Negro, living together in the community will continue. As his only book wholly concerned with the war and Reconstruction, *The Unvanquished* must always be an important source for anyone seeking to understand Faulkner's thinking. With it, he virtually concluded his treatment of the fictional Sartoris family whose resemblances to the real Colonel William Clark Falkner and his descendants are too close to be ignored by students of Yoknapatawpha County. Thus, the Colonel and Bayard depart from Faulkner's books, but in his fiction the strange times in which they lived cannot be forgotten, since they anchor Faulkner's examination of southern history.

Faulkner's First Trilogy:
Sartoris, Sanctuary, and *Requiem for a Nun*

MICHAEL MILLGATE

I want to use the three novels mentioned in my title as the starting point rather than as the exclusive subject matter of this paper, not because a close and comprehensive examination of
those texts, of their genesis and interrelationships, would not
constitute a proper and potentially illuminating contribution to
Faulkner studies, but because it might well prove to demand
book-length treatment and would certainly be beyond the reasonable range and scope of an occasion such as this. In any case,
the questions I want to address are sufficiently and indeed
chiefly prompted by obvious features of the published texts
themselves—questions relating to Faulkner's use of recurrent
characters and situations in these three novels and to the
broader implications that his practice in this instance, or these
instances, may carry for the interrelationship of novels and short
stories within the entire body of his work.

My invocation of the term "trilogy" is partly intended to
shock. When I was asked to speak at this conference I took a
little time out and speculated what an audience in Mississippi
would believe to be current trends, chose what I thought was
the right answer, and invented the most outrageous critical conception I could imagine. More seriously, I think you will readily
allow that there is an obvious continuity between *Flags in the
Dust* and *Sanctuary,* and a no less obvious overlap between
Sanctuary and *Requiem for a Nun.* That there is any substantial

connection between the published *Sartoris* of 1929 and the published *Requiem* of 1951 may not be so clear, but there has also to be fitted into the picture the novel entitled *Requiem for a Nun* which Faulkner projected, and actually started, in 1933.

The chronology is perhaps the first thing to get straight, although as always in Faulkner studies one must try to avoid overconfident pronouncements on the basis of what may be an entirely accidental and unrepresentative survival of documentary evidence. We at any rate know that Faulkner wrote a novel entitled *Flags in the Dust* which in November, 1927, was declined by Liveright, the publisher who had taken his first two novels, *Soldiers' Pay* and *Mosquitoes*. After adventures at which we can do little more than guess, that same novel was eventually accepted by Harcourt, Brace in September, 1928, and published by them in January, 1929, in a shortened form and under the new title of *Sartoris*. I should perhaps note here that because *Sartoris* was the only version of the text published during Faulkner's lifetime, it is the version to which I shall most often refer in this paper—thus conveniently dodging the awkwardness of *Flags/Sartoris*. Since the publication of the Random House edition, of course, that formulation should properly be expanded still further to *Flags/Sartoris/Flags*—or some might prefer *Flags/Sartoris/Dust*. The cutting down of *Flags in the Dust* was done by Faulkner's friend and agent Ben Wasson, although it seems clear from the numerous passages of characteristically Faulknerian prose which appear in *Sartoris* but not in *Flags* that Faulkner had either rewritten parts of the novel before Wasson went to work on it or made additions to the cut-down typescript, or to the galleys, before publication. The typescript sent to the printer seems not to have survived; if it had done so, of course, these and many other uncertainties surrounding the text could almost certainly have been resolved.

At just the time when *Sartoris* was being published, Faulkner began writing the manuscript of *Sanctuary*, which carries the dates January–May, 1929. There is also a typescript bearing essentially the same dates, suggesting that Faulkner (as seems to have been his usual practice) typed up his work as he went along.[1] Between *Flags* and *Sanctuary* Faulkner had of course written *The Sound and the Fury*; by the time he got the galleys of *Sanctuary* he had also written *As I Lay Dying*, and it was his sense of his creative achievement in those other two texts that he subsequently offered as the explanation for the radical rewriting and restructuring of *Sanctuary* in which he engaged before the novel was finally published in February, 1931. Curiously enough, the kind of surgery he performed was closely comparable to what Wasson had done to *Flags*, in that the tendency of the revision in both instances was to reduce the quantity and importance of the material relating to the Benbow family and hence shift the emphasis much more to the other major figure—Bayard Sartoris in *Sartoris*, Temple Drake in the published *Sanctuary*.

These two quite distinct acts of revision have together served to obscure the full intimacy of the connection between the original *Flags in the Dust* text and the original *Sanctuary* text—although "original" is of course a risky term to use in such a context. One must allow for the possibility that all the Benbow material once formed part of a larger pool of Sartoris-related material, comparable to Faulkner's early pool of Snopes material and at some level connected with it. Such an hypothesis allows for the further possibility that *Sanctuary*, although written after *The Sound and the Fury*, had its origins—its conception and perhaps some preliminary sketching out—before that momentous creative event. Faulkner said quite specifically on one oc-

1. The manuscript and typescript are both in the Alderman Library of the University of Virginia. See James B. Meriwether, *The Literary Career of William Faulkner: A Bibliographical Study* (Princeton, N.J., 1961), 66; Michael Millgate, *The Achievement of William Faulkner* (New York, 1966). 113–17; and Gerald Langford, *Faulkner's Revision of "Sanctuary": A Collation of the Unrevised Galleys and the Published Book* (Austin, Tex., 1972). I am especially grateful to Professor Noel Polk for making available to me his transcription of the *Sanctuary* typescript.

casion that he had written *Sanctuary* before *The Sound and the Fury*,[2] and while the context of that remark does not encourage one to think of it as one of Faulkner's most deliberate statements there are other, vaguer references to the same effect.[3] There are certainly reasons to believe that some of the central ideas of the novel—the bizarre rape, for example—were already in Faulkner's mind by the middle 1920s,[4] and the final scene of Temple in the Luxembourg Gardens perhaps bore some relation to a short story written in Paris in 1925.[5] It is, as I say, no more than a hypothesis but it offers a way of accounting for that technical conventionality of *Sanctuary* that is otherwise so surprising in a work written in the immediate aftermath of *The Sound and the Fury*. On the other hand, *The Sound and the Fury* had not yet been accepted at the moment in January, 1929, when Faulkner began work on the one *Sanctuary* manuscript that has actually survived, and he may well have returned to the mode and materials of *Sartoris* in the belief that that was the best available road to commercial success—investing them now with a new and transforming creative exuberance that flowed directly from the experience of writing *The Sound and the Fury*.

It is at all events clear that Faulkner was ready to embark upon another Horace Benbow narrative—for the 1929 version of *Sanctuary* is essentially that—just as soon as he had finished with *The Sound and the Fury* and seen *Sartoris* published. However commercial some of his motives may have been, it appears that they did not include a thrifty desire to use up material recently deleted from *Flags in the Dust*. There are indeed in the *Sanctuary* typescript several direct references back to the world of *Flags/Sartoris*, many of which did not find their way into the

2. James B. Meriwether and Michael Millgate (eds.), *Lion in the Garden: Interviews with William Faulkner 1926–1962* (New York, 1968), 132–33.

3. See, e.g., *ibid.*, 135.

4. Carvel Collins, "A Note on *Sanctuary*," *Harvard Advocate*, CXXXV, November, 1951), 16.

5. Joseph Blotner (ed.), *Selected Letters of William Faulkner* (New York, 1977), 17.

novel as finally published; almost without exception, however, they allude to aspects of that world which had, so to speak, been made public in *Sartoris*. Like any novelist beginning a book that was in some sense a sequel to an earlier one, Faulkner wanted to provide sufficient introductory information to new readers, those who had not read the earlier book, in order that they would be able to approach this text without difficulty or handicap. At the same time he seems to have wanted those who had read *Sartoris* not only to be aware of Horace, Narcissa, and so on as continuing characters but actually to be reminded of specific episodes in which they had been involved.

Early in the *Sanctuary* typescript, for example, we are told that Horace had returned home in the rain one day after Narcissa's marriage to Bayard and found her waiting for him:

> "Narcy," he said, "has that surly blackguard—?"
> "You fool! You fool! You haven't even an umbrella!" she said.[6]

This is obviously a condensation of a slightly longer scene at the end of the second chapter of part 4 of *Sartoris*, where Horace speaks precisely the words I have quoted but Narcissa calls him "idiot" twice instead of "fool" and complains that he has forgotten his raincoat instead of his umbrella.[7] It is an early instance of that phenomenon which recurs again and again in the later works: Faulkner, making a deliberate retrospective allusion, either does not trouble to ensure its verbal accuracy or consciously chooses to adapt it, in language and content, to his current purposes. So Miss Quentin climbs down a pear tree in *The Sound and the Fury* and down a rainpipe in the "Compson Appendix." Faulkner of course defended such "inconsistencies" by declaring, in the prefatory note to *The Mansion*, that he learned

6. *Sanctuary* typescript, f.20; textually identical with the unrevised galleys (Langford, *Faulkner's Revision*, 45).
7. William Faulkner, *Sartoris* (New York, 1929), 302–3.

to know his characters better over the course of the years, and the practice was certainly in line with his profound sense, as man and artist, that life was motion, and motion life, that he must perpetually be posing and meeting new challenges rather than brooding upon the failures (as he always considered them) of the past.

In the particular instance of *Sanctuary* it is conceivable that Faulkner, distressed at the abandonment of the original conception of *Flags in the Dust* and especially at the deletion of so much Benbow family material, was actively concerned to make good some of the deficiencies of the published *Sartoris* by spelling out certain aspects of Horace's relationships with Narcissa and with Belle Mitchell far more directly than had been done in *Sartoris*, or indeed in the uncut *Flags*. At one point in the *Sanctuary* typescript, for example, Horace recalls Belle's telling him that he was in love with his sister and adding: "What do the books call it? What sort of complex?" Horace characteristically dodges the question by means of a feeble joke— "'Not complex,' he said. 'Do you think that any relation with her could be complex?'"[8]—but it is nevertheless possible to read the exchange not just as a summing-up for the reader's benefit ("New readers begin here"), nor as a simple reminder of the earlier book, but actually as a commentary upon it, a retrospective explanation and clarification not entirely dissimilar to that "case-study" of Popeye which Faulkner inserted into the final version of *Sanctuary* itself.

But *Sanctuary* also comments, enlarges, depends upon *Sartoris* in a broader and deeper sense. If it did not it would be hard to see why Faulkner should have chosen to link the two novels as closely and as obviously as he did. One of the central oppositions in *Sartoris* is between the American Civil War and World War I, between a specific time past and a no less precisely

8. *Sanctuary* typescript, f. 18; identical with unrevised galleys (Langford, *Faulkner's Revision*, 43).

dated time present, the latter extending from the spring of 1919 to the early summer of 1920. In *Sanctuary*, insofar as it focuses on Horace (and let me repeat again that the 1929 version contained far more Benbow material than the version with which you are all familiar)—in *Sanctuary* there is a corresponding tension between past and present, in which the present is identical with the date of composition of the novel, the immediate here and now, and the past with the nearer of those two perspectives in *Sartoris*, the postwar period when Bayard Sartoris came home and married Narcissa and died and when Horace left Jefferson to go and live at Kinston in the Delta with Belle Mitchell.

Since the vision of existence that emerges from *Sanctuary* is much darker than the one that emerges from *Sartoris* it is possible to argue that Faulkner is offering in the later novel a statement about the deterioration of the world of Yoknapatawpha—and by implication of the actual world—during the period of the 1920s. But it might be equally feasible to argue that Faulkner, writing in 1929, was simply finding in the contemporary scene—specifically, in bootlegging and its connection with violence and organized crime—a convenient point of departure for a presentation of what might be called the other side of the world of *Sartoris*, a deliberate undercutting of the middle-class and agrarian values which the earlier novel had appeared to offer as positives. I find my warrant for invoking such terms in a passage in the *Sanctuary* typescript in which Horace, overjoyed that Temple's disappearance from Miss Reba's has relieved him of the distressing responsibility of calling her as a witness, "realised again that furious homogeneity of the middle classes when opposed to the proletariat from which it so recently sprung and by which it is so often threatened."[9] Faulkner did not choose to expose Horace's class attitudes so directly in the novel as published, but it seems clear that he intended the psychological and

9. *Sanctuary* typescript, f. 321; identical with unrevised galleys (Langford, *Faulkner's Revision*, 113), except that the latter read "realized" for "realised."

moral breakdown of Bayard Sartoris to find its necessary counterpart not just in the poor white Byron Snopes but in such representative middle-class figures as the well-fed and well-educated lawyer Horace Benbow and the pampered coed Temple Drake. (Why Horace and Temple should be given the surnames of British admirals I do not know; Horace, indeed, also has the first name of an even more famous admiral, Nelson, and there was an earlier British admiral called Sartorius. There is also, of course, Admiral Dewey Snopes. Perhaps Faulkner took private pleasure in thinking of the spring in the opening scene of *Sanctuary* as a miniature sea across which Admiral Horace Nelson Benbow found himself rudely confronted by Popeye the Sailor.)

Some of the impetus towards the composition of *Sanctuary* may again have derived from Faulkner's dissatisfaction with *Sartoris*, from which Horace emerges with rather more credit, or with less emphasized discredit, than he does from *Flags*. But the main thrust is towards a deliberate revaluation and even inversion of the entire world of *Sartoris*, showing the Sartorises and Benbows and Drakes in their shabby and sometimes squalid relationships with each other, with people less fortunately born than themselves, and with the tentacular forces of corruption and violence. Horace, looking for a hill to lie on, might perhaps have been expected to find his way to the MacCallums. Instead he arrives at the old Frenchman Place and finds there a grotesque parody not just of the family farm but of the family itself: all the units necessary to a family are present, but all are in some way physically or socially maimed.[10] (I recognize that there are, as Albert Devlin has pointed out,[11] some odd things about the MacCallums too.) What the reader learns to recognize is that

10. This point is fully explored in Judith Bryant Wittenberg, *Faulkner: The Transfiguration of Biography* (Lincoln, Nebraska, 1979), 94–95. Arthur F. Kinney, in *Faulkner's Narrative Poetics: Style As Vision* (Amherst, Mass., 1978), 192, speaks of Popeye as seeking a family at the old Frenchman Place.

11. Albert Devlin, "*Sartoris*: Rereading the MacCallum Episode," *Twentieth Century Literature*, XVII (1971), 83–90.

however grotesque the ad hoc family at the old Frenchman Place may be—however offensive to the moral susceptibilities of the ladies of Jefferson—it nevertheless displays, through the person of Ruby Lamar, more vitality, more love, and certainly more warmth than anything Horace and Narcissa are capable of generating. Narcissa, like Belle Mitchell, emerges badly damaged from the comparison with Ruby and Miss Reba which is enforced throughout *Sanctuary* (e.g., in the link between the "rose colored shade" in Belle's bedroom and the "fluted shade of rose-colored paper" in Temple's room at Miss Reba's brothel),[12] and the later novel thus complements the earlier by making explicit, or at any rate evident, what had formerly only been hinted at. Taken together, the two novels present an essentially unitary view of a world increasingly subject to social corruption and moral decay in which the young men are characteristically bent on self-destruction and the young women are technically or, what is worse, effectively whores—although it is true that a judgment of Narcissa on such terms must be partly dependent upon the short story "There Was a Queen," published after *Sanctuary* but perhaps anticipated in the allusion to "the dead tranquil queens in stained marble"[13] in the novel's final paragraph, and possibly intended at one time to be incorporated into the body of the text as an ironic parallel to Ruby's giving herself to Goodwin's lawyer and similarly offering herself to Horace.

The events of "There Was a Queen" take place three years after those of *Sanctuary*; the events of the published *Requiem for a Nun* are placed eight years after those of *Sanctuary*. I'd like to be able to make the point that this is roughly the same chronological gap as occurs between *Sartoris* and *Sanctuary*, but Faulkner seems at times to have thought of the interval as

---

12. William Faulkner, *Sanctuary* (New York, 1931), 358, 185.

13. *Ibid*., 380, The original title of the story, however, appears to have been "Through the Window": see James B. Meriwether, "The Short Fiction of William Faulkner: A Bibliography," *Proof*, I (1971), 309.

six rather than eight years[14] and there is, in any case, no doubt
that he intended the time present of *Requiem* to be absolutely
contemporary and hence something like twenty-two actual years
after the 1929 dating of *Sanctuary*. (By putting the Goodwin
trial six years before 1951 Faulkner would have just managed to
miss World War II, and that is conceivably what he originally
had in mind.) I think I have already made it clear that I do not
wish to claim too much for the degree of integration of *Requiem*
into an overall trilogy structure. Even so, it does seem to me
reasonable to posit some kind of special relationship between
two texts, *Requiem* and *Sartoris*, which are both intimately related to a third text, in this instance *Sanctuary*.

Relevant here are the three surviving manuscript pages of
the novel called *Requiem for a Nun* which Faulkner began in
1933[15] and which, he told Hal Smith, would center on a black
woman and be "a little on the esoteric side, like AS I LAY
DYING."[16] The reference to *As I Lay Dying* suggests that Faulkner expected the work to be rendered inaccessible to the unini-
tiated by some kind of technical difficulty; the three manuscript
pages, which actually constitute two separate openings, are certainly written in a fairly dense prose, but it does not look as
though there were to be any particularly spectacular manipula-
tions of point of view. One of the openings consists of a description of the Jefferson jail, a major setting both in *Sanctuary* and
in the 1951 *Requiem*; the other opening is set in Gavin Stevens's
office, where Stevens is interviewing a youngish black man and
his wife about an attempt to cut the wife's throat which had apparently been made by another black woman, named Eunice,
the previous day. There is no obvious narrative link with the

14. See, for example, the correction to p. 208 of the *Requiem* page-proofs at the
University of Virginia and the surviving "six years" on p. 88 of the published text.
15. See Noel Polk, "The Textual History of Faulkner's *Requiem for a Nun*," *Proof*,
IV (1975), 113. I am grateful to Professor Polk for making available to me his transcription of these pages.
16. Blotner (ed.), *Selected Letters*, 75.

world of *Sartoris* and *Sanctuary*—it is probably not relevant that Eunice is the name of the Benbows' black cook. On the other hand, the jail, a brief port of call for young Bayard in *Sartoris*, had already become an important physical and symbolic location in *Sanctuary* and, what is even more to the point, there is ample evidence in other texts to suggest that Horace Benbow gradually "became" Gavin Stevens in Faulkner's imagination, passing on many of his personal characteristics and even some of his personal history—including his participation in the trial of Lee Goodwin. As late as the 1951 *Requiem* there is at least one instance of Gavin's voicing some thoughts about Popeye which were once Horace's, and which were actually omitted from *Sanctuary* as published.[17] One can almost watch the transition— or transmigration—taking place during the revision of *Sanctuary*, as Faulkner strips Horace of most of his self-conscious aestheticism and gives far more emphasis to his well-meaning but ineffectual idealism. By the time the three *Requiem* pages were written in December, 1933 (all on the same day, incidentally), Stevens had already been created in print—first in "Smoke," published in *Harper's Monthly* for April, 1932, and then in *Light in August*, published in October, 1932—and Faulkner's invariable choice of creative evolution over retrospective consistency would have precluded the revival of a character he had finished and done with.

The projected subject matter, plot, and themes of that 1933 *Requiem* can scarcely even be guessed at. Thrashing around for clues one thinks of the Nancy of "That Evening Sun" and of the way the earlier version of *Sanctuary* had opened with the black murderer, the best baritone in north Mississippi, singing from the jail window—but nothing seems quite to fit. Given the presence of Gavin Stevens, however, and the fact that he speaks to the black couple as though they were children, there seems to

17. *Sanctuary* typescript, f. 28 (identical with Langford, *Faulkner's Revision*, 51); Faulkner, *Requiem for a Nun* (New York, 1951), 146.

be the potential for a situation akin to that in *Intruder in the Dust* or in the final chapter of *Go Down, Moses*. If, despite the shift from Benbow to Stevens, the concerns of *Sartoris* and *Sanctuary* were somehow to have been sustained, it could conceivably have been in terms of the trial of a black woman for whom the ineffectual idealist—Stevens standing in for Benbow and race now reinforcing class—would feel the reverse of that instinctive identification he had once felt with Temple Drake. Which is perhaps only to say that *Light in August* and *Intruder in the Dust* might well be reckoned alternative candidates for the third spot in the shadowy trilogy I have been attempting to conjure up.

Perhaps I shall have to settle for some such term as "abortive trilogy" to describe the relationship between *Sartoris*, *Sanctuary*, and *Requiem*. There are cross-references between them—for example, the first of the prose prologues of *Requiem* returns to that early history of Jefferson which had received so much attention in *Flags/Sartoris* and even to the figure of Colonel John Sartoris himself—and it would seem feasible to think of the three novels as corresponding to that "trinity of conscience"[18] Faulkner perceived in *Moby-Dick* and sought to project in *A Fable*. Young Bayard, Horace, and Gavin would thus fall respectively into the three moral categories of knowing nothing, knowing but not caring (or not caring enough), and knowing and caring. If that suggests a rather positive evaluation of Gavin it is necessary to remember that Faulkner's moral activists, including the battalion runner in *A Fable* itself, are almost always precipitators of disaster. But there is no evidence that Faulkner was thinking in such terms as early as *Sartoris* or *Sanctuary*, though he had certainly read *Moby-Dick* by then, and one could not in any case argue that the series is closed by the 1951 *Requiem* either as specifically or as elegantly as the Snopes trilogy is con-

18. Meriwether and Millgate (eds.), *Lion in the Garden*, 247.

101

cluded by *The Mansion*, which not only alternates essentially *Hamlet* material with essentially *Town* material but also shifts technically between the points of view used in the two earlier novels.

There is, of course, a profound difference between a planned trilogy, as I take "Snopes" essentially to be, and the kind of gradually evolved or (less politely) ad hoc trilogy into which I have tried to fit *Sartoris*, *Sanctuary*, and *Requiem*, but I do not think we should necessarily be deterred from perceiving—or projecting—relationships between works in the Faulkner canon simply because the author himself invoked the term "trilogy" on only the one occasion. Indeed, I think we are at a point at which we can properly ask whether or not there are other paired novels, trilogies, abortive trilogies, or significant groupings of otherwise discrete texts anywhere else among Faulkner's works. And, if so, how are we to read such interconnected fictions? Does Faulkner allow himself to assume that the reader of novel B will already have read novel A, or quite the reverse? Does he reward the reader who is extensively familiar with his work over and above the reader who is not?

Once such questions are asked, it is immediately clear that there are, at any rate, a number of novels and stories which do stand in a particularly close or suggestive relationship to each other. Carvel Collins taught us many years ago to think in terms of a "pairing" of *The Sound and the Fury* and *As I Lay Dying*,[19] and I have myself suggested that they might be linked with *Absalom, Absalom!* as a kind of trilogy on the multivalence of truth.[20] The stories in *Knight's Gambit*, to choose a very different example, somehow demand to be linked, through Gavin Stevens, to that more extended "detective" fiction *Intruder in the Dust*—which itself seems clearly to constitute some sort of

---

19. Carvel Collins, "The Pairing of *The Sound and the Fury* and *As I Lay Dying*," *Princeton University Library Chronicle*, XVIII (1957), 114–23.
20. Millgate, *Achievement of William Faulkner*, 106.

extension and commentary upon the final chapter of *Go Down, Moses*. *Big Woods*, simply by existing as a work in the Faulkner canon, also offers some kind of implicit comment upon *Go Down, Moses* as a whole, and there is perhaps something yet to be better understood about the relationship between *Absalom* and *Pylon*, the novel which Faulkner wrote when he ran into difficulties with the more ambitious undertaking. There are arguably elements common to *Pylon* and to Faulkner's other New Orleans novels, *Mosquitoes* and *The Wild Palms* (they all deal, for example, with varieties of permanent or temporary deracination), and there can be no doubt that some of the finest short stories are narrative or emotional spin-offs from the creative surges which generated major novels—that "Barn Burning" is intimately related to *The Hamlet* (of which it once formed the opening chapter), "That Evening Sun" to *The Sound and the Fury*, and perhaps "Dry September" to *Light in August*.

Clearly, Faulkner's texts often fall into very special patterns of relationship that simply cannot be accommodated by such conventional terms as trilogy, tetralogy, and so on. The many appearances of Gavin Stevens present just such a problem—especially if he is given retroactive credit for the activities of his secret sharer Horace Benbow—and in making out my case for a *Sartoris, Sanctuary, Requiem* trilogy I conveniently left out of account not only *The Unvanquished*, which fills in so much of the early background to *Sartoris*, but also *The Reivers*, which returns to the world of Miss Reba's even more directly than does *Requiem* itself. Interestingly enough, it is set at a point in time roughly a decade earlier than the events of *Sartoris*, so that one can, if one wishes, set up *The Reivers, Sartoris, Sanctuary*, and *Requiem* as a more or less regularly spaced chronicle of the Jefferson middle classes—with *The Unvanquished* as a rather more distant historical complement. Or perhaps the central sequence runs through *The Reivers, Sanctuary, Requiem*—Faulkner's Memphis or cathouse trilogy, richly commented upon by the semifictional "Mississippi" essay and by the fact that Faulkner, who once said that the best job ever offered him was that of landlord of a brothel,[21] evidently identified with Mr. Binford.

Even the Snopes trilogy itself is by no means entirely self-contained: I suspect that it is partly because we have already formed such a favorable impression of Charles Mallison from *Intruder in the Dust* that we are prepared to be more patient with him in *The Town* and *The Mansion* than his rather smart-alecky language and attitudes might otherwise permit. Similarly—though I am conscious of venturing into dangerous waters here—there seems little doubt that we carry over into *Absalom, Absalom!* a good deal of what we have learned of Quentin and of Mr. Compson from our reading of *The Sound and the Fury*, although I think it extravagant to argue, as has recently been done,[22] that *Absalom* is scarcely comprehensible to those who are not in possession of such prior knowledge. I'm not at all sure, indeed, that the temptation to import the "incest-motif" from *The Sound and the Fury* isn't another of the multiple false leads in *Absalom*, another of the ways in which Faulkner prevents us from seeing what ought to have been obvious or any rate guessable enough from the start. What Quentin and Shreve imagine Sutpen saying to Henry—"So it's the miscegenation, not the incest, which you can't bear"[23]—may be no less applicable to the Quentin of *Absalom, Absalom!*, and there seems no compelling reason to consider the novel as anything other than a self-sufficient text, although one that is left deliberately open to different readings by different readers who bring different qualifications to it—above all, perhaps, differing degrees of exposure to other Faulknerian texts.

21. Meriwether and Millgate (eds.), *Lion in the Garden*, 239.
22. Estella Schoenberg, *Old Tales and Talking: Quentin Compson in William Faulkner's "Absalom, Absalom!" and Related Works* (Jackson, Miss., 1977), 4–5; she may well be right, however, to suggest that *The Sound and the Fury* and *Absalom, Absalom!* together constitute "a multi-novel or dual-novel" (p. 120).
23. William Faulkner, *Absalom, Absalom!* (New York, 1936), 356.

Whether it is useful, or critically permissible, to work backwards in Faulkner's career is another question. I have never, for example, found it very illuminating to think of *Absalom* as fitted into the temporal framework of *The Sound and the Fury*, to try to feed into Quentin's act of suicide the supplemental motivation that might be reckoned to flow from his recent exposure to the final stages of the Sutpen tragedy. Given that he wanted to use Quentin in *Absalom*, Faulkner in order to avoid absurdity had to place the Harvard portions within Quentin's lifetime as already established by *The Sound and the Fury*, but the ghost of *Absalom* seems simply not to be there in *The Sound and the Fury*, even if the earlier novel cannot help but be a shadowy presence on the sidelines of the later.

My argument has led me towards some particular answers to the questions I raised earlier, but it now seems necessary to attempt a few general propositions. It seems to me, then, that each Faulkner text must be considered a unique, independent, and self-sufficient work of art, not only capable of being read and contemplated in isolation but actually demanding such treatment. Even in his one acknowledged trilogy Faulkner is at pains to reintroduce his characters and reevoke the central situations, often in terms that subtly modify them to suit the purposes of that particular text: hence the different accounts of Mink's murder of Houston and his subsequent expectation of assistance from Flem.

The use of recurrent characters and of the whole Yoknapatawphan apparatus nevertheless encourages the reader to bring to bear at some point and in some fashion—these are matters I frankly find very elusive of definition—the experience gained from reading other Faulkner works. At one level, of course, the process is not unlike that involved in the recognition of any allusion being made from one work to another, except that in Faulkner the experience to be gained from other texts comprises not only a familiarity with particular characters and locations

105

(the old Frenchman Place, after all, is as vital a linking device as any of Faulkner's human figures) but also an awareness of how a Faulkner text is to be approached, engaged, and ultimately possessed—grappled, boarded, and seized I had almost said, remembering those curious nautical allusions in *Sanctuary*. Faulkner, that is to say, gradually teaches his audience how to read him, and while such an assertion could no doubt be made of many innovative novelists, in Faulkner's case the instructional process is unusually deliberate and direct, repeatedly drawing our attention to those other works which will in some way illuminate the thematic or technical complexities of the text with which we are immediately concerned. Perhaps I need scarcely add that this is also an essential element in the process by which the solidity and continuity of Yoknapatawpha County is constantly being enforced.

Despite the power of the Yoknapatawphan idea and the limitations implicit in the fixed chronological sequence of Faulkner's career, there is doubtless a sense in which the Faulknerian fictions can be collectively viewed in terms of infinitely variable patterns of interrelationships, as susceptible to kaleidoscopic shifts of perspective untrammelled by considerations of chronology, undeterred by the pedantries of biographers and textual scholars. As a simple literary historian I find it difficult to think in such terms, to resist the pull of the chronological, of the discoverable and demonstrable structure of the total career. And yet there is no doubt, as I argued in my earlier lecture, that Faulkner did from an early stage project large-scale creative undertakings on into the future, that his imagination was capable of ranging forward in both a general and a detailed fashion over works he had not yet begun to write. To argue, in short, that Yoknapatawpha was a vast imaginative conception which Faulkner only fragmentarily realized on paper is in effect to acknowledge the possibility that a given text may contain deliberate references forward in addition to the kind of retrospective references discussed earlier in this paper. *The Unvanquished* is a striking case in point. Retrospectively, it expands upon and modifies the Civil War narratives earlier incorporated into *Flags/Sartoris*, provides a radically new perspective upon the treatment in *Light in August* of the deaths of the two abolitionists, Miss Burden's father and brother, and offers an extraordinarily concise and cogent summary of the character of Thomas Sutpen as revealed in *Absalom*, the immediately preceding novel. But it can also be said that *The Unvanquished* creates prospectively, in advance of their far more significant roles in *Go Down, Moses*, the figures of Uncles Buck and Buddy McCaslin. Conceivably, too, there are instances of what might be called negative anticipation in particular Faulkner texts: as the limited characterization of Eula Varner in *The Hamlet* is subsequently seen to have depended upon Faulkner's intentions for *The Town*, so certain aspects of Narcissa's character were perhaps held back in *Sartoris* for subsequent release in *Sanctuary* and "There Was a Queen"— so the obviously incomplete presentation of the trial scene in *Sanctuary* may have been related to an expectation on Faulkner's part that he would return to it again in a later novel.

We are of course familiar with the notion, most famously articulated by T. S. Eliot, that each new work of art modifies all of its predecessors. We can probably also agree that there is a sense in which each individual work of any writer modifies, conditions our response to, every other work by that same writer. Our reading of *Typee* is obviously affected by our awareness of Melville as the author of *Moby-Dick*; even our reading of *Moby-Dick* at some level takes into account the existence of *Typee*. But Faulkner's deliberate use of recurrent characters, locations, and situations seems a way of insisting that in reading any one of his novels we take consciously into account, first, a set of specifically linked novels and stories and, secondly, virtually the entire range of his published work. The public face, so to speak, of this design is the pseudogeographical system that Faulkner called

Yoknapatawpha County, and yet the kind of interaction between separate texts to which I am now referring goes beyond the limits of what Yoknapatawpha can reasonably be held to represent. What simultaneously separates and unites such novels as *The Unvanquished* and *Sartoris*, or *Sanctuary* and *The Reivers*, or indeed *The Sound and the Fury* and *Absalom, Absalom!*, is something analogous to what occurs *within* such novels as *The Sound and the Fury* and *Absalom, Absalom!* and *Go Down, Moses*—a shift of perspective, a change in narrative point of view, the presentation of a different facet of human experience, which obliges us to modify our initial assumptions about a character, a situation, or a set of attitudes and beliefs.

Faulkner seems characteristically to have found his resolutions not precisely in irresolution but in the recognition of alternatives, of opposing truths, rather in the manner of that Andersonian Book of the Grotesque, the opening section of *Winesburg, Ohio*, which was so important to his early self-realization as an artist. In my previous paper I spoke of Faulkner's fiction as constituting "a Doomsday Book" of the regional imagination, "a vast compendium of narrated tales and lives, of legends and speaking fables." An alternative way of contemplating his work as a whole—indeed, of seeing all the texts on a single plane, in time as well as in space—might be to think of each novel, and even each story, as a separate chapter in a Faulknerian Book of the Grotesque, an independent fable of human experience ("the old verities and truths of the heart")[24] which will nonetheless reveal its full meaning and implications only when read in the context of all the others. In a curious way *The Wild Palms*, which has so often seemed to lie outside the Faulknerian mainstream, has a special claim to be considered the paradigmatic Faulknerian text, the one which most absolutely dramatizes and depends upon that juxtaposition of discontinuous, contradictory, and yet

24. James B. Meriwether (ed.), *William Faulkner: Essays, Speeches and Public Letters* (New York, 1965), 120.

in some sense complementary narratives which is recognizable as the fundamental principle running through the whole of Faulkner's infinitely rich and various life's work. *Sartoris, Sanctuary*, and *Requiem for a Nun* may not make much of a trilogy, but they can certainly be spoken of—like the two narratives of *The Wild Palms*, like the chapters of *Go Down, Moses*, like *The Sound and the Fury* and *Absalom, Absalom!*, like the entire Faulknerian corpus—as contrapuntal in integration.[25]

25. Malcolm Cowley, *The Faulkner-Cowley File: Letters and Memories, 1944–1962* (New York, 1966), 116.

Faulkner and Respectability

NOEL POLK

We are all aware of the importance of the theme of respectability in Faulkner's work. At very nearly every turn his characters concern themselves in one way or another with how they or their actions are going to be perceived by someone else; it is difficult to overemphasize how important to Faulkner's world the eyes and the ears of the Jefferson community actually are.[1] We may think with a tolerant smile of the country women who want to get out of the wagon and walk into town so people will think they live in Jefferson; or with a more serious brow of Narcissa Benbow's fear that someone will find out Byron Snopes has written amorous letters to her, or that public opinion of Horace's dealings with Lee and Ruby Goodwin is somehow going to besmirch her own good name.

Faulkner went on record time and time again as being devoutly opposed to the kind of anesthetizing conformity that has characterized American urban and suburban life in the twentieth century, because conformity of any kind placed serious limitations on the free human spirit. In *Flags in the Dust*, for example, he describes Jefferson's "shady streets" as being like "green tunnels along which tight lives accomplished their peace-

---

1. See, for example, Cleanth Brooks's discussion of *The Town* and of *Light in August* in *William Faulkner: The Yoknapatawpha Country* (New Haven: Yale University Press, 1963).

ful tragedies,"[2] and later in the same novel he refers to Jefferson's "new tight little houses with minimum of lawn" (*Flags*, 148). In *Requiem for a Nun* those same houses are "new minute glass-walled houses set as neat and orderly and antiseptic as cribs in a nursery ward, in new subdivisions named Fairfield or Longwood or Halcyon Acres which had once been the lawn or back yard or kitchen garden of the old residences."[3] Clearly, these houses do little to enhance the quality or even the quantity of life.

Yet Faulkner also made clear his conviction that human values are both generated by and supported by the stability and the security that social institutions offer. There is in this not so much a contradiction as there are simply two opposite ends of one of Faulkner's thematic spectrums, simplified for the purpose of nonfictional discussion. His fictional treatments of these themes are far more complex.

My starting point, then, is to suggest that in Faulkner's created world, as in our real one, respectability is not necessarily a bad thing. That's not quite the same thing as saying that it's always a good thing, however. We have all enjoyed seeing Oxford's gorgeous old antebellum and Victorian homes, all different from each other and sitting on huge shaded lots and bearing the individualized names of their builders or names like Rowan Oak, Ammadelle, Fiddler's Folly, or Shadow Lawn. But also in Oxford, as in our own home towns, are the mass-produced houses of the modern housing developments, each sitting on its treeless postage stamp of lawn, and each one looking just like its neighbor. These quintessential symbols of modern mass culture are a considerable step down from houses like Rowan Oak. But they are at the same time a considerable step up from ghetto slums and from the ramshackle dogtrot and shotgun houses so many

2. William Faulkner, *Flags in the Dust* (New York: Random House, 1973), 107–108.
3. William Faulkner, *Requiem for a Nun* (New York: Random House, 1951), 249.

people have lived in, and they are affordable precisely because they are mass-produced and virtually identical. Whether these housing developments are good or bad for the spirit, then, depends largely on which direction you are looking at them from. At one point in *Intruder in the Dust* Chick Mallison takes a sneering look at one house in Jefferson which he describes as "a small neat shoebox of a house built last year between two other houses already close enough together to hear one another's toilets flush." His uncle Gavin tries to make him understand how anybody could live in such a crowded neighborhood: "When you were born and raised and lived all your life where you cant hear anything but owls at night and roosters at dawn . . . you like to live where you can hear and smell people on either side of you every time they flush a drain or open a can of salmon or of soup."[4]

Respectability, then, is a condition which works both for us and against us. The "condition" embodies a nebulous and fairly fluid set of rules governing social intercourse, which vary from town to town and even from neighborhood to neighborhood. Insofar as respectability works to render people mindless, unreflective, and submissive, insofar as it levels us, forces us to accept mediocrity as both our best and our due, it is of course pernicious. Insofar as it creates a stable, working framework within which we can live our lives, it is not just a good thing, but a necessary.

At its most obvious and least harmful level, respectability has to do simply with appearances. At its most pernicious it takes the form of repression—most frequently it is sexual repression, but any form of aberrant behavior can find itself proscribed. The obsessively "respectable" person tries to repress in others what he is himself most afraid of, what he has worked so hard to repress in himself, and so the repression is usually only partially

4. William Faulkner, *Intruder in the Dust* (New York: Random House, 1949), 47.

successful. Over and over again there lurks in the bosoms of respectable people a combination of sympathy for and fear and envy of those whose lives are not as uneventful as their own. You'll remember the prissy, respectable little old ladies in "Dry September" who cluster around Miss Minnie Cooper after she has claimed that she has been raped. Their sexual excitement runs high as they talk, as does Miss Minnie's:

As she dressed for supper on that Saturday evening, her own flesh felt like fever. Her hands trembled among the hooks and eyes, and her eyes had a feverish look, and her hair swirled crisp and crackling under the comb. While she was still dressing the friends called for her and sat while she donned her sheerest underthings and stockings and a new voile dress. "Do you feel strong enough to go out?" they said, their eyes bright too, with a dark glitter. "When you have had time to get over the shock, you must tell us what happened. What he said and did; everything."[5]

Clearly their interest in Miss Minnie's "rape" is a combination of fear and envy, and they hope somehow for some release—vicarious, of course—of their own frustrated sexual energies, which they have kept so neatly hidden under their veils of respectability.

A more dramatic example of the same thing occurs in *Light in August*, where the imagination of the Jefferson townfolks exercises itself in a sexual release, almost an orgy, at the burning house of Joanna Burden. The spectacular murder-immolation and supposed (hoped) rape of Miss Burden supplies them with what Faulkner calls an "emotional barbecue, a Roman holiday." The women come "in bright and sometimes hurried garments, with secret and passionate and glittering looks and with secret frustrated breasts . . . to print with a myriad small hard heels to the constant murmur *Who did it? Who did it?* periods such as

5. William Faulkner, "Dry September," in *These 13* (New York: Jonathan Cape and Harrison Smith, 1931), 276.

perhaps *Is he still free? Ah. Is he? Is he?*[6] They want and need the peace and security that their normal lives give them, and would not for anything live out by themselves away from town, the way Joanna Burden has. But they also long for the sexual and emotional excitement provided by scenes such as this, and like Temple Drake and so many of Faulkner's characters, they are both attracted to and repelled by the prospect of violence. An act of violence, of which they are, in the eyes of the world, unwilling and helpless victims, or in which they participate vicariously and sympathetically, is their only means of satisfying both their deepest emotional and physical needs and their sense of social and moral right, and thereby of absolving themselves in advance of any guilt that might accompany voluntary and deliberate sexual fulfillment or defiance of the community.

I would like to address the theme of respectability by looking at two of Faulkner's works, one relatively early, one late—the short story "Uncle Willy," published in 1935, and *The Town*, published in 1957—in order to suggest some of the changes that Faulkner's own attitudes toward respectability may have undergone over the years. I'm not unaware of the theme's importance in such works as *Sanctuary* and *Light in August*, but the treatment of the community in those novels seems to me in some ways much less complex than its treatment in "Uncle Willy."

"Uncle Willy" is one of Faulkner's most Andersonesque stories. It is worth our attention here, for the peculiar terms in which the little boy tells his story help to illustrate the ways in which the claims of the community and those of the individual continually rasp against each other. As the child narrator tells it, "Uncle Willy" is a story very much like Eudora Welty's "Lily Daw and the Three Ladies," in which the forces for "good" in the community—three busybodies—team up against the slightly feebleminded Lily Daw in order to save her from her own sexual

6. William Faulkner, *Light in August* (New York: Harrison Smith and Robert Haas, 1932), 273.

self. "Lily Daw" is a comic story in which Lily finally beats the three ladies. "Uncle Willy" is quite the opposite; although some of it is quite funny indeed, there are no clear-cut victories.

In the eyes of the narrator, Uncle Willy Christian (and the irony of his name is not lost on the reader) is a model human being and a hero:

> . . . he was the finest man I ever knew, because he had had fun all his life in spite of what they had tried to do to him or with him, and I hoped that maybe if I could stay with him a while I could learn how to, so I could still have fun too when I had to get old. . . . I knew . . . that, no matter what might happen to him, he wouldn't ever die and I thought that if I could just learn to live like he lived, no matter what might happen to me I wouldn't ever die either.[7]

The narrator draws the battle lines clearly: Uncle Willy's free spirit against his chief nemesis Mrs. Merridew, and "all the old terrified and timid clinging to dull and rule-ridden breathing which Jefferson was to him" (CS, 239). Mrs. Merridew is particularly self-righteous and shrewish and unattractive, and she naturally makes us cheer for Uncle Willy, whom we already like because the narrator likes him so much.

But Faulkner doesn't leave it at that; he plays havoc with our sympathies in this story, because Uncle Willy is also a dope addict who feeds his habit in his own drug store. That in itself would not be so bad, if you believe that people ought to have the right to destroy themselves if they want to. The problem is that Uncle Willy is open with his addiction, even to the point of allowing the narrator and the other children to watch him give himself his daily "fix": "And we would eat the ice cream and then we would all go behind the prescription case and watch Uncle Willy light the little alcohol stove and fill the needle and roll his sleeve up over the little blue myriad punctures starting at his

---

7. William Faulkner, "Uncle Willy," in *Collected Stories* (New York: Random House, 1950), 239, 242.

elbow and going right on up into his shirt" (CS, 226). We realize, but the narrator obviously does not, that this kind of influence on those youngsters simply cannot be tolerated by a community with any concern whatsoever for its children.

The story, then, concerns Uncle Willy's various flights from Mrs. Merridew and her minions. They make him quit dope. In a typically involved Faulknerian sequence of events, Mrs. Merridew and others decide Uncle Willy should go "cold turkey." They whisk him away from his drug store and his needle, lock him in his own house, and take turns standing guard. Uncle Willy escapes three days later when Mrs. Merridew at last falls asleep; he comes straight to the drug store, where the children are waiting for him. He is shaking so badly that they have to help him light the stove and fill the needle for his long overdue fix. When Mrs. Merridew and her posse—the marshal and Reverend Shulz and three more ladies—finally catch him, he grabs him "by the back of the neck and [shakes] him and [says to him in a kind of whisper], 'You little wretch! You little wretch! Slip off from *me*, will you?'" (CS, 230). They take him back to his home and hold him in bed. The boys hear him through the window, a defeated man: "Wait," he pleads with them. "Wait! I will ask it one more time. Won't you please quit? Won't you please go away? Won't you please go to hell and just let me come at my own gait?" Mrs. Merridew quashes any hope of that: "No, Mr. Christian," she says. "We are doing this to save you." The rest of the passage suggests how completely the narrator feels that Uncle Willy is being immolated on the altar of respectability:

> For a minute we didn't hear anything. Then we heard Uncle Willy lay back in the bed, kind of flop back.
> "All right," he said. "All right."
> It was like one of those sheep they would sacrifice back in the Bible. It was like it had climbed up onto the altar itself and flopped onto its back with its throat held up and said: "All right. Come on and

get it over with. Cut my damn throat and go away and let me lay quiet in the fire." (*CS*, 231)

But this is only a skirmish, not the entire war. Uncle Willy is what the narrator calls "sick for a long time" in Memphis, obviously undergoing the cure. He comes home finally, a man apparently broken, "his skin the color of tallow and weighing about ninety pounds now and with his eyes like broken eggs still but dead eggs, eggs that had been broken so long now that they didn't even smell dead any more—until you looked at them and saw that they were anything in the world except dead" (*CS*, 233). After relearning the boys' names, Uncle Willy quite selfishly involves them in a series of unsavory activities: they help him convert from the religion of dope to the religion of whiskey. The boys help him steal three gallons of alcohol. Then he gets the narrator to write a letter to his sister, lying about Uncle Willy's health and conning her into buying Uncle Willy an automobile. He uses the car to make regular trips to the bootleggers in the area and weekly trips to Memphis. He brings back from one of these trips to Memphis a wife, whose sole purpose is to outrage Jefferson, to demonstrate his contempt for its values, and, not least, to irritate Mrs. Merridew: "a woman twice as big as Uncle Willy, in a red hat and a pink dress and a dirty white fur coat over the back of the seat and two straw suitcases on the fenders, with hair the color of a brand new brass hydrant bib and her cheeks streaked with mascara and caked powder where she had sweated" (*CS*, 236). Mrs. Merridew is sufficiently irritated. "It was," the narrator tells us, "worse than if he had started dope again. You would have thought he had brought smallpox to town" (*CS*, 236). They manage to "save" Uncle Willy from her too, by convincing the woman that Uncle Willy doesn't have any money. But Mrs. Merridew has had enough: "You're crazy, Mr. Christian; crazy," she tells him. "I have tried to save you and make something out of you besides a beast but now my patience is exhausted. I am going to give you one more chance. I am going to take you to Keeley and if that fails, I am going to take you myself to your sister and force her to commit you to an asylum" (*CS*, 238).

Uncle Willy escapes also from the Keeley Institute and enlists the narrator's assistance in his suicide, which he accomplishes by trying to fly a ramshackle airplane. The story ends as it began, with the narrator trying to explain his full and deliberate complicity in what has happened. The adults have absolved him in advance, claiming that Uncle Willy "tolled" him away; they refuse to believe that the child is anything but an innocent victim. Part of the impact of the story, as Joseph Reed has pointed out,[8] lies precisely in our perception that the adults are right, that the young narrator does not understand that Uncle Willy has in fact betrayed him, has in fact "tolled" him away and used him to his own ends.

"Uncle Willy" is a funny story, on the surface, because of the narrative point of view. The little boy presents Mrs. Merridew and the other members of her posse in caricature, and we want to and do laugh at Uncle Willy's battle tactics, since we want Mrs. Merridew to be beaten and Uncle Willy to be let alone. But it gets less and less funny as we realize how pernicious an influence Uncle Willy is on the children: he deliberately and selfishly involves them in crime; he distorts all of their values, virtually equating ice cream cones and heroin injections and making them believe that having "fun" is the only important thing in life; and he makes them help him commit suicide. He is a grotesquely unhealthy influence. But Mrs. Merridew, representing the best interests of the community in saving those children from Uncle Willy, is in many ways an even less attractive model; with her gestapo tactics, she is arguably an even

8. Joseph W. Reed, Jr., *Faulkner's Narrative* (New Haven: Yale University Press, 1973), 38–41.

more pernicious influence. Faulkner does nothing to resolve the tension established by the conflict between these two polar extremes.

In *The Town*, Flem and Eula Snopes are transported from the fabulous, vast, and mythical world of *The Hamlet* into the more domestic and more real world of Jefferson. They are no longer the slightly preposterous symbols that they were in Frenchman's Bend; they no longer represent anything: they are simply human beings. Cleanth Brooks sees this as one of the failings of *The Town*: "In spite of Ratliff's remark on respectability as an irresistible passion, Flem will seem to us less portentous. He becomes more despicable but more vulnerable as he begins to pay attention to what people may think of him. He must acquire a certain kind of house with certain kinds of furnishings, not because he wants them or cares for them, but because he believes they are what is expected of him."[9] Again, Brooks suggests that "as long as Flem represented pure acquisitiveness . . . he could count in the novel almost as an elemental force." Flem's "failing" in *The Town*, his respectability, "brings him closer to the breed of human beings that we know and are."[10] Brooks is precisely right; but whereas he finds in it the novel's relative failure, this seems to me in one sense to be the entire point of the Snopes trilogy. Flem *is* one of the "breed of human beings that we know and are," and we shall miss some of the trilogy's profundities is we do not recognize that at the start.

To a large degree, however, Flem does remain the "pure acquirer" of *The Hamlet*. Although Ratliff accuses Stevens of "missing it completely" when the lawyer keeps on discussing Flem as if money were his only motive, and although we are temperamentally inclined to agree with the sensible Ratliff when he and Stevens disagree, it is important to remember that during the months immediately following the publication of *The*

9. Brooks, *William Faulkner*, 214.
10. *Ibid*.

119

Town, Faulkner consistently maintained that money was indeed what Flem was after, that respectability became a necessary tool to that end. Nevertheless, Flem is not the completely dishonest, evil person he has been depicted by most critics. In fact, Flem is probably scrupulously honest in his financial dealings: the folks in Frenchman's Bend, you'll recall, were considerably better off dealing with Flem than with Jody Varner, because Jody regularly cheated them at both the store and the gin; and in the "Centaur in Brass" episode of *The Town* Flem learns how easily he can get caught—and ruined—if his hand is in the till for the wrong reasons. His drive toward a huge bank account makes it necessary for him to appear perfectly proper in the eyes of the people of Jefferson, and since he can never be sure who is watching or when he is being watched, he must not only *appear*, but *be* proper: he feels he must purge himself of all taint of corruption, concupiscence, cupidity, and any of the various forms of vulgarity that might sling mud on his name and position, and thereby reduce his earning power. He must, in other words, rid himself of all the things we have come to identify as "Snopesism." This is no more than a lot of people do, who aren't insidious forces.

It is important to keep this perspective on Flem as a human being, because, as I've suggested, much of the meaning of the trilogy may be lost without it. For we get only minimal insight directly into Flem's mind—and, in all fairness I must point out here that Brooks's complaint with *The Town* is based on his feeling that we don't get enough insight into Flem's mind to support the more human and complex character of Flem that Faulkner is striving for, though it seems to me entirely sufficient. Even so, we don't get very much. We get all our information from Ratliff, Stevens, and from Charles Mallison, who is the principal narrator, and who tells us at the beginning of the book that he is, in effect, the voice of the community: "So when I say 'we' and 'we thought' what I mean is Jefferson and what Jefferson thought."[11] He thereby stresses the relationship between the characters in this novel and the community. Ratliff is able to speculate fairly accurately about some things that Stevens finds out to be true; Stevens never understands some of the things he learns; and Charles tells us what is more or less public knowledge. The disparity between the appearance, as Charles tells it and as Jefferson sees it, and the reality, which we finally extrapolate from the speculations of all three narrators, provides the book's narrative tension.

In *The Town*, then, Flem and Eula are housebroken, as it were: the degree of their domestication may be suggested to the reader by the simple fact that Chick Mallison refers to them as *Mr.* and *Mrs.* Snopes—terms that somehow don't go together euphoniously, and which continue to grate strangely on our ears long after we realize, admit, that the Snopeses are adult, respected citizens of Jefferson, and Charles is a child. The townfolk gossip about Flem and Eula as they would gossip about any respected and successful citizen whose wife they suspect of irregular conduct, and just as they probably gossip about Gavin and Linda, though of course out of range of Chick's ears, so naturally we don't hear it.

Since there is little they can do about the Flem–Eula–Manfred de Spain triangle, even if they would, they content themselves with gossip, titillating themselves with a vicarious sort of participation in the adultery and a not-so-vicarious libidinous consternation as they watch this magnificent lady simply walk across the square:

. . . not, as far as we knew, going anywhere: just moving, walking in that aura of decorum and modesty and solitariness ten times more immodest and a hundred times more disturbing than one of the bathing suits young women would begin to wear about 1920 or so, as if in the second just before you looked, her garments had managed in one

11. William Faulkner, *The Town* (New York: Random House, 1957), 3.

last frantic pell-mell scurry to overtake and cover her. Though only for a moment because in the next one, if only you followed long enough, they would wilt and fail from that mere plain and simple striding which would shred them away like the wheel of a constellation through a wisp and cling of trivial scud. (*Town*, 9–10)

Describing the town's reaction to Eula and Manfred at the Cotillion Ball, Chick suggests some of the complexities of the public attitudes toward the whole business: of course it has to do with Eula's beauty and vitality, and the allurement of a woman who is so completely outside the range of their experience and even the scope of their imaginations; but it has more to do with what Eula makes them realize about themselves:

. . . Mrs Snopes was dancing that way, letting Mr de Spain get her into dancing that way in public, simply because she was alive and not ashamed of it . . . was what she was and looked the way she looked and wasn't ashamed of it and not afraid or ashamed of being glad of it, nor even of doing this to prove it, since this appeared to be the only way of proving it, not being afraid or ashamed, that the little puny people fallen back speechless and aghast in a shocked circle around them, could understand; all the other little doomed mean cowardly married and unmarried husbands looking aghast and outraged in order to keep one another from seeing that what they really wanted to do was cry, weep because they were not that brave, each one knowing that even if there was no other man on earth, let alone in that ball room, they still could not have survived, let alone matched or coped with, that splendor, that splendid unshame. (*Town*, 75)

Thus, they are all on de Spain's side, Chick tells us: "We were his allies, his confederates; our whole town was accessory to that cuckolding—that cuckolding which for any proof we had, we had invented ourselves" (*Town*, 15). They are proud to partake, even vicariously, of the splendor which is Eula Varner Snopes.

In some ways this attitude is natural enough, and harmless enough. Later in the novel Eula in fact points out to Stevens just how tolerant and kind people have been over the years, since they have not interfered, for her good or for the good of the community, by telling her mother or her father about her affair with de Spain (*Town*, 329). This is a far different Jefferson from the one that routed Uncle Willy, and Eula's appreciation of those folks may give us a better sense of the essential health of Jefferson society than we usually allow. To be sure, the town's interest may indicate the sexual repression that we've discussed as being part of "respectability." Montgomery Ward Snopes's "atelier" peep show is a *booming* success, apparently, in this respectable little town; his patrons obviously seek in his shop some form of excitement they do not find at home. Nevertheless, there is nothing essentially prurient about Jefferson—at least nothing unhealthily prurient, I should say.

The relationship of Charles, Sr. and Maggie Mallison, for example, is a warm and healthy one—one of the few "normal" marriages in Faulkner's work—and it is not without significance that they stand right at the center of this most domestic of all his novels. They are sensible and unshamed and not only good-humored but also witty, especially Maggie, who has an abundant sense of life. Charles, Sr.'s caustic bedeviling of Gavin makes for some of the finest humor in the book and provides us with a useful brake on Gavin's high-gear eloquent justifications for his interest in Linda Snopes: forming her mind indeed! Charles and Maggie help us view the phenomenon of Eula and de Spain from a sensible perspective and in this they represent the main element of Jefferson. Maggie, with her good-humored knowledge of sexuality and sexual attraction, readily understands why Eula has all the men in town panting after her, and when she says she understands, Charles, with a typical male's reluctance to let his wife know he is attracted to another woman, responds defensively: "Speak for your brother. . . . I never looked at her in her life." "Then so much the worse for me," Maggie replies, wittily to the point, "with a mole for a husband. No: moles have warm blood; a Mammoth Cave fish—" (*Town*, 48).

It is, in fact, only Gavin Stevens in all of Jefferson who tries to do anything about Eula and Manfred. He is the Mrs. Merridew of *The Town*, although his motives and goals are different and although he pursues his quarry with much less competence than she. Stevens is one of the biggest old maids in Yoknapatawpha County, one of the primmest and most easily shocked citizens in Faulkner's world. Remember how upset he is, in France, when he discovers what kind of canteen Montgomery Ward Snopes is running? When he is queried in one of Chick's letters about Monty, he writes back, frantic even in the letter, *"Dont mention that name to me again. I wont discuss it. I will not"* (*Town*, 107). This is the same sort of sensibility that makes him believe, in *Requiem for a Nun*, that "there is a corruption even in just looking at evil, even by accident; . . . you can't haggle, traffic, with putrefaction—you can't, you don't dare" (*Requiem*, 129). This attitude is precisely why he helps Flem close the peep show in Jefferson. Both claim to do it "for Jefferson," but both have different motives.

Stevens fights de Spain after the controversial dance at the cotillion for a number of reasons: his sexual desire for Eula, his jealousy of de Spain, and his sense that such goings-on debase not just the Helen and the Semiramis which Stevens believes Eula to be, but also the entire stage upon which his and her lives are being played out. It is also probable that Gavin Stevens himself feels corrupted, tainted, *tempted*, by its presence in Jefferson, because Eula constantly reminds him, like the other men in Jefferson, of his own sexual nature, a part of him that he obviously fears. He is shocked when Eula bluntly offers herself to him; he later runs away from sexual involvement with Linda, and is shocked yet again when Linda, in *The Mansion*, offers herself to him even more bluntly than her mother had, using the harsh, four-letter Anglo-Saxon word which he will not repeat: he blocks the very word from the line of type on which he

is reporting the conversation.[12] This helps to explain why in *The
Mansion* Stevens retreats almost completely from his sexual nature, runs from it into marriage with an old girlfriend, Melisandre Backus Harriss, in what Professor Millgate has correctly
called a "sadly middle-aged affair."[13] With Melisandre, who has
two grown children, he can expect to be relieved of a too-de-
manding sexual responsibility, both with Melisandre and with
Linda. The irony is hardly lost on the reader, though Stevens
does not appear to notice, that, having married Melisandre, he
reaps the benefits of the fortune left to her by her deceased
bootlegger husband, a *real* gangster, a flesh and blood criminal,
compared to whom Flem is small fry indeed, even if Flem is all
that Gavin believes him to be. Stevens's failure to see this irony
is one measure of his grasp of the situation he helps to create in
The Town.

One significant character in *The Town* who has not received
much attention is Manfred de Spain, Eula's paramour. He carries a full share of the novel's complexities, however, because in
his peculiar relationship with the town itself he becomes one of
the touchstones of the novel's themes. Even though, like Stevens Stevens, he is the descendant of one of the area's oldest
families, he is, like Flem, virtually an outsider. He is a West
Point graduate and a veteran of the Cuban conflict; and he bears
a battle-scar of dubious origin. And, Chick tells us: "he had not
been long at home and out of his blue Yankee coat before we
realised that he and Jefferson were incorrigibly and invincibly
awry to one another, and that one of them was going to have to
give. And that it would not be him: that he would neither flee
Jefferson nor try to alter himself to fit Jefferson, but instead
would try to wrench Jefferson until the town fitted him, and—

12. William Faulkner, *The Mansion* (New York: Random House, 1959), 238.
13. Michael Millgate, *The Achievement of William Faulkner* (New York: Random House, 1966), 247.

the young people hoped—would succeed" (*Town*, 10). Part of
the reason he is finally vanquished by Flem (though it takes
eighteen years) is that Flem's methods are precisely the opposite. Whereas de Spain goes out of his way to defy the city's
mores, Flem does everything he can to ingratiate himself. De
Spain flaunts his differences, Flem obliterates his, melts into the
fabric of the town's life as smoothly as he can. De Spain is child-
ish and obtuse, especially during the early years of his affair with
Eula; he buys Flem, or allows himself to be bought by Flem,
with the newly created job of superintendent of the power-
plant, in order to keep up his relationship with Eula. Most com-
mentators have assumed that in this Flem is blackmailing de
Spain; but I would point out that de Spain is no babe in the
woods, and, considering the other elements in his relationship
with Jefferson, I suspect that he may not be so much a victim of
Flem's villainy as has been thought: he would hardly be the first
politician to use his political power to get in bed with a beautiful
woman. De Spain flaunts his illicit affair with Eula publicly at
the cotillion ball and privately, to Stevens, when he drives by
his house with the cut-out wide open and when he cruelly sends
him the used condom. He is so much an outsider to the community and the community spirit that when the business about
the brass in the watertower is exposed and he is asked to resign
from the mayorship, he agrees only if by doing so he can hu-
miliate Stevens: not for the sake of the city, he says, but only if
Stevens will ask him to (*Town*, 98).

When Gavin tries to influence his sister Maggie not to invite
the mayor to the Cotillion Club dance, Charles, Sr. objects, saying that they can't not invite the mayor. Maggie argues that they
certainly can exclude de Spain if they want to, and tells us exactly how the town feels about de Spain: "The mayor of a town
is a servant," she says. "He's the head servant of course: the
butler. You dont invite a butler to a party because he's a butler.
You invite him in spite of it." De Spain is, of course, invited; and

126

Charles explains that the Cotillion Club "didn't have to invite him because he was the Mayor, and so they invited him just to show it" (*Town*, 57).

But there is another side to de Spain, too. He grows considerably during the eighteen years he and Eula have together. In the beginning they are, like Stevens, young and callous, and de Spain flaunts his relationship with Flem's wife as a sexual victory. But he is not entirely irreclaimable at any time: after his disgraceful performance at the dance, after he has whipped Stevens in order to protect himself, he leaves the alley quietly. Charles expects to hear the cut-out, but doesn't; there is only silence (*Town*, 76). Even de Spain, it would seem, is ashamed of what he has done. Later, he replaces the money Byron Snopes steals, a clear reminder that he does have some integrity at least as a banker if not as a citizen. Finally, after Eula kills herself, with the shot Chick tells us "finished [de Spain] too" (*Town*, 339), he shows up at the graveside, which Charles thinks perfectly proper, since de Spain was a business associate of the new widower. Charles says de Spain "turned from the grave when we all did except that he was the first one" and an hour later he left town (*Town*, 339). Nobody has yet accused de Spain of the virtue of simple grief. But de Spain is not one to make gestures toward propriety, and so I'd suggest that critics have failed to understand the simple fact that Eula and de Spain have been in love with each other; any affair, even marriage, lasting eighteen years must have something more than just sex to sustain it. Eula, at least, loves de Spain (*Town*, 329); there's no reason to think de Spain doesn't return that love, and every reason to think he does. Granted, their sterile relationship prompts Charles to accuse them of "outrag[ing] the economy of marriage which is the production of children, by making public display of the fact that you can be barren by choice with impunity" (*Town*, 338). Discounting the probability that Chick may be wrong, that Eula is not barren "by choice with impunity," their barrenness is doubtless Eula's, rather than de Spain's, decision. She already has one hostage to fortune; Flem already has one rope around her neck: why should she present him with another?

Eula too grows considerably during this novel. Like de Spain, she at first flaunts herself at Jefferson, in defiance or despair or both. De Spain doesn't dance by himself. The Eula who comes to Gavin Stevens's office the evening following the ball to reward him is neither a very healthy nor a very likable person. She is instead a sad, cynical, dispirited—and very real—human being. Stevens expects his Helen to enter on a wave of Wagnerian brasses, and is disconcerted to hear her clump loudly up the stairs: he is amazed at how real she is, how small she is in proportion to how much of his own peace she has displaced. She offers herself to him crudely: Let's "do it here" she says, pulling down the curtain.

The conversation following his consternation and his refusal reveals a Eula without compassion for others or hope for herself; she places no value on herself, and therefore even less value on the sexual favor she has offered. Among the many complicated reasons Gavin refuses her is the simple one that it would not mean anything to her. Why did you come here? he wants to know: "Because you are unhappy," she says. "I dont like unhappy people. They're a nuisance." Especially when it can be remedied so easily (*Town*, 93). In this she sounds very much like Uncle Willy. "You spend too much time expecting," she tells Gavin. "Dont expect. You just are, and you need, and you must, and so you do. That's all. Dont waste time expecting" (*Town*, 94). That sounds pragmatic, and it is; but it is also soulless and eventually lifeless, and for that reason runs a poor second as a philosophy of life even to Stevens's fatuous idealizing, and an even poorer third to the more practical, everyday pursuit of their own hopes and dreams by the middle-class, respectable people of Jefferson.

By the end of the novel, Eula has undergone a tremendous

growth in character, partly because of her and de Spain's love, partly because of her response to Stevens's chivalric defense of her after the dance—the full meaning of which dawns on her only gradually, one expects, though she concedes immediately that he may have refused her "because you're a gentleman and I never knew one before" (*Town*, 94). But mostly she grows because of her love of her daughter, and in response to Linda's needs. She stays married to Flem Snopes for eighteen years in order to preserve Linda's faith not just in the morality of marriage but in the morality of *normalcy*. She does this for Linda, not for the community, but she does it to assert the value of the family and the community, and she dies in the belief that Linda will be better able to deal with the world if she thinks her mother was a suicide than if she thinks she was merely a whore. In this sacrifice Eula is very much *un*like Caddy Compson, unlike Laverne Schumann, and unlike Charlotte Rittenmeyer, all of whom abandon their children in order to free themselves from responsibility. The mindless earth-mother of *The Hamlet* becomes, in *The Town*, the steady and faithful defender of order and decorum. The most respectable person in *The Town*, then, is Eula Varner Snopes, who defends the values of the Jefferson community with her very life. Her trip to the beauty parlor on her last day alive, who had never been before because she had never needed to go, is a final affirmation of her solidarity with other Jefferson women.

V. K. Ratliff, I believe, understands this, and this may be what he means when he contends that Flem was the only one who understood Eula (*Town*, 99).[14] It is clear from the beginning of the trilogy that Flem's power over everybody derives from his superior understanding of human nature: he knows what makes everybody tick and uses that knowledge to his advantage. What makes him particularly despicable in *The Town* is the way he

14. See Faulkner's confirmation of Ratliff's opinion in Frederick L. Gwynn and Joseph L. Blotner (eds.), *Faulkner in the University* (New York: Vintage, 1965), 108.

uses Eula and Linda. One of the serious errors Gavin Stevens makes in his dealings with the Snopeses—and it is an error born of his incredible arrogance and his equally incredible ignorance—is in believing that Linda must hate Flem as much as he does; he does not realize, in his childless-bachelor wisdom, that in spite of everything Linda in fact loves Flem, whom she believes to be her father: a girl "dont really hate your father," Eula tries to tell Stevens, "no matter how much you think you do or should or should want to because people expect you to" (*Town*, 322). And it is a powerful scene indeed that Eula describes a few pages later when she relates to Stevens how Flem finally agreed to allow Linda to go to the university:

She threw the book, she didn't put it down at all: she just threw it, flung it as she stood up out of the chair and said:
"Daddy." I had never seen her touch him. He was her father, she never refused to speak to him or to speak any way except respectfully. But he was her enemy; she had to keep him reminded always that although he had beaten her about the schools, she still hadn't surrendered. But I had never seen her touch him until now, sprawled, flung across his lap, clutching him around the shoulders, her face against his collar, crying, saying, "Daddy! Daddy! Daddy! Daddy!" (*Town*, 325–26)

Flem uses the greed and the sexual appetites of others to his advantage, and by and large we feel that they get what they deserve, since he is merely using their own folly against them. What he does to Linda is far different, far more reprehensible: he uses a daughter's natural love for a father, *Linda's own love for him*, against her; and that is wicked indeed.

One of the many tragedies of the Snopes trilogy is the error Eula makes in calculating Linda's response to her mother's life and death, even in calculating the necessity for her sacrifice, since we know that Linda is not blind and that she knows about her mother and Manfred de Spain. Eula's sacrifice does not seem to "take" on Linda, as acts of sacrifice often do not. In *The Mansion* Linda returns to Jefferson a widow with a Jewish name, a communist, and a "nigger-lover," not necessarily in that order. Like Manfred de Spain she is a wounded war veteran; also like Manfred she tries to force Jefferson to change to suit her, and, like de Spain, she lives in complete disregard of community values. Professor Millgate quite correctly speaks of her "decline" as a human being.[15] Just as Flem uses her love for him so calculatedly for his own purposes, so does she coldbloodedly use Gavin Stevens's love for her to work her vengeance on Flem. It is not at all a pretty thing she does to Stevens.

What Linda becomes, however, in no way diminishes either the magnificence of Eula's gesture or the significance of her sacrifice. In his address to the graduating class of Pine Manor Junior College in June of 1953, Faulkner discussed the modern world's tendency to dehumanize people by making it difficult to be an individual. He concludes this fine speech by suggesting that one gains a sense of one's self not by being belligerently and automatically different from everybody else: self-knowledge begins at home, he says:

Because it begins at home. We all know what "home" means. Home is not necessarily a place fixed in geography. It can be moved, provided the old proven values which made it home and lacking which it cannot be home, are taken along too. It does not necessarily mean or demand physical ease, least of all, never in fact, physical security for the spirit, for love and fidelity to have peace and security in which to love and be faithful, for the devotion and sacrifice. Home means not just today, but tomorrow and tomorrow, and then again tomorrow and tomorrow. It means someone to offer the love and fidelity and respect to who is worthy of it, someone to be compatible with, whose dreams and hopes are your dreams and hopes, who wants and will work and sacrifice also that the thing which the two of you have together shall last forever; someone whom you not only love but like too, which is

15. Millgate, *Achievement of William Faulkner*, 246.

more, since it must outlast what when we are young we mean by love because without the liking and the respect, the love itself will not last.[16]

Eula does not have anyone save Linda worthy of her love and fidelity and respect, and so in these terms the idea of "home" must have been a mockery to her. Yet she manages, courageously and compassionately, to look beyond her own problems. She thinks love and fidelity and respect important enough as ideals to want Linda to value them too, important enough, indeed, to die for them.

Faulkner continues in that lecture to define "home" more broadly:

Let us think first of, work first toward, saving the integer, association, collection which we call home. In fact, we must break ourselves of thinking in the terms foisted on us by the split-offs of that old dark spirit's ambition and ruthlessness: the empty clanging terms of "nation" and "fatherland" or "race" or "color" or "creed." We need look no further than home; we need only work for what we want and deserve here. Home—the house or even the rented room so long as it includes all the houses and rented rooms in which hope and aspire the same hopes and aspirations—the street, then all the streets where dwell that voluntary association of people, simple men and women mutually confederated by identical hopes and aspirations and problems and duties and needs, to that point where they can say, "These simple things—security and freedom and peace—are not only possible, not only can and must be, but they shall be." Home: not where *I* live or *it* lives, but where *we* live: a thousand then tens of thousands of little integers scattered and fixed firmer and more impregnable and more solid than rocks or citadels about the earth, so that the ruthless and ambitious split-offs of the ancient dark spirit shall look at the one and say, "There is nothing for us here."[17]

16. James B. Meriwether (ed.), *Essays, Speeches, and Public Letters of William Faulkner* (New York: Random House, 1966), 140.
17. *Ibid.*, 141–42.

More in her life than in her death, but also in that final sacrifice, Eula affirms those values of home and community that Faulkner speaks of in this lecture. *The Town*, Faulkner's most complex fictional treatment of this theme, is for me a wonderful book, immoderately funny, wise, and heartbreaking. Eula Varner Snopes stands at the center of its humor, its wisdom, and its heartbreak. Along with the town itself, she is the novel's life-giver.

Faulkner:
The House of Fiction

JAMES G. WATSON

William Faulkner's fiction, we might agree, is characterized by a profound sense of place. This is rendered, in part, by the southern regional material in his books and stories: by actual places that are the settings of action, events, and situations; by the kinds of characters who populate such places; and by the ideas and attitudes those characters share and the language in which they express themselves. It is rendered, too, by Faulkner's profound and no less enigmatic sense of fictional form. Place, I think, is a function of form. No matter how familiar the setting, the sense of place depends upon the quality and kind of its construction, and this is true whether the place be a county, a town, a hamlet, or a separate dwelling. Especially it is true of imaginary places, such as Yoknapatawpha County or Jefferson or Frenchman's Bend, which have no palpable existence outside the boundaries of the fiction. The reality of such places depends upon the imaginative integrity of their builder, the kind of integrity that Cash Bundren describes in this passage late in *As I Lay Dying*:

Folks seems to get away from the olden right teaching that says to drive the nails down and trim the edges well always like it was for your own use and comfort you were making it. It's like some folks has the smooth, pretty boards to build a courthouse with and others dont have no more than rough lumber fitten to build a chicken coop. But it's better to build a tight chicken coop than a shoddy courthouse, and

134

when they both build shoddy or build well, neither because it's one or tother is going to make a man feel the better nor the worse.[1]

Henry James would have understood. The "house of fiction," he said in the Preface to *The Portrait of a Lady*, might be a square and spacious edifice or something less imposing, but it was nothing without the integrity that he called "the conscious- ness of the artist." He too thought of the novelist as a builder, and in his retrospective judgment he found *Portrait* a "neat and careful and proportioned pile of bricks . . . a structure reared with an 'architectural' competence."[2] That structure is heavily dependent upon place for the depiction of Isabel Archer's dis- placement abroad, and to build the novel James used real and imaginary houses in America and Europe. Isabel's sheltered life in Albany is portrayed by her double house there, her self-de- lusions about personal freedom are uncovered in the open spaces of the house at Gardencourt, and her imprisoned life with Gilbert Osmond is symbolized by the Palazzo Roccanero, their "black rock" villa in Rome.[3] No less than those of James, Faulk- ner's novels are tightly nailed and neatly trimmed buildings, housing real and imaginary places as well as flesh and blood characters. And like James, Faulkner uses houses to build with—not merely as picturesque regional backdrops or stage sets but as complex symbolic forms fully integrated into the structure of the novels. I want to say some things about the ways in which specific houses serve Faulkner's sense of place and form in *As I Lay Dying, The Sound and the Fury*, and *Sanctuary*. In

1. William Faulkner, *As I Lay Daying* (New York: Random House, 1964), 224; here- after cited in the text as *AILD*.

2. Henry James, "Preface," *The Portrait of a Lady*, in *The Novels and Tales of Henry James* (New York: Scribner's, 1936), III, x, xi, xvi.

3. For discussions of houses in James's fiction, I am indebted to two sources in par- ticular: Robert L. Gale, *The Caught Image: Figurative Language in the Fiction of Henry James* (Chapel Hill: University of North Carolina Press, 1964), 218–25; and R. W. Stall- man, "The House That James Built—*The Portrait of a Lady*," in Stallman, *The Houses That James Built and Other Literary Essays* (East Lansing: Michigan State University Press, 1961), 3–33.

those books houses so profoundly render the reality of place because they are so closely tied to and expressive of the characters'
own sense of place—not just as a physical but as a spiritual,
psychological, and moral reality. If you will permit me one more
turn of this screw, the sense of place in Faulkner's house of fiction depends in no small degree on the houses of Faulkner's
fictions.

Or rather, since I willingly accede to the experts in matters
of local lore, it depends on the fictional houses of his fictions.
Addressing this conference in 1977 on the subject "Faulkner's
Localism," Professor Calvin Brown identified houses as the one
notable exception to the topographical and geographical parallels that he was tracing between Lafayette and Yoknapatawpha
counties. Railways and roadways, ditches and streets, reservoirs
and rivers and streams he found to be pretty much each in their
ordered places, but actual houses, he said, there are none. Let
me quote him:

> One matter in which Faulkner very definitely does *not* use the
> local scene is that of houses. Even without his maps, we could easily
> tell the approximate location of the Benbow, Compson, and Sartoris
> houses, for example, but we cannot point to any actual buildings that
> inspired them. The identifications that we now hear have their basis
> in tourist-promotion, not responsible scholarship. I suppose it is prob-
> ably much easier to put invented people into invented houses than it
> is mentally to evict one's neighbors and move strangers into their
> houses. At any rate, Faulkner never tried to do this.[4]

Why actual houses cannot have changed location to meet the
needs of the fiction, as the entire campus of the University of
Mississippi apparently did according to Professor Brown, is not
entirely clear to me. But as a tourist from Oklahoma lecturing in

4. Calvin S. Brown, "Faulkner's Localism," in *The Maker and the Myth: Faulkner
and Yoknapatawpha, 1977,* ed. Evans Harrington and Ann J. Abadie (Jackson: University Press of Mississippi, 1978), 13–14. A version of the same is "Faulkner's Geography
and Topography," *PMLA,* LXXVII (December, 1962), 652–59.

Mississippi on Yoknapatawpha County, I am not seriously in-clined to argue. One can find in *The Cofield Collection* and other photographic essays houses that are close enough to Faulkner's fictional ones to have served as his models. Moreover, whether real or imaginary, they tend to identify themselves for us: if we do not recognize them on the streets of Oxford, we assuredly do on the streets of Jefferson.

I do not mean only that we recognize the easy stereotypes of farm houses and antebellum mansions, although there are shot-gun cabins and stately homes enough in Yoknapatawpha County. I mean that Faulkner's houses are nearly as many, as varied, and as unique in form and function as the individuals who dwell in them. The house at Sutpen's Hundred, Hubert and Sophonsiba Beauchamp's Warwick, and Ikkemotubbe's steamboat are all southern mansions, all decidedly different. And they all signify. The twin beach cottages in *The Wild Palms* are as significant to the contrapuntal form of that novel and to its themes as they are to place, though place is strongly evoked,[5] and the same might be said of the contrasted big house and tenant cabin in "Barn Burning" or "Wash." Such houses often embody their own sets of social rules and exemptions and may mirror the characters of their inhabitants. In "A Rose for Emily," to take a well-known case, the Grierson house is described in images that explicitly portray Emily's stubborn pride and forbode her secret. "It was a big, squarish frame house," the narrator begins, "that had once been white, decorated with cupolas and spires and scrolled bal-conies in the heavily lightsome style of the seventies, set on what had once been our most select street." To this portrait of fallen status and faded beauty, he adds that the house is a picture of "stubborn and coquettish *decay*."[6]

5. The most cogent discussion of these and other houses in *The Wild Palms* is Thomas L. McHaney, *William Faulkner's The Wild Palms: A Study* (Jackson: University Press of Mississippi, 1975).
6. William Faulkner, "A Rose for Emily," in *Collected Stories of William Faulkner* (New York: Random House, 1950), 119. (Italics mine.)

In addition to condition and location, Faulkner's houses express themselves also by their type, their construction, and their history. Some family houses, like the Sartoris house, are monuments to the living traditions of the past and refuges in the present, but in *Sanctuary* the locked and boarded Benbow house suggests that the traditions of home and family are anachronistic. Horace opens the house but he occupies only one room before he returns to Belle and the "stucco house"[7] in Kinston with its unpaid mortgage. Like Horace's Kinston residence, Gowan and Temple Stevens's "new bungalow on the right street"[8] in *Requiem for a Nun* represents the façade of respectability they have erected around their marriage. Finally, Faulkner actually names some of his characters for houses or, as with Gail Hightower, for parts of them. In the story "Artist at Home" Roger and Anne Howes's surname reinforces the several ironic distinctions between *house* and *home*; Homer Barron's name suggests the barren home in which Emily Grierson lives; and on June 2, 1910, Quentin Compson is reminded of home by Gerald Bland's companion, Miss Holmes. Perhaps the extreme of this practice is *Idyll in the Desert* where a character named Darrel Howes— or Dorry House, as the narrator calls him—abandons his aging mistress at a camp for tuberculars in the Arizona mountains. Their house is called "Sivgut" because, the narrator explains, it is a *sieve* through which patients pass as fast as a week's food can pass through their *guts*. Unhappily, Dorry's maternalistic mistress contracts his disease and is left no exit. What Sigmund Freud would make of houses such as these is not altogether beside the point; what William Faulkner made were clearly distinguishable places populated by distinguishable people in usually (but not always) distinguished fictions.

Like the absence of actual Lafayette County houses from

7. William Faulkner, *Sanctuary* (New York: Vintage, 1975), 114; hereafter cited in the text as *S*.
8. William Faulkner, *Requiem for a Nun* (New York: Vintage, 1975), 136.

Yoknapatawpha County, the presence of so many apocryphal ones might prove nothing worthy of note were it not for the fact that houses generally, and the ones most special to us in particular, are so deeply involved with our sense of place. Our houses are the most familiar and significant settings of our intimate lives, endlessly evocative of the cruxes of association by which we locate ourselves in space and time. House implies home, and inevitably home is a definite and particular locale. In addition, as a geometric object more or less standard in its elements and configuration, the generic house may function as an archetypal symbol. The dialectics of outside and inside, upstairs and downstairs, for example, render the house not only a localized refuge but a universal mode of self-definition and expression. Particular rooms, too, are frequently charged with meaning. In the vertical figure of the self-as-house, an attic—or high tower—is the realm of the intellect and idealism, the cellar of the physical body; private rooms house one's secret self and public rooms the social. To be *unhoused*, in these terms, is to be isolated potentially not only from a particular place in space and time but from fundamental referents of human identity. For Faulkner, houses and architectural images were a habitual mode of expression and a characteristic vehicle of extended metaphors for fictional form. And for place. The French phenomenologist Gaston Bachelard calls such figures "images of *felicitous space*,"[9] and Faulkner's descriptions of Yokanapatawpha County were larded with them. On the *Absalom, Absalom!* map he wrote, "William Faulkner: Sole Owner and Proprietor," and he spoke of the "little postage stamp of native soil" from which, as he said, "I created a cosmos of my own . . . a kind of keystone in the Universe."[10] Tantalizingly—but as far as I know coincidentally—Bachelard echoes

9. Gaston Bachelard, *The Poetics of Space*, trans. Maria Jolas (Boston: Beacon Press, 1969), xxxi.
10. James B. Meriwether and Michael Millgate (eds.), *Lion in the Garden: Interviews with William Faulkner, 1926–1962* (New York: Random House, 1968), 255.

that phrasing when he writes, in *The Poetics of Space*, "our house is our corner of the world . . . it is our first universe, a real cosmos in every sense of the word."[11]

In *As I Lay Dying*, the Bundren's corner of the world is both setting and symbol for their situation in just these terms. With the house at the top of a high bluff and a barn at the base, the farm is a clearly distinguishable place. It is particularized, however, by that verticality emblematic of the archetypal house. Human at its upper elevation, it is animal at its lower extreme. The positioning of house and barn defines the Bundrens' existence as a duality of flesh and spirit, mind and body—what Addie will call words and deeds. From the vantage point of the Bundren hilltop, Doctor Peabody employs the mind-body principle to define dying, and he illustrates with a suitable architectural image: "I can remember," he says, "how when I was young I believed death to be a phenomenon of the body; now I know it to be merely a function of the mind—and that of the minds of the ones who suffer the bereavement. The nihilists say it is the end; the fundamentalists, the beginning; when in reality it is no more than a single tenant or family moving out of a tenement or a town" (*AILD*, 42–43). Peabody's hilltop idealism, like some of Anse's proclamations, is not for the long road. But it illustrates one way in which the physical configuration of house and barn supplies the novel with a symbolic standard against which Faulkner measures characters and situations, working similarities and deviations, parallels and inversions against the standard pattern much as he does with mythic and legendary structures elsewhere. This includes inner as well as outer space. Entering the back door of the house early in the book, Darl hears Cora Tull's voice carried down the hall to him from the front room where his mother lies dying, her mind set on death and revenge. Here is the way he describes it:

11. Bachelard, *Poetics of Space*, 4.

140

I enter the hall, hearing the voices before I reach the door. Tilting a little down the hill, as our house does, a breeze draws through the hall all the time, upslanting. A feather dropped near the front door will rise and brush along the ceiling, slanting backward, until it reaches the down-turning current at the back door: so with voices. As you enter the hall, they sound as though they were speaking out of the air about your head. (*AILD*, 19)

The description is precise and detailed, accurate even to the aerodynamics of the feather's flight. And it is highly suggestive. The image of voices "speaking out of the air," for example, has obvious reference to Darl himself, who does hear voices and speaks a voiceless language. Like the house-barn figure that defines the exterior parameters of experience, the elements of this description—the tilting hallway, the breeze, the feather, and disembodied voices—are the terms of a recurrent and accretive metaphor for the private self. By the similarities and differences between outside and inside, the full humanity of the characters and the full range of humanity in the novel are approximated.

In *As I Lay Dying*, André Bleikasten has said, "Metaphor is the figure of figures. . . . Through the multiplicity of unexpected connections and reverberations they introduce into the book, metaphors reinforce the interrelatedness of its parts. . . . [They] are intended to transmute the factual-objective into the poetic."[12] In the case of Darl's description, the tilted house is an image for humpbacked Anse Bundren and the feather establishes his proprietorship. Anse is repeatedly described as a bird: he is a rooster (*AILD*, 43) and an awry-feathered owl (*AILD*, 48). His name suggests the word *anserine*, or gooselike, and he comes to Addie like the wild geese in the spring "looking already like a tall bird hunched in the cold weather, on the wagon seat" (*AILD*, 162), a description that pictures his buzzardlikeness on the wagon journey to Jefferson. He considers it God's plan that

12. André Bleikasten, *Faulkner's As I Lay Dying*, trans. Roger Little (Bloomington: Indiana University Press, 1973), 39.

men, like houses and trees, are made "up-and-down ways" (*AILD*, 35), and as goose and buzzard, rooster and owl, his life from birth to death and from dawn to dark conforms immutably to that vertical plan. Though he feels flaunted by the horizontal road, he is certain that "Old Marster will care for me as for ere a sparrow that falls" (*AILD*, 37).

The metaphors that link Anse's life and house fix him as an ironic referent for the two opposed lives of Cora Tull and Addie, each of whom has her own sense of involvement in a divine plan. Cora's likeness to Anse-as-house lies in her association with birds—she is a buzzard (*AILD*, 14) who raises chickens—and her disembodied voice. It is her voice that floats featherlike, "speaking out of the air" about Darl's head, and she is one of the singing women at Addie's funeral whose voices, Tull says, come from the house as if "out of the air, flowing together and on in the sad, comforting tunes. When they cease it's like they hadn't gone away. It's like they had just disappeared into the air and when we moved we would loose them again out of the air around us, sad and comforting" (*AILD*, 86). Cora is a fundamentalist, and she properly values the spirit above the flesh, but she is as self-righteous as sour milk. Tull houses her in a house as tight as a jar (*AILD*, 132), but he imagines that she is a bodiless soul, "with that singing look in her face like she had done give up folks and all their foolishness and had done went on ahead of them, marching up the sky, singing" (*AILD*, 146). As the metaphors of the novel accumulate connections, Cora is increasingly defined in terms of the vertical leg of the figure of which Addie is the horizontal.

It is worth reminding ourselves here that the extremes of vertical and horizontal that Addie calls words and deeds have been fixed in the texture of *As I Lay Dying* by the house symbol well before her own climactic chapter, two-thirds of the way through the book. Like Cora, she is gradually defined in terms of the upstairs-downstairs, soul-body dichotomy, but instead of

"marching up the sky" Addie is "planted" in the physical world
(*AILD*, 162). The identity she finds in the agonies of the flesh is
prefigured by her metaphoric association with the barn, where
Jewel's horse-mother is stabled and where Vardaman runs to
find her when, as he says, "the other one laid down in her bed
and drew the quilt up" (*AILD*, 63). Nor are the voices that Addie
hears in the air prayers and hymns but the disembodied voices
of the wild geese, "coming faint and high and wild out of the
wild darkness" (*AILD*, 162).

The addition of Addie's sexual longing to the crux of associations surrounding birds and voices is itself prepared for by another element of the interior house. Early in the book the
breeze that Darl says "draws through the hall all the time" cools
his sexual longing: he remembers lying "with my shirt-tail up,
hearing them asleep, feeling myself without touching myself,
feeling the cool silence blowing upon my parts and wondering if
Cash was yonder in the darkness doing it too, had been doing it
perhaps for the last two years before I could have wanted to or
could have" (*AILD*, 11). The same breeze is used as a figure in
the longer, poetic passage where Dewey Dell describes her
emergence from adolescence. She says, "*it was wind blowing
over me it was like the wind came and blew me back from where
it was I was not blowing the room and Vardaman asleep and all
of them back under me again and going on like a piece of cool
silk dragging across my naked legs*" (*AILD*, 115–16). For Addie,
as indeed for Cora, sexuality is a direct and present threat to
salvation in a world governed by the fundamentalist doctrine
that "the reason for living is getting ready to stay dead" (*AILD*,
167). Cora abjures the flesh and marches up the sky alone; Addie
resolves the conflict for herself by leaving the school house,
where she whips children, for Anse's house, where she bears
them. The conjunction of house and husband is rendered at
their first meeting when his humped back prompts her to in-
quire three times about his house: "But you've got a house," she

143

says, "They tell me you've got a house and a good farm. . . . A new house. . . . Are you going to get married?" (*AILD*, 163). When the humped man in the tilted hilltop house betrays her with words, she dismisses him as a factor in her life: she calls him "a significant shape profoundly without life like an empty door frame" (*AILD*, 165) and denies him access to her. Speaking of herself as a self-contained house with an empty door, she says of her body:

I would think: The shape of my body where I used to be a virgin is in the shape of a   and I couldn't think *Anse*, couldn't remember *Anse*. It was not that I could think of myself as no longer unvirgin, because I was three now. And when I would think *Cash* and *Darl* that way until their names would die and solidify into a shape and then fade away, I would say, All right. It doesn't matter. It doesn't matter what they call them. (*AILD*, 165)

When Jewel is born, the conflict between body and soul is resolved for Addie: he is the word become flesh through an act of flesh, simultaneously her cross and the means of her salvation. Now Addie repairs the imbalance in her life with Anse by giving him Dewey Dell and Vardaman, "And so," she says, "I have cleaned my house. . . . And then I could get ready to die" (*AILD*, 168).

In many respects *As I Lay Dying* is a great comic novel, and it is one of the great comic ironies in Faulkner's work that the balance Addie achieves in her life is destroyed at her death by her ironic counterpart, Cora Tull. The bevelled coffin that Cash builds her is horizontal, half house and half bed as Cash says (*AILD*, 77), but Cora imposes upon that horizontal house the social and religious proprieties of the vertical archetype. Even though Addie achieves her balanced identity outside her marriage, she is buried in her wedding dress, her head to the foot of the only house in her life built to her unique individual specifications. Thus the novel ends as it began, with verticality restored as a principle of order in the Bundren household. The house where funeral music floats disembodied in the air gives way to the house in Jefferson that the new Mrs. Bundren fills with gramophone music. Addie's journey ends when she is planted again, this time in the Jefferson cemetery with her people, and Dewey Dell, who is likewise "a wet seed wild in the hot blind earth" (*AILD*, 61), is likewise replanted: tricked by Skeets McGowan's words, she submits to him, suitably enough, in a locked cellar underground. Only Darl, who lies "beneath rain on a strange roof, thinking of home" (*AILD*, 76) on the night of his mother's death, is *unhoused* of the fundamental referents of his identity. He accomplishes the destiny he prophesies for himself when he says, "How do our lives ravel out into the no-wind, no-sound, the weary gestures wearily recapitulant: echoes of old compulsions with no-hand on no-strings: in sunset we fall into furious attitudes, dead gestures of dolls" (*AILD*, 196–97). The passage owes something to the confusions that beset Gerontion in the "cunning passages and contrived corridors" of Eliot's poem, where Gerontion's incapacity to act makes him "An old man in a draughty house/Under a windy knob."[13] In Darl's case, the tilted house where he was conceived by a trick of words gives way to the madhouse and "a cage in Jackson where, his grimed hands lying light in the quiet interstices, looking out he foams. 'Yes yes yes yes yes yes yes yes'" (*AILD*, 244).

With respect to the primary settings and events of the book, *As I Lay Dying* is perhaps the least likely of Faulkner's early Yoknapatawpha novels to seriously employ architectural images. Three-fifths of the book, after all, takes place on the rural road to Jefferson. Yet all of it takes place in the minds of the characters, where inner and outer realities both are portrayed in lan-

13. T. S. Eliot, "Gerontion," in *T. S. Eliot: The Complete Poems and Plays* (New York: Harcourt, Brace and World, 1952), 22. For Faulkner's use of "Gerontion" in *As I Lay Dying* and *Absalom, Absalom!*, see James G. Watson, "If *Was* Existed: Faulkner's Prophets and the Patterns of History," *Modern Fiction Studies*, XXII (Winter, 1975–1976), 499–507.

guage, whether poetic or prosaic, pervaded by architectural images and references. Place in this example is unquestionably a matter of form. The word *house* is used 98 times in *As I Lay Dying*,[14] more than half of them occurring after Anse has locked his door and the journey is begun. *House* is the seventh most common noun in the novel and the single most common place noun. In addition, *house* is directly evoked another 150 times by house synonyms and parts such as *door/doorway* (57), *home* (27), *window* (26), *room* (17), *wall/walls* (14) and *roof* (9). These, like *house*, may be used factually-objectively ("We got to get your leg fixed so we can start *home* tomorrow" [*AILD*, 248; my emphasis]), or poetically ("How often have I lain beneath rain on a strange *roof*, thinking of *home*" [*AILD*, 76; my emphasis]). In the sections of the novel narrated by the Bundrens, *house* occurs 61 times, 28 of which are in Darl's sections, where his recurrence to that word in his own speech and the reported speech of others expresses his longing for a secure identity tied to place. I suspect that this usage, like some of the other metaphors of the novel—Darl's raveling out into time, for example, or his description of Cash as a doll stuffed with sawdust—carried into *As I Lay Dying* from its immediate predecessor, *The Sound and the Fury*. There the Compson house is the focal point for the identities of many of the major characters, not as an archetypal standard but as a refuge in fact or in memory. Although Jason's locked upstairs room and the peering into and crawling out of windows in the book may justifiably invite psychological interpretation, the Compson house is first a fully realized and particularized place-as-home. As home and refuge it is what Bachelard calls "the human being's first world"[15] and we can see something of its function by examining it in relation to Ben and

14. This figure and the following statistics on word frequency in *As I Lay Dying* are from Jack L. Capps (ed.), *As I Lay Dying: A Concordance to the Novel* (Ann Arbor: University Microfilms International, for the Faulkner Concordance Advisory Board, 1977).

15. Bachelard, *Poetics of Space*, 7.

Quentin who are, respectively, housed and unhoused prisoners of their house.

Fifty years of close reading and scholarship have uncovered numerous similarities between these first two narrators of the book, and I have no intention of rehearsing them all here, except to say that Ben's forced location at the Compson house contrasts with Quentin's forced dislocation from it and to remind you that the sale of Ben's pasture is the means by which Quentin's year-long lodgment at Harvard is accomplished. Properly speaking, *home* to Ben is the house and the garden circumscribed by the fence: it is his own, quite literal postage stamp of soil, his first and only world, his cosmos. By the landmarks that he uses in his wanderings, we learn that world as he knows it, both outside and inside. The position of his late afternoon shadow, for example, tells us that his graveyard in the cedar trees behind the house is south and east of the kitchen. The house faces north and the pasture is probably on its western boundary. These and other landmarks such as Dilsey's house, the barn, the branch, the flowering tree and the swing exist for Ben, like the events that occur there, not only in space but in time too. They are the exterior referents of his universe. The house itself is equally well particularized according to Ben's life in it. Upstairs are four bedrooms, occupied in 1928 by Mother, Jason, Miss Quentin, and Ben himself, but distinguished for Ben by the various traumas that occurred there over thirty years. Mother's room is where his name was changed, and it smells of sickness from *"a cloth folded on Mother's head"*[16] another is where Caddy used perfume after she left Ben to sleep alone. At least three of the bedrooms are associated in Ben's mind with sickness and death: Damuddy's, Mr. and Mrs. Compson's, and the room where the children sleep on the night Damuddy dies that Caddy says is "where we have the measles" (*SF*,

16. William Faulkner, *The Sound and the Fury* (New York: Modern Library, 1967), 75; hereafter cited in the text as *SF*.

89). In *The Sound and the Fury*, as we know, sickness and death are the frequent metaphors for sexual love, which like a locked bedroom is yet another sphere of experience from which Ben is barred.[17] Downstairs Ben's life is somewhat more secure, confined as it is to the kitchen, where Dilsey feeds and celebrates him, and the parlor, where he is succored by Mother's cushion and Caddy's slipper. Both rooms contain the smooth shapes of fire, but in the parlor on April 7, 1928, the mirror that was once Ben's doorway to peace and refuge from conflict is closed to him. When Luster turns on the lights on Saturday evening, "The windows went black, and the dark tall place on the wall came and I went and touched it. It was like a door, only it wasn't a door" (*SF*, 74). As Ben knows the maze of his house, with its locks and limits, its secure and its terrifying corners, so we know Ben. Or rather, through them we know Ben, for they are the referents of his wordless and otherwise inexpressible self.

That Ben should be a prisoner of the house and garden is a practical necessity, and of course he is not even a knowing prisoner since he is incapable of knowing in any usual sense of that word. Yet housed as he is, he defines himself for us in terms of the elements that define his captivity: in his section of the novel there are more than fifty references to fences and gates, twelve of them in the opening scene where he peers "through the fence, between the curling flower spaces," holds to the fence, goes along the fence, and sees his shadow on the garden fence at the end of the yard (*SF*, 1–2).[18] His isolation from the world is

17. Ben recognizes sickness, death, and sexuality by smell: he can smell his father's death, for example, and of course he smells Caddy's virginity and its loss. Quentin's obsession with sexuality as sickness or death expands on Ben's metaphor. He remembers Caddy saying of her lovers, "*When they touched me I died*" (*SF*, 185), and of her pregnancy, "*There was something terrible in me sometimes at night I could see it grinning at me I could see it through them grinning at me through their faces it's gone now and I'm sick*" (*SF*, 130).

18. André Bleikasten makes this same point in a different context in *The Most Splendid Failure: Faulkner's The Sound and the Fury* (Bloomington: Indiana University Press, 1976). 80–83. Bleikasten argues that Ben's fences and gates are Freudian symbols of his longing for Caddy, from whom he is forever separated.

as complete as—and rendered in the same terms as—that of the speaker of *The Waste Land* who says:

> . . . I have heard the key
> Turn in the door once and turn once only
> We think of the key, each in his prison
> Thinking of the key, each confirms a prison.[19]

Ben confirms his own prison for the reader in just this way by recurring to the physical boundaries of his world. Faulkner may also have had in mind the note with which Eliot glossed these lines when he created Ben's tightly bounded universe. Eliot quotes F. H. Bradley, *Appearance and Reality*, in his note to line 412; although Ben cannot "think," the same passage might well gloss him.

My external sensations are no less private to myself than are my thoughts or my feelings. In either case my experience falls within my own circle, a circle closed on the outside; and, with all its elements alike, every sphere is opaque to the others which surround it. . . . In brief, regarded as an existence which appears in a soul, the whole world for each is peculiar and private to that soul.[20]

In *The Sound and the Fury* the fenced house and garden are analogous to the closed circle of Ben's private sensations and associations. He is a prisoner of both home and self, as incapable of passing alone through the fence with Uncle Maury's love letter to Mrs. Patterson as he is of expressing his love to the Burgess girl, to whom he is "trying to say" (*SF*, 64) when he passes through the open gate. Against the terrors of the world beyond the fence, the familiar symmetry of house and home sustains Ben, even if only barely so. When Luster so terrifyingly dis-

19. T. S. Eliot, *The Waste Land*, in *T. S. Eliot: The Complete Poems and Plays*, lines 412–15.
20. *Ibid.*, 54.

orients him in the Jefferson square, therefore, it is appropriately the architectural symmetry of his counterclockwise ride that restores the world to him: "The broken flower drooped over Ben's fist and his eyes were empty and blue and serene again as *cornice* and *facade* flowed smoothly once more from left to right; *post* and tree, *window* and *doorway*, and signboard, each in its ordered place" (*SF*, 401; my emphasis).

Although Ben's world is restricted to the Compson house and grounds and Quentin's extends from Mississippi to Massachusetts, Quentin inhabits the house in memory in nearly the same way that Ben does in fact. Whereas Ben is locked in, however, Quentin is locked out: his recurrence to house and home is a mode by which he expresses his dilemma as the ironically outcast favorite son. Unhoused in fact by his residence at Harvard and psychologically by his broken family, he is captive to the images that swarm his mind on June 2, 1910, bound to a place that he can neither inhabit nor escape. In this plethora of associations, however, the Compson house itself remains largely in shadow. Unlike Ben, whose physical captivity compels him to describe his prison, Quentin seldom particularizes its characteristics. Once again, Gaston Bachelard offers an explanation why this might be so. According to Bachelard, the chief benefit of one's house is that it "shelters daydreaming": he calls the house "one of the greatest powers of integration for the thoughts, memories, and dreams of mankind."[21] But such houses, he points out, need not be described in detail. On the contrary,

> Over-picturesqueness in a house can conceal its intimacy. This is also true in life. But it is truer still in daydreams. For the real houses of memory, the houses to which we return in dreams, the houses that are rich in unalterable oneirism, do not readily lend themselves to description. To describe them would be like showing them to visitors. We can perhaps tell everything about the present, but [never] about

21. Bachelard, *Poetics of Space*, 6.

the past! The first, the oneirically definitive house, must retain its shadows.[22]

Here Bachelard states as theory what Faulkner does in practice. Quentin's real house of memory is detailed only insofar as physical detail is necessary to locate him in the remembered scene: at the branch, for example, or the ditch or in the pasture. More often, physical setting evokes the quality or theme of a scene. With Natalie, Quentin's combined sexual urgency and shame are conveyed by the separation of the barn from the house: "*Did Caddy go away did she go to the house you cant see the barn from our house did you ever try to see the barn from*" (*SF*, 167). If the house of the past conveys intimacy by its unspecified geometry, the houses of the present hide intimacy behind meticulously detailed façades. Wandering with Julio's sister on June 2, 1910, Quentin describes this scene:

We reached the station and crossed the tracks, where the river was. A bridge crossed it, and a street of jumbled frame houses followed the river, backed onto it. A shabby street, but with an air heterogeneous and vivid too. In the center of an untrimmed plot enclosed by a fence of gaping and broken pickets stood an ancient lopsided surrey and a weathered house from an upper window of which hung a garment of vivid pink. (*SF*, 162–63)

A moment later his mind turns to interiors:

The houses all seemed empty. Not a soul in sight. A sort of breathlessness that empty houses have. Yet they couldn't all be empty. All the different rooms, if you could just slice the walls away all of a sudden Madam, your daughter, if you please. No Madam, for God's sake, your daughter. (*SF*, 164)

The nature of these details—the fenced plot, the surrey, and the undergarment—and the fact that Quentin is in company with a

22. *Ibid.*, 12–13.

girl he calls *sister*, suggests this house outside Boston as an analogue of the Compson house where the fenced yard contains a dilapidated carriage and where Caddy's soiled undergarment is a major issue in Quentin's emotional life. Yet nowhere in *The Sound and the Fury*, let alone in Quentin's twilit reveries, are the Compson house and grounds so precisely described as the house in Boston. Conversely, this imagined interior scene— "Madam, your daughter, if you please"—is far less vivid than Quentin's memories of the actual interiors of home.

Perhaps Quentin need not describe the exterior of his own house in detail because it is his home. Perhaps, too, his physical removal from the house in Mississippi removes any necessity for him to describe particular aspects of it as he does of present houses and landscapes. Whatever the case with exteriors, the interiors of houses—their stairways, corridors, and private rooms—frequently provide him with the metaphors by which he expresses his interior life. On the eve of Caddy's wedding, for example, his words against Herbert Head, the pistol that he could not use against Dalton Ames, and Caddy's symbolically forbidden bedroom combine in a single anguished cry by which he metaphorically avenges himself on his sister's lovers and penetrates her body: *"Quentin has shot Herbert he shot his voice through the floor of Caddy's room"* (SF, 130).

In a related scene, a picture in a children's book becomes a figurative room that has the same dreamlike lack of specification as so many of Quentin's own memories, and like his obsessive memories of his house, the picture too imprisons him. This is what he recalls:

When I was little there was a picture in one of our books, a dark place into which a single weak ray of light came slanting upon two faces lifted out of the shadow. *You know what I'd do if I were King?* she never was a queen or a fairy she was always a king or a giant or a general *I'd break that place open and drag them out and I'd whip them good* It was torn out, jagged out. I was glad. I'd have to turn back to it until the dungeon was Mother herself she and Father upward into weak light holding hands and us lost somewhere below even them without even a ray of light. (*SF,* 215)

As king, giant, and general, Caddy clearly dominates Quentin in this scene. The "dark place" that he says is inhabited by Mother and Father is a room housing sexual knowledge—Quentin calls it "Mother herself"—and Caddy's readiness to break into that room prefigures her own violation by the giantlike army man, Dalton Ames. Quentin's fear of sexuality leaves him "lost somewhere below even them" in the dark prisonhouse of his own inescapable virginity.

In the following scene, the corridor to the dormitory latrine merges with another frightening memory of home, this one set in the upstairs hallway of the Compson house where Quentin walks toward the bathroom. By this conjunction of memories, the dark dungeon in the picture becomes the darkened house itself. The extended metaphor is enriched by the addition of doors to water. As the present gives way to the past, Quentin walks with the "sad generations seeking water" at Harvard (*SF,* 215) and simultaneously stumbles through the hallway at home *"where a misstep in the darkness filled with sleeping Mother Father Caddy Jason Maury getting so far ahead sleeping I will sleep fast when I door Door door"* (*SF,* 216). The interior of Quentin's oneiric house is constituted of the elements that define his dilemma and his solution to it: the hallway that imprisons him isolates him from his sleeping family, but at its end is the door beyond which he will "sleep fast." Earlier, Quentin had said that after the Dalton Ames affair "I seemed to be lying neither asleep nor awake looking down a long corridor of grey halflight where all stable things had become shadowy paradoxical all I had done shadows all I had felt suffered taking visible form antic and perverse mocking without relevance inherent themselves with the denial of significance they should have affirmed thinking I was I was not who was not was not who" (*SF*, 211). Now, like the tilted hallway that leads Darl Bundren to a madhouse, Quentin's dark corridor leads him beyond night and unrest to "the sea and the peaceful grottoes" (*SF*, 139) of the House of Death where, as he says, "I will look down and see my murmuring bones and the deep water like wind, like a *roof* of wind" (*SF*, 98; my emphasis).

Faulkner's fondness for such interiors and his poetic use of them can be documented in his early poetry, his stories, and his novels. Of work predating *The Sound and the Fury*, the imagery of several poems from *A Green Bough* suggests that they may have prepared the way for the metaphoric interiors of the novel. Poem XIX, for example, combines erotic love with death-by-water in a Prufrock-like passage set in the "slow cathedralled corridors" under the sea where a drowned man is caressed by "seamaids red and brown."[23] One working title of *The Sound and the Fury* was "Twilight," and in Poem XXII the shadowed half-light of memory leads the speaker to a door to remembered love:

> I see your face through the twilight of my mind,
> A dusk of forgotten things, remembered things;
> It is a corridor dark and cool with music
> And too dim for sight,
> That leads me to a door which brings
> You, clothed in quiet sound for my delight.[24]

These and similar images prefigure the poetry of *The Sound and the Fury* where, in the fuller context of the fictional world, architectural metaphors of house and home firmly root characters in a specific place and time. The metamorphosis from poetic

23. William Faulkner, *A Green Bough*, in *The Marble Faun and A Green Bough* (New York: Random House, 1965). The typescript of Poem XIX is dated "2 April, 1925"; see Keen Butterworth, "A Census of Manuscripts and Typescripts of William Faulkner's Poetry," *Mississippi Quarterly*, XXVI (Summer, 1973), 338.
24. Faulkner, *A Green Bough*, 44.

image to actual physical setting continued from novel to novel as Yoknapatawpha County evolved, but Faulkner never entirely abandoned his figurative houses for merely literal ones. In *Sanctuary*, the book that immediately followed *As I Lay Dying*, there are actual houses that we might immediately recognize—in or out of the fiction—but they are employed in new and even startling ways. I want to conclude with two of these: the Old Frenchman Place in the country outside Jefferson and Miss Reba Rivers's sporting house in Memphis. They are the scenes of Temple Drake's violation and corruption respectively, and each is a carefully particularized place well suited to its symbolic function in the novel.

The Old Frenchman Place, which lifts "its stark square bulk against the failing sky" (*S*, 7) in the opening pages of *Sanctuary*, is certainly a picturesque enough setting for the crimes committed there, and Faulkner valued it enough to return to the antebellum house for major scenes in *The Hamlet* and *Requiem for a Nun*. But for all of its foreboding dilapidation, the characteristic of the house that Faulkner repeatedly stresses in *Sanctuary* is its unrestricted and unrestrained openness. The house offers no one sanctuary because it has no dimension to distinguish inside from outside. The dominant feature is a center hall, "open through the house" (*S*, 41, 8, 86), and on Saturday night and Sunday morning Temple rushes again and again into, out of, and through that hall, searching for the refuge conventionally associated with houses. A house without locks, however, and frequently without even doors, can offer no interior sanctuary. Temple's bedroom is invaded at will on Saturday night, not only by Popeye but also by Lee Goodwin, Van, Gowan, Tommy, and Ruby Lamar. Popeye calls the Frenchman Place a "goofy house" (*S*, 94) and so it is, for it is architecturally indistinguishable from the barn where Ruby takes Temple for the night and in no sense safer. Like the house, the barn has an open center hall (*S*, 88, 95) and Temple's corn crib hideaway, like her bedroom, is located just inside the front entrance (S, 86, 96–98). When Popeye comes for her on Saturday morning, he easily circumvents the doglike Tommy at the door, and the violation begun in a room in the house the night before is completed in an analogous room in the barn. On Saturday evening Temple appeals for sanctuary to a vision of her own home where her father, Judge Drake, would be "sitting on the veranda, in a linen suit, a palm leaf fan in his hand, watching the Negro mow the lawn" (S, 52). On Sunday morning, in the corn crib with Popeye, her father is replaced in her imagination by Lee Goodwin's father, Pap, and she screams to him for help as he sits on the ruined porch in blind and force-less judgment, "his hands crossed on top of the stick" (S, 99). In the sanctuary of the Luxembourg Gardens at the end of the novel, the two fathers are again ironically superimposed: as Judge Drake sits with "his hands crossed on the head of his stick" (S, 309) Temple yawns into her mirror.

The corruption of spirit that affects this change in Temple Drake is accomplished at Miss Reba's house in Memphis, an edifice perfectly suited to the psychological damage that Faulkner balances against the physical violence at the Frenchman Place. Whereas the Frenchman Place is characterized by un-checked freedom, Reba's is an entirely closed house of shadowed corridors, locked doors, and drawn shades—an urban rather than a rural house, decrepit rather than a historic ruin. That Temple should be raped at the open house and made captive to lust in the closed one is appropriate to the outer-inner aspect of her predicament. The houses are complementary and represent demoniac extremes of the archetypal home: each is a figurative underworld where the temple of family is desecrated by the re-versal of conventional family roles. The Lee Goodwin family with its dying child is replicated in Memphis where Popeye is a satanic "Daddy" (S, 229), Reba the Mother-as-Madam, and Temple their Child and Victim.

Further, each house is a concrete symbol of the kind of desecration wrought upon Temple herself. At the Old Frenchman Place, the symbolic association of barn with body functions is reinforced by the fact that the bootleggers use a back stall in the barn as an outhouse. Temple fastidiously refuses to use the stall herself, is spied on in the weeds outside the barn by Lee Goodwin, and runs from him into the barn where Popeye rapes her. The association of female sexuality with excrement is repeated in Memphis where the Snopes cousins comically confuse the front of Reba's whorehouse with the back when they mistake its "lattice-work false entry" (S, 185) for an outhouse. That metaphor extends one of the darker motifs of *The Sound and the Fury* where Quentin is obsessed with Caddy's muddy underdrawers and describes her body in terms of blood and excrement: "Delicate equilibrium of periodical filth between two moons balanced. Moons he said full and yellow as harvest moons her hips thighs" (SF, 159). In *Sanctuary* Miss Reba's house with its "false entry" is perversely suggestive of the aberrant sexual violations that are the cause and the means of Temple's corruption. In addition the house with no front makes concrete the figure for sexual intercourse that Darl Bundren alludes to and Quentin Compson names "*The beast with two backs*" (AILD, 244; SF, 184). Reba's is a temple of prostitution—the house that Virgil Snopes says cannot be a hotel because it has no sign is itself the sign and symbol of its function.

Those are ideas that Henry James might not have understood. But he almost certainly would have understood—and approved—Faulkner's own "architectural competence" in rendering those ideas fictionally. I have no doubt that there are times in his fictions when the South is Faulkner's subject and when the gallantry or the tragedy of the South is represented by its architecture. Some passages in *Requiem for a Nun* describing the courthouse and the jail come first to mind. But there are very few instances, and certainly *Requiem* is not one such, when the South is Faulkner's only subject or when his fictional houses

157

are only picturesque backdrops, two-dimensional stage sets without human depth and perspective. Like Yoknapatawpha County itself, the houses of Faulkner's fictions project a sense of place by their regional characteristics and by the full range of human attachments to them—the tendernesses with the savageries, the psychological realities with the physical ones. Dream house or real one, historic relic or antiquarian refuge, the houses of Faulkner's fictions are complex and expressive symbolic figures: fictional places that are fictional forms. And no wonder that this should be so in the house of fiction. "The carpenter don't build a house just to drive nails," Faulkner said at Virginia. "He drives nails to build a house."[25]

25. Frederick L. Gwynn and Joseph Blotner (eds.), *Faulkner in the University: Class Conferences at the University of Virginia, 1957–1958* (Charlottesville: University of Virginia Press, 1959), 50.

"I Taken an Oath of Office Too":
Faulkner and the Law

NOEL POLK

The two chief features of Jefferson, Mississippi's, architectural landscape are the courthouse and the jail: they stand throughout most of William Faulkner's fiction as the central axis of his narrative and thematic concerns, and they are connected to each other by the strongest and most irresolvable ties. Between these two poles run the currents of Faulkner's most powerful characters and his most significant themes: the eternal conflicts between good and evil, between power and weakness, between passion and impotence, between justice and injustice, and between freedom and bondage. Some of his most memorable scenes take place in or around these two buildings, and some of his most profound analyses of the human condition emerge from his descriptions of and meditations upon the buildings and their relationships.

The courthouse is of course the actual and metaphorical center, the hub, of Faulkner's created world. Invested in it is the history not just of Yoknapatawpha County, but of the entire race of civilized man, of the splendid dream that conquered wildernesses and dethroned kings—the dream of freedom, justice, peace, security, of progress, of hope. When the courthouse was first built it was "the biggest edifice in the country"; the original settlers, who built it, saw it as belonging to them, but at the same time as being "bigger than any because it was the sum of all and, being the sum of all, it must raise all of their hopes and

159

aspirations level with its own aspirant and soaring cupola."[1] It is at once the repository of man's dreams, the symbol of his aspirations, and the inspiration for his labor.

If the courthouse is the symbol of man's image of himself as a creature capable of choosing good over evil, capable of freedom—if the courthouse is the symbol of man's ideal state—the jail is, by contrast, the symbol of the other part of his nature. What the jail symbolizes is that anarchic part of man's personality that insists upon breaking laws, that refuses to be shackled by any rule or convention. Paradoxically, this impulse toward chaos is to a large degree the same impulse toward freedom that keeps man building courthouses.

In a deeper sense, then, the courthouse represents the rights and privileges that civilization confers upon man; the jail represents the responsibility, the price in suffering and anxiety, that civilization exacts from him: the price he must pay for those rights and privileges. If the courthouse is the repository of man's dreams and hopes, the jailhouse is the record of his failures; and because it is a record of failure, it is a chronicle of longing and despair, of suffering and of pain, and is therefore a much more moving portrait of the human heart in conflict than that found in the courthouse, in the history of man's successes. Indeed, in *Requiem for a Nun* Gavin Stevens tells us that

. . . if you would peruse in unbroken—ay, overlapping—continuity the history of a community, look not in the church registers and the courthouse records, but beneath the successive layers of calcimine and creosote and whitewash on the walls of the jail, since only in that forcible carceration does man find the idleness in which to compose, in the gross and simple terms of his gross and simple lusts and yearnings, the gross and simple recapitulations of his gross and simple heart. (*Requiem*, 214)

1. William Faulkner, *Requiem for a Nun* (New York: Random House, 1951), 42.

And I can't resist quoting a similar passage from *Intruder in the Dust*:

. . . not courthouses nor even churches but jails were the true records of a county's, a community's history, since not only the cryptic forgotten initials and words and even phrases cries of defiance and indictment scratched into the walls but the very bricks and stones themselves held, not in solution but in suspension, intact and biding and potent and indestructible, the agonies and shames and griefs with which hearts long since unmarked and unremembered dust had strained and perhaps burst.[2]

In attempting to treat "Faulkner and the Law" then, it is also necessary to deal with Faulkner and lawbreakers, because of the ways in which laws and lawbreakers are inextricably related to one another in Faulkner's complex vision of the world. At the beginning we must confront a series of problems, having to do not just with the nature of civilization but also to a certain extent with the nature of fiction. All teachers of literature are asked to explain why Faulkner and others insist upon dealing with "sordid" subject matter. Why don't they, we are asked, deal with the good side of life? We respond in a variety of ways, mostly inadequately, since there is no good answer. But the simple truth is, and the explanation that my students finally buy, is that Good Unproblemed People who obey all the rules are generally pretty dull, while those unprincipled scoundrels who run the countryside just minutes ahead of the posse are likely to be fascinating, if only for the possiblity of violence they may do to others or have done to them. There's something important in us that wants to admire and romanticize the lawbreaker—especially, particularly, if the criminal is a criminal with a bit of class or skill and is extraordinarily clever. Thus we make room in our national

2. William Faulkner, *Intruder in the Dust* (New York: Random House, 1949), 49–50.

pantheon for the likes of such thugs as Billy the Kid, Jesse James, and Bonnie and Clyde, and for people even more recent than that. Remember not too long ago the young man who hijacked a jetliner, extorted an enormous amount of money from the airline, then bailed out of the plane over the Rocky Mountains in the middle of the night and was never heard from again? He became almost a national hero, and was instantly apotheosized with the nearest thing to canonization our protestant culture has to offer: his name and deeds emblazoned on T-shirts! And, finally, I hope that you were as pleased as I by the group of French bandits a year or so ago who tunnelled their way into the safe-deposit room of a Marseilles bank, made themselves comfortably at home for the weekend with picnic baskets full of wine and food and, with girly pictures taped to the wall, proceeded, at their leisure, to open the boxes and loot the bank. Of course, none of us would have been very happy with these antics had it been our money they stole!

Why do we respond to these people, whose example, if everybody followed suit, would bring to ruin the order, peace, and security we all cherish and need? Perhaps it is too simple to say that we respond because they were not caught, or because they were striking out against the establishment, though that's probably a good part of it. In a perverse sort of way, however, those criminals, be they vicious or classy, remind us that laws *can* be broken. If we choose *not* to break them, we thereby assert the very freedom the laws deny us. Whatever grief and problem lawbreakers cause us, they are nothing compared to the serious trouble we would be in if no laws could be broken or, indeed, if nobody wanted to break any.

We can understand the law, and our relationship to it—at least as Faulkner analyzed that relationship—by looking for a moment at the origins of the Yoknapatawpha County courthouse and jail, as related in the opening prologue of *Requiem for a Nun*. This is material that I've commented on elsewhere in some detail,[3] but a brief reminder of some of the significant events during the days of Jefferson's founding will be useful to us.

Jefferson's original settlers, you will recall, come to the north Mississippi wilderness in order to escape the trials and tribulations of an East Coast that has been overrun by people and by government, two necessary concomitants of each other, although the settlers don't know that yet. They settle in an area as completely uncivilized as they can find, an area midway between the Natchez Trace and the Mississippi River, telling themselves that what they want is to avoid evil—they want "no part of the underworld of either" the Trace or the River (*Requiem*, 6). What in fact they are after is freedom; what they want more than anything else is to escape from the legal bonds and social pressures that living in civilization entails. Like Huck Finn, they light out for the territory, running from all those folks who insist that they be, or at least act, civilized. They believe that they can escape human nature, and hope to re-establish connections with their lost innocent selves in a North Mississippi Wilderness Eden.

Being human, however, they bring with them the very condition they are trying to escape; they bring it in the form of Alec Holston's gigantic lock, which, like the jail itself, comes to symbolize what may have been William Faulkner's only orthodox Protestant belief: original sin—the human condition of sinfulness which makes locks and jails necessary. The settlers do realize that they must have a jail, even if they have no other public buildings to identify themselves as a social unit, to hold those who break what few rules they do have. In their pseudoprelapsarian state, however, our future Jeffersonians figure to need it only for "amateurs"—runaway slaves and such—and so make it a ramshackle, insubstantial structure that costs them very little time or money. They do not prepare themselves adequately,

3. Noel Polk, "Alec Holston's Lock and the Founding of Jefferson," *Mississippi Quarterly*, XXIV (Summer, 1971), 247–69.

then, to deal effectively with evil when it does, as it must, finally, appear; the jail is simply no match for the Natchez Trace hoodlums they put in it. These "professionals" break out easily and disappear, taking with them not just old Alec's lock, but one entire wall of the building.

The settlers learn a quick and relatively painless lesson that makes them aware of their vulnerability to thugs like these; they decide that they will be safer, more secure, more able to pursue life, liberty, and happiness if they organize themselves to provide for their mutual protection. They confederate and create a town. First they rebuild the jail, replacing the one missing wall; but they also add three more walls to that one they had to build anyway and thereby make another room which they will use as the courthouse. Thus at the beginning the courthouse and the jail are not just *contained* in one building, they *are* one building. The original structure emphasizes the similar purposes of their origins and their relationships to each other.

Among the many things that follow their incorporation, two are important for our purposes here: first, in order to organize, each of the settlers gives up certain of his freedoms, as we all must if we are to control the forces of anarchy. In *Requiem* Faulkner equates freedom, *absolute* freedom, with anarchy: "for these were frontier, pioneer times, when personal liberty and freedom were almost a physical condition like fire or flood" (*Requiem*, 6). That is, to have the security necessary to their happiness they must give up some of the freedom they came West to find. Thus they discover that freedom must be defined in terms of its limits. As soon as they organize themselves they are, in political terms, no longer free; this is proven thirty years later when they try to leave the Union, fight the Civil War to prove they are free, and are defeated in the attempt.

The second thing worth noting is that over the years the settlers abandon the responsibility in the very pursuit of the dream.[4] When the early townsfolk decide to build another, bigger courthouse, one big enough to contain their dream, they make no provision for rebuilding the jail. Soon, in fact, they repudiate the jail altogether because it is the uncomfortable reminder of the price they no longer are willing to pay for the purchase of the dream. They pick up the entire town, as it were, and move it—the town, not the jail—one block south (*Requiem*, 213), leaving the jail in a cul-de-sac backwash, one block insulated from the town's governmental and commercial pursuit of happiness; they regard it, Faulkner tells us, as they regard a "public comfort-station" (*Requiem*, 228). It is the fact that they separate the jail from the courthouse—that is, separate the responsibility from the dream—that makes them, us, vulnerable to the rascals and demagogues who have ever gained their way into the courthouses and statehouses by promising us what we wanted to be promised.

Faulkner begins one of his best speeches by taking his audience back to the time when God was creating mankind. God "didn't merely believe in man," Faulkner suggests: "He knew that man was competent for a soul because he was . . . capable of teaching himself to be civilized, to live with his fellow man in amity, without anguish to himself or causing anguish and grief to others, and of appreciating the value of security and peace and freedom."[5] Faulkner then describes the angels who watched while God made man: all but one "merely looked on and watched—the serene and blameless seraphim, that white and shining congeries who . . . were content merely to bask for eternity in the reflected glory of the miracle of man, content merely to watch." These are very much like the content, sheeplike

4. Faulkner's "Address to the Delta Council" treats these ideas in nonfiction form. See James B. Meriwether (ed.), *William Faulkner: Essays, Speeches and Public Letters* (New York: Random House, 1966), 126–34.

5. "Address to the Graduating Class Pine Manor Junior College," in Meriwether (ed.), *Essays, Speeches and Public Letters*. All quotations are from pages 135–38.

masses that populate our world: "white, immaculate, negative, without past, without thought or grief or regrets or hopes."

The one angelic exception to this was, of course, Satan himself, the archcriminal, *the* lawbreaker, whose opinion of the human race was even worse than that of the "others," the "negative and shining ones." Satan not only "believed that man was incapable of anything but baseness, this one believed that baseness had been inculcated in man to be used for base personal aggrandizement by them of a higher and more ruthless baseness." Satan is described in heroic terms. He is "the splendid dark incorrigible one, who possessed the arrogance and pride to demand with, and the temerity to object with, and the ambition to substitute with—not only to decline to accept a condition just because it was a fact, but to want to substitute another condition in its place." Faulkner further declares that God then "used the dark spirit" to His purposes; He made rebelliousness an integral part of the human spirit (among other reasons, doubtless, in order to keep His heaven from becoming the paradise of Mark Twain's vision, filled with the good and faithful and eternally boring cherubim who do nothing but sing His praises all day long).

God knew the risks He would run, however: "He already presaw the long roster of the ambition's ruthless avatars— Genghis and Caesar and William and Hitler and Barca and Stalin and Bonaparte and Huey Long." But He was willing to risk all of that ugly crew because He also presaw "the long roster of other avatars of that rebellious and uncompromising pride also," the other aspect of that darker spirit, those who have "not only the ambition and the ruthlessness and the arrogance to show man what to revolt against, but also the temerity to revolt and the will to change what one does not like." These "other avatars" are the "artists and philosophers," the creators, who remind us constantly of "the tremendous shape of our godhead."

The idea that God actually used, and even admired, the dark spirit of rebelliousness is purely Faustian, and it may be that in

166

writing this passage Faulkner was drawing upon the lines in the "Prologue in Heaven" of Goethe's great poem, in which, after making His wager, God says to Mephistopheles,

> I have never hated the likes of you.
> Of all the spirits of denial
> The joker is the last that I eschew.
> Man finds relaxation too attractive—
> Too fond too soon of unconditional rest;
> Which is why I am pleased to give him a companion
> Who lures and thrusts and must, as devil, be active.[6]

If Satan is our nemesis, he is also, to a profound degree, our salvation, in that it is he who, "luring and thrusting" man, invests him with the spirit of freedom—the simultaneously creative and destructive spirit that makes us break laws just because they are laws, without regard to whether they are good laws or bad.

Precisely there is the rub. Because that same spirit of freedom is, as Faulkner tells us, also the spirit of anarchy. If it is curbed and bitted, it is no longer freedom. Too strong a curb and bit, too much peace and security, and we become sheep. One Faulknerian index to the spiritual vitality of a people is the degree to which and the frequency with which they kick against the pricks: a people who never question or challenge the laws that govern them can hardly be very vital or, alas, very much alive.

Civilization cannot depend entirely upon the good will and idealism of its most civic-minded and cooperative citizens. It must also depend upon the aggressiveness and ruthlessness, even the rapacity, of that old dark spirit. Faulkner illustrates this in *Requiem for a Nun* in the person of Compson, who, unlike the other settlers, is no altruistic dreamer; he has not come to

---

6. *Faust*, "Prologue in Heaven," lines 97–103, of the Louis MacNeice translation.

northern Mississippi seeking peace and freedom; he has come seeking profit. He has swapped Ikkemotubbe a racehorse for a "square mile of what was to be the most valuable land in the future town of Jefferson" (*Requiem*, 13), and has contrived (we are not told how) to sell this square mile to the city fathers *for his own price*. He is ruthless and opportunistic, and not at all highminded. But he is the only one of the settlers who is able to act in a crisis; he alone saves the community (and his investment) from dissolution when factions disagree over what to do with the Natchez Trace bandits. In the name of what he calls a "crisis in the public peace and welfare" (*Requiem*, 15), he dictatorially takes laudanum from Dr. Peabody's bag, mixes it with whiskey, and gives it to the faction he opposes. Later, when the same hopeful and idealistic citizens are working on the courthouse building—or at least they are holding shovels and hammers—they pause in a moment which is almost an epiphany for them, to contemplate the dream which the courthouse and their new town represent:

"By God. Jefferson," [one says].
    "Jefferson, Mississippi," a second added.
    "Jefferson, Yoknapatawpha County, Mississippi," a third corrected; who, which one, didn't matter this time either since it was still one conjoined breathing, one compound dream-state, mused and static, well capable of lasting on past sunrise too. (*Requiem*, 32–33)

Compson, however, knows that if they spend all their time in a "dream-state, mused and static," they will never get the actual courthouse off the ground—or ON the ground, rather. So he shakes them, crudely, out of their reverie: "It aint [Jefferson or anything else] until we finish the goddamned thing. . . . Come on. Let's get at it" (*Requiem*, 33). Compson does what he does in order to protect his own interests, rather than out of any altruistic spirit. But Jefferson would not have come into existence had it not been for that ruthless, aggressive spirit. Rapacity and altruism stroll hand in hand down the primrose path to civilization.

Even if a proper "balance" between freedom and order could be found, I suspect that even in the very idea of balance is something inimical to the human spirit. We worship passion, in almost any form, if it is sufficiently passionate and expressive. That is why we are so moved, over and over again, in *Sanctuary*, at the sight of the hands of the Negro murderer gripping the bars of the jail window, even though we know that he has murdered his wife, slashed her throat in the moonlight. The tension that is caused in us by the simultaneous pull, in opposite directions, of the desire for order and the desire for freedom, of the desire for peace and the desire for stimulation—that essential and irresolvable tension—is the matrix of the creative urge. The civilized person, the artist, channels his anarchic urges into creativity. But the desire to smash, to break free, and do something uncontrollable, is very much a part of our nature. To put it in well-known Faulknerian terms, man's supreme desire is to mark the earth some way, whether by building or destroying, to put his "Kilroy was here" on the wall of oblivion: that is his only immortality.

The law is in Faulkner a large and clumsy and needlessly complex institution. In *The Town* the venerable V. K. Ratliff opines that "federal folks were not interested in whether anything worked or not, all they were interested in was that you did it exactly like their rules said to do it."[7] Later, in the same novel, Ratliff pounces on Gavin Stevens as representative of the tribe of lawyers and government officials: "He's a lawyer," he says, "and to a lawyer . . . if it aint complicated up enough it aint right and so even if it works, you dont believe it" (*Town*, 296). This attitude manifests itself more elaborately, though no less satirically, in *Requiem*, in the passage where Faulkner declares that

7. William Faulkner, *The Town* (New York: Random House, 1957), 155–56.

Cecilia Farmer's father has his job as jailer not at all because he is competent for the job; rather, the jail itself has become just one more "moveable pawn on the county's political board," and he is hired

. . . not for work or capability for work, but for political fidelity and the numerality of votable kin by blood or marriage—a jailor or turnkey, himself someone's cousin and with enough other cousins and inlaws of his own to have assured the election of sheriff or chancery- or circuit-clerk—a failed farmer who was not at all the victim of his time but, on the contrary, was its master, since his inherited and inescapable incapacity to support his family by his own efforts had matched him with an era and a land where government was founded on the working premise of being primarily an asylum for ineptitude and indigence, for the private business failures among your or your wife's kin whom otherwise you yourself would have to support. (*Requiem*, 228)

The law in Faulkner is also a corrupt institution, because it invests power in the hands of corruptible human beings who use their power to their own ends; and one need only point to deputies like the nameless one in *Pylon* and the redoubtable Butch Lovemaiden in *The Reivers*, not to mention rascals and scalawags like Senator Clarence Snopes and District Attorney Eustace Graham, to illustrate the misuse of legal power. The settlers who believed that because the courthouse is the sum of all it must therefore *raise* all were wrong, at least in the short run. The Jefferson courthouse becomes, in the twentieth century, a government so corrupt that it differs from the governments of Chicago and Kansas City only in size and in the scope of its opportunity (*Requiem*, 243–44).

Faulkner's most sinister and cynical portrait of the law in its relationship to society is, without question, *Sanctuary*; it is there depicted not merely as corrupt but as a foul and pestilential system that allows no room for justice or mercy. It is one of the chief tools of the forces of darkness. In *Sanctuary* the law always does exactly what it should not do. It protects the guilty and punishes the innocent; when it does punish the guilty, it does so for the wrong reason, and almost accidentally. The earnest advocate of the law's ideals, Horace Benbow, is easily defeated by the corruption that he sees and hears about, so pervasive is it: the police chiefs and detectives who frequent Miss Reba's Memphis whorehouse, especially the grotesquely overweight chief of police who has to have a special bed brought in; the Memphis Jew lawyers who are obviously manipulators of the law in the employ of the Memphis underworld; the lawyers whom Ruby has to sleep with in order to try to keep Lee out of prison; the politically ambitious Eustace Graham, who preys on everyone's sentimental sensitivity to his crippled leg, and who is more than willing to sacrifice Lee Goodwin and Ruby Lamar and Horace and Temple and everybody else to get what he wants; the clownish and incompetent Senator Clarence Snopes, who because of his clownishness and incompetence is surely representative of all that can go wrong with our system of government. (Some intelligent person might be fooled once or twice into voting for Eustace Graham, but how could anybody even slightly more intelligent than a chipmunk vote for Clarence? The fact that Clarences continue to be elected to responsible positions—in Mississippi and other states—is perhaps indicative of the glaring defect in our system of government, a cause for shame.)

The law is perverted many times in *Sanctuary*. We are amused, if exasperated, to hear Clarence Snopes opine that "there ought to be a law" to keep people like himself—that is, a white American—from being misused by those Memphis Jew lawyers. But amusement turns to savage irony when Popeye says, in all seriousness, that "there ought to be a law" to keep people from making and drinking whiskey, because he makes his own living as a bootlegger; the irony takes a quantum leap when we realize that Popeye is, can be, needs to be, a bootlegger, precisely because there *is* such a law (called Prohibition) which he has been flouting for years with complete impunity!

The law in *Sanctuary* frequently *becomes* a sanctuary, and in more ways than one. If Temple and Judge Drake use it to protect themselves from prosecution or public disgrace, if Clarence uses it to hide his incompetence for anything else, if the tall convict in *The Wild Palms* cannot wait to get back to Parchman's benevolent arms, others in Faulkner use the law to protect themselves from moral deliberation and choice. This, I rather suspect, might be the worst of all the misuses of the law, the most debilitating to the human spirit. And now I'm speaking not just of civil law, but also of moral law, any law which we accept without question or challenge. Two examples will suffice.

The first is Thomas Jefferson Pettigrew, the mail-rider in *Requiem for a Nun*, the frail, irascible little man who does not "represent" but, Faulkner tells us, actually *is* the United States. As the United States it is right that he have a mouth full of law, even if it is a pettifogging legalese that he speaks. When the settlers lose the lock that has become the United States' property, Pettigrew threatens them with maximum punishment for a crime that hardly amounts to a respectable misdemeanor: you've committed, he tells the settlers,

. . . a violation of act of Congress as especially made and provided for the defacement of government property, penalty of five thousand dollars or not less than one year in a Federal jail or both. For whoever cut them two slits in the [mail] bag to put the lock in, act of Congress as especially made and provided for the injury or destruction of government property, penalty of ten thousand dollars or not less than five years in a Federal jail or both. (*Requiem*, 23–24)

The settlers are wrong when they accuse Pettigrew of wanting "confusion. Just damned confusion" (*Requiem* 25). What he wants and needs is the order that a strict adherence to the law

172

gives him. Like many of Faulkner's characters, he tries to impose his own abstract formulations of his ideals upon a situation in life which they will not fit. Like the settlers, he is unprepared to deal with any situation not covered by his rules. That, doubtless, is why he capitulates so easily to the settlers' bribe.

The other example of this kind of mentality that I shall note here is General Gragnon, the ruthlessly military commanding officer in *A Fable* who insists upon executing all members of the mutinous regiment, because that is what the laws of his profession state that he must do. And he dies, accepts execution himself, rather than admit that those rules are insufficient to deal with the mutiny.

The significant thing about the legal system as Faulkner presents it to us, however, is that in spite of all these flaws—its potential for misuse, its tendency to create elephants to deal with fleas, its frequent injustices and gross inequities—in spite of all this, it *works*. Over the long haul it does manage to find a creative balance between man's natural desire for order and his equally natural drive toward freedom. For every Gragnon who insists that the law must be obeyed to preserve civilization, there is a corporal who insists that the law must be broken in order to free men's spirits; for every both of them there is an Old Marshal who recognizes the symbolic values in each of their opposing positions, and who finds a way, not to compromise them, but to *use* them both as necessary and desirable, if extreme, philosophical positions, in order to keep the world going. In *A Fable*, the corporal symbolizes the eternally free spirit of the human race—man's duty to himself—and General Gragnon symbolizes man's equally eternal responsibility to his community.

So, taking the long view, the system of laws works; it is essentially sound and healthy, from the bottom to the top; from, in *Requiem*, for example, the governor to the jailer, who are at

173

opposite ends of just about every scale you can think of, but who are very much alike in their commitment to justice and in their compassion for the suffering of both Nancy Mannigoe and Temple Stevens. It is worth noting that the popular conception—or at least my own conception before I started working seriously on this paper—the popular conception of Faulkner's law enforcement officers as having stepped right out of a Dodge commercial simply does not hold water. There are the Butch Lovemaidens, of course: we will ever have them with us. But most of the sheriffs and deputies in Faulkner are competent, honorable, sensible and even courageous men who take their jobs seriously. Recall the sheriff in *The Sound and the Fury* who handles Jason Compson precisely as he deserves to be handled, and the steady, tough Hope Hampton in *Intruder in the Dust*; even the bumbling deputy Grover Cleveland Winbush in *The Town* is balanced by the sensible and competent Sheriff Hub Hampton. The list could be extended. And it is very much worth remembering that the lynchings in "Dry September" and *Light in August* are not done or condoned by law officers, but by vigilantes, self-appointed purveyors of the public weal who choose to follow their own rather than the established legal procedures.

One of the two central characters in "Pantaloon in Black" is the unnamed deputy who in the second part of the story comes home nearly in a state of hysteria and tries to tell his wife what has happened at the jail. This story has had me puzzled for years. Rider's part of the story is powerful and moving: in grief over his wife's death, the Negro tries to kill himself; he succeeds by killing a white man and getting himself lynched. But the deputy's part of the story had seemed somewhat flat in what I took to be its obvious and conventional "meaning," which was contained in the cheap and easy irony of having a stereotypical redneck Mississippi lawman look with totally uncomprehending eyes at Rider's struggle in the jail before being taken out:

174

"Them damn niggers," [he tells his wife]. "I swear to godfrey, it's a wonder we have as little trouble with them as we do. Because why? Because they aint human. They look like a man and they walk on their hind legs like a man, and they can talk and you can understand them and you think they are understanding you, at least now and then. But when it comes to the normal human feelings and sentiments of human beings, they might just as well be a damn herd of wild buffaloes."[8]

The deputy proceeds with his bitter story, interpreting all the facts in precisely the wrong way, and ends with the tremendously moving description of Rider on the jail floor, after his struggle, "laughing, with tears big as glass marbles running across his face and down past his ears and making a kind of popping sound on the floor like somebody dropping bird eggs, laughing and laughing and saying, 'Hit look lack Ah just cant quit thinking. Look lack Ah just cant quit'" (*Moses*, 159). He concludes by asking his wife: "And what do you think of that?"

His card-cheating wife, however, who has been busy getting ready to go out, is not the least interested in what he is saying; she is only remotely aware that he is talking at all, much less that he is describing to her the events preliminary to a lynching. What puzzled me most about this story was why the deputy even bothered to tell this to anybody, much less to one so completely uninterested, until finally it dawned on me that he is not talking to her at all: he is talking only to himself, trying to sort out what he has seen. He has been overwhelmed by something which neither his background nor his legal training has prepared him for—and I don't mean the lynching: I mean Rider's agonizing, unassuageable grief. This deputy, who has not before now thought Negroes capable of such a normal human emotion, has seen a Negro suffer. Thus he talks desperately, trying to describe what has happened in terms of his old patterns of understanding; but his cliché-ridden redneck vocabulary is insufficient. He is

8. William Faulkner, *Go Down, Moses* (New York: Random House, 1952), 154.

not trying to explain Rider away; he is, simply, profoundly, trying to understand. He is, then, an educable man, and as such he represents one of the most important elements in Faulkner's system of values: the capacity for growth, the ability to change.

It may not be significant that this man is a law officer, but I think it is, and it might be useful to look quickly at another low-ranking lawman, the jailer in *Intruder in the Dust* who takes seriously his official duty to protect Lucas Beauchamp, while nervously and in near panic awaiting the arrival of the Gowries, who, he fears, will kill him in order to get Lucas:

"Dont mind me," [he tells Gavin Stevens]. "I'm going to do the best I can; I taken an oath of office too." His voice rose a little, still calm, just louder: "But dont think nobody's going to make me admit I like it. I got a wife and two children; what good am I going to be to them if I get myself killed protecting a goddamn stinking nigger?" His voice rose again; it was not calm now: "And how am I going to live with myself if I let a passel of nogood sonabitches take a prisoner away from me?" (*Intruder*, 54)[9]

Both of these men are very much a part of their culture; neither entertains the remotest notion of the actual or even potential equality of the races. But both are, I would suggest, in their own ways, ennobled by the law they serve, respond properly to the ideals that law represents.

I would like to close with a very few words about Faulkner's best-known lawyer and public servant, Gavin Stevens, who is central to an understanding of Faulkner. After writing *Sanctuary*, Faulkner abandoned completely the effete and nihilistic Horace Benbow, and replaced him with Stevens. They are virtually identical, except that Stevens is endowed with more resilience; he has the capacity to maintain his belief in the ideals of his profession in spite of his repeated mistakes and defeats.

9. See Warren Beck's comments on this passage in *Intruder* in his *Faulkner* (Madison: University of Wisconsin Press, 1976), 94–97.

He seems to me in many ways to epitomize the essential Faulknerian man, and it is no accident that for all his shortcomings
Stevens is the central figure in Faulkner's late work. Time and
time again he is the touchstone for, if not the actual carrier of,
Faulkner's assessment of human capacities; and in that lies the
reason, I believe, why Faulkner returned to him over and over
again. It is possible, probable even, that we may never completely establish peace and harmony on earth; what is certain is
that we will never do it if we quit trying, quit believing in those
ideals. For all his many faults, for all his chuckleheadedness,
Stevens keeps us reminded of that fact: he never drops the
gauntlet.

Just before he goes to meet Eula Varner Snopes for their
third and final conversation in *The Town*, Stevens takes a ride
out to the top of Seminary Hill, a place that affords him an almost aerial view of Jefferson and the surrounding countryside.
What he describes is a complex world bound together by the
inextricable strands of man's belief in progress and of his simple,
inevitable, rapacity. I'm not at all sure that Faulkner would
agree completely with Stevens's vision, especially since Stevens
claims to look out over Yoknapatawpha County "detached as God
Himself," and believes he presides "unanguished and immune"
over that world. He is, of course, fooling himself if he believes
that even he can do so; there is never a suggestion that Faulkner
felt himself "detached" from his world or was ever "unanguished" by or "immune" to the sufferings and failings and the
relatively few victories of his people. But what Stevens describes must surely be at least partly what Faulkner saw when
he surveyed, at this late point in his long career, his own teeming created world:

. . . you stand suzerain and solitary above the whole sum of your life
beneath that incessant ephemeral spangling. First is Jefferson, the
center, radiating weakly its puny glow into space; beyond it, enclosing

177

it, spreads the County, tied by the diverging roads to that center as is
the rim to the hub by its spokes, yourself detached as God Himself for
this moment above the cradle of your nativity and of the men and
women who made you, the record and chronicle of your native land
proffered for your perusal in ring by concentric ring like the ripples on
living water above the dreamless slumber of your past; you to preside
unanguished and immune above this miniature of man's passions and
hopes and disasters—ambition and fear and lust and courage and ab-
negation and pity and honor and sin and pride—all bound, precarious
and ramshackle, held together by the web, the iron-thin warp and
woof of his rapacity but withal yet dedicated to his dreams. (*Town*,
315–16)

The last lines, which for me crystallize Faulkner's complex conception of the nature and function of civilization and of law, are
central to what I've been trying to say, and bear repeating:
". . . all bound, precarious and ramshackle, held together by the
web, the iron-thin warp and woof of his rapacity but withal yet
dedicated to his dreams."

The law, then, works, in spite of its many and obvious de-
fects, not just because it holds anarchy at bay, but because it
declares that man can be better than he is, holds out the possibility that the ideal might in fact be made actual one day, and
provides the means to make the ideal real.

178

Faulkner's Curious Tools

THOMAS L. McHANEY

You recognize the striking phrase in my title. "Curious tools" comes, with minor translation, from *The Sound and the Fury*, the moving scene where Dilsey sits with the remnant of her own family and the thirty-three-year-old Benjy Compson, waiting for the Easter sermon in Dilsey's church. They are expecting a big guest preacher from St. Louis, and they suppose he will be literally a large and imposing man, but they are astonished and disappointed when the visitor appears: "undersized, in a shabby alpaca coat," his face like that of a "small, aged monkey."[1] The local minister's oratorical introduction only seems to diminish this insignificant man, and Dilsey's daughter Frony whispers sarcastically, "En dey brung dat all de way fum Saint Looey." Her mother replies, "I've knowed de Lawd to use cuiser tools dan dat" (366). For all the privation and failure in her own life, Dilsey once again is right. Reverend Shegog is a spellbinder even when he begins speaking in a white man's voice; but when he breaks into the language of his hearers with "Brethren," he makes a music that goes right to their hearts. In the course of his simple but powerful sermon about death defeated by resurrection, despair refuted by hope, he and the congregation become as nothing, "and there was not even a voice but instead

1. William Faulkner, *The Sound and the Fury* (New York: Cape & Smith, 1929), 365.

179

their hearts were speaking to one another in chanting measures beyond the need for words" (367).

One tragedy of Faulkner's brilliant novel is that not enough of the right people hear or heed that sermon. Though perhaps I am wrong. Perhaps the right people do hear it, since the novel is only fiction; for we hear it, the readers, and whether we heed it or not is a matter of the soundness and receptivity of our own hearts. We not only hear a proper message, we see, in full irony, what is wrong with a world that does not hear, a world lost in the unpardonable sin, despair.

We do not know much about Reverend Shegog. (One thing we do know is not found in the novel: Shegog is the name of the early settler of Lafayette, not Yoknapatawpha, County, who built the house Faulkner would begin purchasing only a few months after *The Sound and the Fury* appeared, a house Faulkner gave the magical name Rowan Oak.) Shegog is from St. Louis, a far piece from Jefferson; why he has been invited, how this small congregation can afford such a visitor, how he has come, these things are not told. His effectiveness is, I think, beyond dispute. His voice may not penetrate the bleak chill of the Compson hearts; but his hearers walk out into a bright noon on that April day, renewed and perhaps, like poor Dilsey, with eyes blurred but spiritual vision clear. His unprepossessing appearance provokes two figures of speech. First he is seen as a "meagre figure, hunched over upon itself like that of one long immured in striving with the implacable earth" (367). He reminds me a little of the deformed figure of conscience that comes to haunt Mark Twain, only too briefly and without success, in "The Recent Carnival of Crime in Connecticut." Is his form, like that of Twain's moldy and twisted conscience, a symptom of disregard? In a world dominated by Compsons, one could well believe it. Second, he is described as "like a small worn rock whelmed by the successive waves of his own voice" (367); this image also suggests disregard, isolation. Both images point forward to Faulkner's later work, which is my reason for beginning with this title and this scene.

Reverend Shegog is my point of entry for discussing what I discern as other "curious tools" in Faulkner's fictions, characters who, in the most unpropitious circumstances, and sometimes unawares, speak to our hearts. Some of these characters remain controversial, and it may be that I will not resolve the controversies about them. Some of them speak and act in novels that are not regarded as among Faulkner's best—quite the contrary, in fact—and it may be that I will not redeem these novels from dispraise. I hope only to illuminate a small corner in the large house of Faulkner's fiction, and to share a bit of a mystery with you in the form of several observations and remarks.

The chief observation is this: particularly in his later novels, Faulkner goes out of his way to use extremely unlikely characters as catalysts for, or even proponents of, noble gestures (while, one might add, he gives noble-seeming but ultimately failing roles to the proper and the well-to-do). One such character, although a minor one, is Nub Gowrie, a one-armed reprobate, father to several worthless sons, in *Intruder in the Dust*. Yet another is that bushwhacking murdering bastard Mink Snopes, especially as he is portrayed in the final volume of the Snopes trilogy, *The Mansion*. The two I am most interested in, however, are the "nigger dope-fiend whore," Nancy Mannigoe, in *Requiem for a Nun* and the obscene vicious groom, Harry, in *A Fable*. These characters are not alone in Faulkner's work as types, nor are they exactly a phenomenon restricted to what I am calling the later novels. Perhaps, with some reflection, you can find someone like them in any of the earlier novels; I am not sure. I do see their roots, if that is the proper word, in the final three books Faulkner wrote before the four-year silence, as far as books were concerned, that coincided with World War II.

In *The Wild Palms*, the figures themselves are invisible. Harry Wilbourne gazes out of his cell window at signs of domestic life going on in the abandoned hulk of an unfinished warship that dates from World War I; the anonymous life seems to signify the kind of human endurance that will help Harry decide to live and keep faith with the preciousness of his memories. In *The Hamlet*, there is of course Mink Snopes, who bears just a little more than a man can bear until he acts, but there is also the idiot, Ike, fleeing with his cow. And while I agree that Faulkner is not endorsing stock-diddling or the life of an idiot, the meaning of Ike's gestures, and their contrast to the loveless and demythologized world around him, is no more lost on us than is Reverend Shegog's sermon. In *Go Down, Moses*, I see Samuel Worsham Beauchamp; he has been too reconstructed in the modern urban mode to speak to us directly, but his grandmother speaks for the "slain wolf," in essence, and so he, too, is a "curious tool," one whose message is also missed by those who need it most, as we comprehend when we hear Gavin Stevens's confident reinterpretation of Molly Beauchamp's love and fidelity.

I find these figures, which serve as foreshadowing, in significant spots in Faulkner's career, though I imagine it is largely a fortuitous significance. But Faulkner's career does divide rather neatly into thirds. First is the period from 1919 to 1928 when he is learning his craft, searching for his subjects, and writing most imitatively, while trying to decide what kind of literary life he will pursue and where and how he will live it. Second, the remarkable span from 1929 to 1942, when he mastered material and style, created an artist's life in an artist's house—compare life in Rowan Oak with any other life in Oxford and, peering deeply enough, you will find that it was significantly different— and let the demon drive him, fiercely begrudging the necessity of Hollywood, even when, as we now know, Hollywood had its compensations. Third, the rest, starting with that four-year hiatus, the period which I call the "later Faulkner."

The points of demarcation in these three cycles are Janus years, years which look both forward and back. Nineteen twenty-nine is such a year; it saw the publication of *Sartoris* (née *Flags in the Dust*), where Faulkner looked backward technically but forward into his material, and *The Sound and the Fury*, where he brought forward so much from his personal and artistic past in a unique form. Nineteen forty-two is another such year, in different terms, concluding and summing up Faulkner's investigation of Yoknapatawpha's great families, with, at the end, a voice that would play important roles in the later years. Gavin Stevens has the last word in *Go Down, Moses* in 1942, almost as if he knew he would have to be silent for a while; but he surfaces in *Intruder in the Dust* (1948), *Knight's Gambit* (1949), and *Requiem for a Nun* (1951), his reputation as a talker, not a doer, augmented almost geometrically, and he reappears, modulated by V. K. Ratliff, in *The Town* and *The Mansion* (1957 and 1959). Obviously Stevens is important to Faulkner's later work, though he is not, I believe, one of the "curious tools." He is too well-off, too promising, too decorous and garrulous for that role. He is important chiefly because he has been a kind of red herring to critics of the later work. This is a matter that needs addressing briefly before we return to look at the legitimate "curious tools."

Here is the trouble. The later Faulkner, as I call it, is largely dispraised, and the presence of Gavin Stevens has had a lot to do with that. He is, as I said, a red herring, though not likely a deliberate one. Gavin appears in 1932 in "Smoke," one of the magazine stories that became a part of *Knight's Gambit*; his characterization in the concluding episode of *Go Down, Moses* is as distinct as it will ever need to be. If we have understood that novel—understood the difference between Ike and Lucas—we understand him. It is of course true that not everyone has understood *Go Down, Moses*, and this was so, to a greater degree, when critics got around to Stevens and discovered that there was a shelf of books in which he appeared. William Faulkner had won the Nobel Prize for literature and he had delivered an eloquent, simple speech in Stockholm that called upon Cold

War youth to quit being afraid of life, that urged young writers to dramatize the human heart and its rich predicaments, that predicted man's ability to prevail by doing his best.

Now it happens that Gavin Stevens is a character very much like the journalists and literary men whom Faulkner, in his Nobel Prize acceptance speech, had presented with an apparent paradox. The paradox was this: Faulkner was *not* a literary man; he couldn't be, because he lived in rural Mississippi, claimed farming as his occupation, wrote peculiarly structured books which earned him no reputation at all, insofar as sales were concerned, or a reputation as the captain of a "cult of cruelty," gratuitously exploiting violence, depravity, and so forth—the wicked, perverse, obsessed Dostoevsky of the Canebrakes. He did not spend enough time in chic cafes talking with the literary boys. It did not seem likely, once you thought about it, that such a man could write such a speech. But Gavin Stevens possessed degrees from Harvard and Heidelberg; he was an intellectual, a bookish humanist, a "bucolic Cincinnatus"—a latter-day Roman whose hobby was the translation of the Old Testament into classical Greek, who sent provincial Mississippi schoolgirls to Greenwich Village to further their spiritual and sexual educations (chiefly, one fears, because he did not have the nerve to undertake that job himself). He would have to be the ghostwriter of the Nobel Prize speech; and he would have to be the elaborator of the ideas behind that document, he or someone like him. Criticism, looking for meaning in the late works, followed Gavin's trail. What was his message? What, therefore, was Faulkner's message?

It is now time for us to decide what Faulkner was saying in the Nobel Prize address. I believe he was asking a question and more or less answering it at the same time. The question is, Is there any hope for mankind? The answer is, Yes, as long as there is hope for the individual. Faulkner had already decided, and demonstrated—sometimes in his own life—that man can bear anything and is often called upon to prove it. Now, in the wake of World War II, he felt impelled to discover whether man could do better. He had matchless models, of course, chief among them the authentic story of Jesus of Nazareth—and I say "authentic" to differentiate from the bogus Christ that Ike McCaslin believes he imitates. But he had the artist too, as we will see, and he had these "curious tools."

We need not rehearse what man, collectively and individually, had lived through between Faulkner's completion of the parts of *Go Down, Moses*, shortly before Pearl Harbor, and his loving revival of Yoknapatawpha in "Appendix: Compson, 1699–1945," completed not many months after the bombing of Hiroshima and Nagasaki. Enough had happened to make Faulkner believe that man needed to hear some good news, and he found ways to bring it. This has been the basis of controversy, for since Faulkner also soon began to make public statements outside the framework of fiction, his later novels have been regarded as polemical too, more concerned with his ideas and opinions than with dramatizing the old truths of the human heart which, he had affirmed in Stockholm, were alone worth writing about.

Did Faulkner fall into the very trap he had warned his readers against in the Nobel Prize speech? Did he so lack faith in his own message that he felt compelled to force it through the fiction, violating the possibilities of the novel and pointing up the artificiality and abstraction of his characters? This is what many critics not partial to what they believe to be Faulkner's ideas have said. And what is worse, critics most disposed to applaud Faulkner because at last, apparently, he had adopted a message—or should we say, thinking of Gavin, a messenger—these critics turned on him as well. Here the shadow of Gavin Stevens falls most heavily. Faulkner, whose spokesman was Stevens, so the argument might run, was either a knee-jerk liberal on southern social matters or, because Stevens was, closely perceived, still talking about Sambo and a failure to boot, he was a fuzzy-minded conservative trying to justify an outmoded way of life, though advocating a minimal, appeasing amelioration. As we know, Faulkner's phones rang in the night with calls from both New York and the Delta.

Portions of this controversy don't really need our attention. Gavin Stevens, as a type, has a fairly long lineage in Faulkner's work—from Horace Benbow—and no reasonable reader of the fiction can believe that one should equate Stevens with Faulkner very closely, if that were ever a very good thing to do between an author and his characters. Nor will any reasonable reader assume Faulkner's complete admiring approval of Stevens's actions—should we say, inactions—or garrulous musings either. Something in Stevens obviously fascinated Faulkner a good deal, and he is important; he dramatizes the role, and the fate, of the soft-minded intellectual in a provincial community (a role one can sometimes see played out, with equal interest, in those provincial societies known as universities). It interests me that Faulkner's own great-grandfather, Colonel W. C. Falkner, though self-educated, was a kind of intellectual: he had written novels, plays, poems, taken the grand tour of Europe, and fostered local cultural and educational institutions in his native Ripley, several leagues and, formerly, three different train rides from where we are now; but Faulkner did not convey any of these intellectual traits to Colonel John Sartoris when he derived that character from his family's real and legendary past. Faulkner's intellectuals are anomalous, though tolerated, and they are, I believe, the only men in Yoknapatawpha County who have hobbies, though you might be generous to Benbow and say that his glassblowing is an art. Stevens's doubtless uncompleted translation of the Bible is the antithesis of Faulkner's own concerns as a writer; classic Greek, which is not the original language of the Old Testament anyway, is not likely to make the

Bible accessible to modern man; nor, finally, is it even the right testament for Faulkner's purposes, the one with a message of salvation and hope.

In Stevens's defense, Lucas Beauchamp doesn't have any hesitation about trusting him; like Molly, who in *Go Down, Moses* goes to Stevens to bring back her grandson's body, Lucas must see Stevens as a symbol of community rectitude and fair play. He knows that Stevens will be kind, helping even when he condemns or condescends. But Lucas also knows Stevens's limitations and faults, and he refuses Stevens's offer of companionship and protection in the jail cell. It is not only because Lucas is not afraid. "I reckon not," he says, declining Stevens's offer. "They kept me up all last night and I'm goneter try to get some sleep. If you stay here you'll talk till morning."[2] In *The Mansion*, Chick thinks of his uncle's ability as a hunter: "he—Gavin— wouldn't be much of a gun even if he stopped talking long enough."[3] And in *Intruder*, he muses upon the "significantless speciosity of his uncle's voice" (80–81). The voice is deceptive, false with the ring of truth, not even significant. Chick recognizes that his uncle's garrulity is a meaningless alternative to action. He closes the door on his uncle and starts upon his dark quest. Chick never really analyzes, except as he takes a different course, because he has too many more important things to do. I also imagine he may have recognized in his uncle at least a mild example of what Addie Bundren is represented as thinking: "how words go straight up in a thin line, quick and harmless, and how terribly doing goes along the earth" (unless one has what T. S. Eliot called knowledge carried to the heart). Addie continues, "doing goes along the earth, clinging to it, so that after a while the two lines are too far apart for the same person to straddle from one to the other; and that sin and love and fear

---

2. William Faulkner, *Intruder in the Dust* (New York: Random House, 1948), 65.
3. William Faulkner, *The Mansion* (New York: Random House, 1959), 206.

are just sounds that people who never sinned nor loved nor
feared have for what they never had and cannot have until they
forget the words."[4]

Reverend Shegog's words have power—they have worn him
like a rock repeatedly overwhelmed by the sea—and they cease
to have separate identity, as he and his listeners commune heart
to heart. Addie is still disillusioned by the "heartbreaking stupidity of words" expressed by the young sculptor Gordon in
Mosquitoes, words which "became mere sounds to be bandied
about until they were dead."[5] It is inevitable, perhaps, that
Chick is to become the victim of words too, given his upbring-
ing, for after World War II he will become a disappointment,
though, like his uncle, not without occasional insight and wisdom. The war, he believes, does something to him: "the tragedy
of war was that you brought nothing away from it but only left
something valuable there; that you carried into war things
which, except for the war, you could have lived out your life in
peace and without ever having to know they were inside you."[6]
His uncle is trapped in rhetoric; he is trapped in self-doubt.
Neither Gavin nor Chick is "curious," as I have indicated. They
are good-looking, well-dressed, well-educated (Chick goes to
Harvard too), and their very status disqualifies them; we expect the best from them, and they also have easy access to the
power and prestige of the community where they never become
leaders.

The "curious" one in *Intruder* is, I think, Nub Gowrie—"a
violent foulmouthed godless old man who had happened to lose
one of the six lazy idle violent more or less lawless a good deal
than just more or less worthless sons."[7] Unawares, he is the
agent by which Chick learns a truth of the human heart: that

4. William Faulkner, *As I Lay Dying* (New York: Random House, 1964), 165–66.
5. William Faulkner, *Mosquitoes* (New York: Boni & Liveright, 1927), 186.
6. William Faulkner, *The Mansion*, 354–55.
7. William Faulkner, *Intruder in the Dust*, 161.

grief can live "where in a sense a heart capable of breaking had no business being" (161), a vision that reflexively illuminates Lucas Beauchamp for him, whose love for an old wife Chick now also perceives. There is a similar lesson in *The Mansion*, where Gavin and Chick have a sufficiently difficult time thwarting the political ambitions of a lesser Snopes, Clarence, whose career is cut short by the dog-thicket device. Chick realizes the import of his uncle's pre–World War II remarks, when he had said that young people would have to save the world; that was empty rhetoric, he realizes, and dangerous indifference. What man had better do, he says, is to "learn how to trust in God without depending on Him."[8]

The contrast between the team of Chick and Gavin and Mink Snopes puts into relief the device I refer to as "curious tool." The message in this case is one only the readers hear, and the language—really, it is image more than *words*—speaks not to the mind but the heart. Like Nub, Mink could hardly be less promising to begin with, and after a lifetime in prison, he has very little command of the world he must traverse to kill Flem, but, as Dilsey says, I've known the Lord to use curiouser tools. Mink is a bushwhacker, a murderer, though he does not act destructively until he is unbearably provoked. He seeks equity when justice, its mouth full of words, denies him and then keeps him immured. Like the meager figure of Shegog—with whom it may seem sacrilegious to compare him—he is small, unprepossessing, and has struggled his whole life with the implacable earth. Literally immured in prison, he escapes finally to accomplish revenge for the violation of family loyalty, and then he hides in a cavelike hole and gives himself up gradually to the earth. He accepts peace; he will join "the folks that had the trouble but were free now," becoming one as good as the rest: "the beautiful, the splendid, the proud and the brave, right on up to the very

8. William Faulkner, *The Mansion*, 321.

top itself among the shining phantoms and dreams which are the milestones of the long human recording—Helen and the bishops, the kings and the unhomed angels, the scornful and the graceless seraphim" (436), words we can't help quoting but just words—"shining phantoms and dreams"—which stand for things Mink knows but cannot, and need not, express.

Intruder and *The Mansion* bracket *Requiem for a Nun* and *A Fable*, and it is in these novels that Faulkner has fashioned his most curious tools. I want to work backward from *A Fable* because I remain less confident about *Requiem*, and I hope to creep up on it from the perspective of a character whose quality seems less arguable than Nancy Mannigoe's.

The form of Faulkner's most controversial later novels, *A Fable* and *Requiem for a Nun*, is unusual, but then it is surely established in the minds of all of us that they are not formally extraordinary, given that Faulkner always juxtaposed—he liked the word himself—contrasting lives, contrasting styles, contrasting fictional elements. Yet the forms of *Requiem* and *A Fable*, each in its different way, have caused more trouble, or inspired less sympathetic reading, than most of Faulkner's earlier strategies, chiefly because both books have been taken too literally for what they appear to be: a drama, on the one hand, a fable on the other. The extent to which these recognizable forms are fictions themselves—fictions of fictions or fictions within fictions—and thus metaphors, has not been grasped. But that is another story.

The meanings of these books have attracted literal attention, attention first misplaced, and then literalized. That is, not simply the dramatic impression they give but the paraphrasable "message," if that is what it is, has seemed unusual for Faulkner and it has been accepted as literally *the* message. But the meaning of these two books is no more extraordinary or unusual, once we have read all Faulkner's works, than their physical forms in the same context. Close analysis of *Requiem for a Nun* and *A Fable* will reveal any number of images and phrases present in earlier work. Because some of these phrases or images also crop up in Faulkner's nonfictional public statements or appear to be similar to such statements, they have been taken, when in the mouths of some of his characters, as the *meanings* of his fictions. This occurs despite modifications of the phrases themselves or, more important, counterstatement and limiting circumstances created by the give and take of the fictional form, where character is played off against character, speech against speech. A complex, indirect writer like Faulkner has been interpreted, in short, as suddenly shifting to the simple and the direct, even convicted of setting up mouthpieces in his fiction.

Are the matters upon which Faulkner lays stress in the later novels so different from what he had emphasized in the earlier ones? I don't think so, though I am not going to try to argue that the later works are as great as the novels produced between 1929 and 1942. I do say that Faulkner's later fiction is no less fiction, no less dependent upon complexity, diversity, a dialectic of images and personalities, and an exploration toward meaning, rather than an argument for it. I also claim that the meanings we derive from the later fiction are not really different from those we derive from the earlier work. Everything we know about Faulkner as man and artist should teach us that his articles of belief formed early and remained consistent, though he learned about human nature and his craft all his life. All we have to do to confirm this, if we cannot immediately find it in the fiction (though I maintain we can), is to look at the writers he always admired, the writers with whom he had the greatest affinity. Do they not all—Shakespeare, Conrad, Mann, Joyce, Flaubert, and the rest, Faulkner's Masters, as Michael Millgate has called them[9]—do they not offer in their way the same kind of hope for man that Faulkner did? Dramatizing man's folly, his evil, don't they still demonstrate conviction about man's fate? The artist,

9. Michael Millgate, "Faulkner's Masters," *Tulane Studies in English*, XXIII (1978), 143–55.

the real artist, can hardly fail to demonstrate conviction, for his profession—and he has better rights than most to that word, *profession*—confirms value even when his work faces some of the horrors of reality. Faulkner would say as much, and often did. Man may, in the current age, need to be reminded about the differences between art and the intellectual, psychological, and sexual pornography that passes for entertainment; he may need to be told that he writes too much from the glands and not enough from the heart.[10] In his public statements Faulkner began to do that. Here is a sampling: The artist writes, he said in his Introduction to *The Faulkner Reader* (1954), to

. . . uplift man's heart; the same for all of us. . . . Some of us don't know that this is what we are writing for. Some of us will know it and deny it, lest we be accused and self-convicted and condemned of sentimentality. . . . This does not mean that we are trying to change man, improve him, though this is the hope—maybe even the intention—of some of us. On the contrary, in its last analysis, this hope and desire to uplift man's heart is completely selfish, completely personal. He would lift up man's heart for his own benefit because in that way he can say No to death.[11]

On the occasion of Albert Camus's death, he wrote,

Camus said that the only true function of man, born into an absurd world, is to live, be aware of one's life, one's revolt, one's freedom. He said that if the only solution to the human dilemma is death, then we are on the wrong road. The right track is the one that leads to life, to the sunlight. . . . The track he followed was the only possible one which could not lead only to death. The track he followed led into the sunlight in being that one devoted to making with our frail powers and our absurd material, something which had not existed in life until we

10. A recent essay by the novelist John Gardner, entitled "Moral Fiction," lays stress on points similar to Faulkner's. *Hudson Review, XXIX (Winter,* 1976–77*),* 497–512; *reprinted in Pushcart Prize, III, Best of the Small Presses,* ed. Bill Henderson (Yonkers, N.Y.: Pushcart Press), 52–68.

11. James B. Meriwether (ed.), *William Faulkner: Essays, Speeches, and Public Letters* (New York: Random House, 1965), 181.

made it. [And he sought answers which, Faulkner said, are not to be found] only to be searched for, constantly, always by some fragile member of the human absurdity. Of which there are never many, but always somewhere at least one, and one will always be enough.[12]

One will always be enough. In *A Fable* the power and necessity of conviction plays an important role. The rationalist who "understands" man, like the Supreme-General, may win many victories; but the inspired seeker, who discovers what man can be at his best, is never absolutely defeated. Faulkner gives the final scene in *A Fable* to the battalion runner, a man paradoxically trapped in words, who must use language to make his gesture of defiance against the rhetoric of war. "You too helped carry the torch of man into that twilight where he shall be no more; these are his epitaphs," he shouts to the crowd that is about to attack him. "They shall not pass. My country right or wrong. Here is a spot which is forever England—"[13] Crippled but indomitable, claiming immortality, he is man's puny inexhaustible voice. But is he altogether one of Faulkner's "curious tools"? I don't think so: at least not quite, for he has learned the things which make him act now, at novel's end, from others. First there is Reverend Tooleyman, the old black preacher from America who participates in the racehorse adventure that is such an important fable within this fable. Like Joan of Arc, Reverend Tooleyman (significantly renamed from Tobe Sutterfield) has heard voices and come to France: "Men and boys, marching for months down into one muddy ditch to kill one another. There was too many of them. There wasn't room to lay quiet and rest. All you can kill is man's meat. You can't kill his voice" (200–201). The conjunction of earth and voice carries us back to the images surrounding Reverend Shegog, but we are no more ready to apply them than the runner, at this point, is ready to understand

12. *Ibid.*, 113–14.
13. William Faulkner, *A Fable* (New York: Random House, 1954), 436.

Tooleyman's words. He remains cynical; can you still hear the voice, he asks, "Even if it's not saying anything but Why?" (201). "What can trouble you more than having a human man saying to you, Tell me why. Tell me how. Show me the way?" is Sutter-field's answer (201). "And you can show him the way," the runner says. "I can believe," the old black preacher replies. But the runner can neither hope nor believe. "You aint ready yet nei-ther," Tooleyman tells him (203); that is, I think, the point of the scene and perhaps of the book, too, though I wouldn't begin to reduce its complexities.

The horserace episode in *A Fable* provides contrast for un-derstanding what it will take to get the runner ready, and that in turn will reveal, without Faulkner ever saying so, what has made soldiers of warring armies quit the war and force the princes of this world to engage in collusion to start it again. The agent of the runner's conversion is a "curious tool": "the morose, savage, foul-mouthed almost inarticulate . . . foreigner who moved, breathed, not merely in an aura of bastardy and bache-lordom but of homelessness too, like a half-wild pedigreeless pariah dog: fatherless, wifeless, sterile and perhaps even impo-tent too, misshapen, savage and foul: the world's portionless and intractable and inconsolable orphan, who brought without warn-ing into that drowsing vacuum an aggregation bizarre, mobile and amazing as a hippodrome built around a comet" (189–90). This is Harry the groom, or Mistairy—mystery—as Tobe Sutter-field, alias Reverend Tooleyman, calls him. Mistairy and Tooley-man and an adolescent black boy race the stolen horse until they are almost caught. They create a legend, and then, as their cap-tors close in, Harry shoots the horse without ever explaining why, uttering only a "single vicious obscene contemptuous epi-thet" when the former deputy tries to explain to himself: "they would have used its ballocks to geld its heart with for the rest of its life"—by putting it to stud, denying its passion—"except that

194

you saved it because any man can be a father, but only the best, the brave—" (163).

Harry has a passion for the horse; the horse has a passion for racing, though it is crippled. Passion is enough. Their adventure is doomed, but "not because passion is ephemeral"—it is not. "Which was why," Faulkner writes, "they never found any better name for it, which was why Eve and the Snake and Mary and the Lamb and Ahab and the Whale and Androcles and Balzac's African deserter, and all the celestial zoology of horse and goat and swan and bull, were the firmament of man's history instead of the mere rubble of his past" (161) and also why, akin to "Adam and Lilith and Paris and Helen and Pyramus and Thisbe and all the other recordless Romeos and their Juliets," the "warp-legged foul-mouthed English horse-groom" and his horse are limned in "the world's oldest and most shining tale" (153). Oh, but their adventure *is* doomed, because there is a reward for their capture. But doom does not destroy passion; it is always reborn, and even Christ can return as a corporal in the Great War. Curious indeed, but "the firmament of man's history" insures us that such things are true. Harry will make the ultimate gesture himself, leaving the trench to defy the powers of the world, "not the first one through because when he rose to his feet, running, the old Negro was panting beside him" and the others, as the runner shows him, "crawling on their hands and knees through the gaps in the wire as though up out of hell itself, faces clothes hands and all stained as though forever one single nameless and identical color from the mud in which they had lived like animals for four years, then rising to their feet as though in that four years they had not stood on earth, but had this moment returned to light and air from purgatory." They are blown up, of course, by their own concerted artillery, German and British, and as it begins to happen, the laconic Harry cries, "Not to us," without realizing that he is saying "we and not *I* for the first time in his life probably" and hearing, as the last thing he hears, the unkillable runner's voice, "They cant kill us!" (321–22). The conjunction of images that surrounds Shegog surrounds these men, too: figures moiling out of the earth toward the light, a voice absurdly crying out its immortality—and all this in the midst of the most pitiless moment of man's most devastating war.

How does the message of this "curious tool" compare with that of the far more Faulknerian-sounding words spoken by the Supreme Commander in the last parts of the novel? The General offers the Corporal his temptations, tries to disillusion him by predicting the behavior of the "disciples," and attempts to sway him from accepting martyrdom through the story of the condemned convict and the bird, a parable of life and its pleasures.[14] The General reveals to him the future—but patently his version: a technocracy where men live and die in vehicles on one all-encompassing highway, where the last battle will be between two machines "wrestling against the final and dying sky robbed even of darkness and filled with the inflectionless uproar of the two mechanical voices bellowing at each other polysyllabic and verbless patriotic nonsense" (354). Man will survive, he adds, and his words seem to be like Reverend Tooleyman's and to echo or paraphrase Faulkner's Nobel Prize acceptance speech. The General explains why:

. . . because he has that in him which will endure even beyond the ultimate worthless tideless rock freezing slowly in the last red and heatless sunset, because already the next star in the blue immensity of space will be already clamorous with the uproar of his debarkation, his puny and inexhaustible voice still talking, still planning; and there too after the last ding-dong of doom has rung and died there will still be one sound more: his voice . . . I don't fear man. I do better. I respect and admire him. And pride: I am ten times prouder of that

14. The General is like Satan, and the Corporal is his son; perhaps it is the mother who is God and this the child of the world's mixed nature; perhaps we have been looking to the wrong heaven all along.

immortality which he does possess than ever he of that heavenly one of his delusion. Because man and his folly—"

"Will endure," the corporal said.

"They will do more," the old general said proudly. "They will prevail." (354)

Similarities to the Nobel Prize speech are clear, but there are important differences: Faulkner said, "It is easy enough to say that man is immortal simply because he will endure: that when the last ding-dong of doom has clanged and faded from the last worthless rock hanging tideless in the last red and dying evening, that even then there will still be one more sound: that of his puny and inexhaustible voice, still talking."[15] The General says "man and his folly," and he has emphasized to the Corporal that man is a seething mass, led easily down the road to death and destruction, with all glory accruing to powerful men like himself, one of whom he invites the Corporal to become. The Corporal, the runner, and Reverend Tooleyman say something else: first, that man's voice is not just talking senseless babble; it is asking Why? or expressing conviction that life has meaning. The groom demonstrates the truth of their belief, for even when operating his curious insurance company, he emphasizes man's absurd hope for continuance. Men bet their lives against a kind of Murphy's Law probability: if they commit themselves to a long-term debt by borrowing against their insurance, the obvious result will be that they will live to need to pay it off. The groom's passion for the racehorse is another demonstration. His rising up out of the trench and crying "we" is yet another.

In the Nobel Prize speech, Faulkner explained that *he* declined to accept the end of man, or the notion that man would only endure: "He is immortal, not because he alone among creatures has an inexhaustible voice, but because he has a soul, a spirit capable of compassion and sacrifice and endurance."[16]

15. Meriwether (ed.), *Essays, Speeches, and Public Letters,* 120.
16. *Ibid.*

These are the qualities which the General tries to dissuade the Corporal from expressing. The hope of the world is such that the envious marplot of Eden sires children who rebel against him!

After the Corporal's execution, his family take the body and bury it in a cave on their farm. All these simple people have is their land and the ability to work it: "the land which was immune even from the blast and sear of war. It would take work of course, it might even take years of work, but . . . their luck was the work they faced, since work is the only anesthetic to which grief is vulnerable. . . . the miniscule integer of the farm would affirm that he had not died for nothing and that it was not for an outrage that they grieved, but for simple grief: the only alternative to which was nothing, and between grief and nothing, only the coward takes nothing" (399). We have heard similar words from Harry Wilbourne at the conclusion of his part of *The Wild Palms* and from Gordon in *Mosquitoes*.[17]

The artillery barrage, which destroys the groom and Reverend Tooleyman and maims the runner and starts the war again, comes directly over this poor farm without hurting it, though one shell hits the cave where the Corporal's body lies, and the body disappears, to end up later, we learn, in the tomb of the Unknown Soldier in Paris, symbol and apotheosis of anonymous sacrifice. The farm episode reminds us that one cannot kill the simple instinct to till the land, and, by extension, you can't kill matchless models of human endeavor. Figures out of the earth and the questioning voice blend, now and again, to create revealing monuments of man's aspirations and his potential. These images are also in Faulkner's famous speech.

In Japan in 1955, Faulkner was asked if he considered human life basically a tragedy. "Actually yes," he said. "But man's im-

---

17. William Faulkner, *The Wild Palms* (New York: Random House, 1939), 324; Faulkner, *Mosquitoes*, 329. See also William Faulkner, *Go Down, Moses* (New York: Random House, 1942), 186.

mortality is that he is faced with a tragedy which he can't beat and he still tries to do something with it." Then he was asked if he had ever thought that man might attain perfection. With some irony, he replied, "Yes, by changing his whole nature, [his] character." But, if man did that, "he would stop being man, stop being the interesting creature that he is. . . . I do believe in man and his capacity for [advancement]. I still believe in man. That he still wishes, desires, wants to do better than he knows he can and occasionally he does do a little better than anybody expects of him. This man [is immortal]."[18] Earlier, Faulkner had told a group of Mississippi farmers: "Sociologists tell us that man's problems are insoluable, that there are too many men." But, he said, he couldn't believe this, "that man's crime against his freedom is that there are too many of him . . . that he cannot hope to cope with his environment and its evils, because he cannot even cope with his own mass." To believe this, he argued, you have written off man's power for responsibility.[19]

Clearly that is something which Faulkner could not do. And in *Requiem for a Nun* he constructs an elaborate parable of that responsibility in which the seemingly inconsequential act of losing a fifteen-pound padlock catapults the men of what will become Jefferson forward into modern institutional society, where justice becomes a building and an inhuman force, simply because no one will take responsibility for that lock, no one wants to pay the price. As a consequence, the world, "in fact the whole race of man, as long as it endured, forever and irrevocably" is "fifteen dollars deficit, fifteen dollars in the red."[20]

The men who have lost the lock mean well, but not too well, and they get themselves into the waiting—not necessarily predatory, just waiting—clutches of a kind of backwoods Satan

18. James B. Meriwether and Michael Millgate (eds.), *Lion in the Garden: Interviews with William Faulkner, 1926–1962* (New York: Random House, 1968), 89.

19. Meriwether (ed.), *Essays, Speeches, and Public Letters*, 133.

20. William Faulkner, *Requiem for a Nun* (New York: Random House, 1951), 36.

named Thomas Jefferson Pettigrew, who tempts them and wins. The result, as noted, is the institution of law, against which Temple Drake will struggle futilely to stop the execution of Nancy Mannigoe, who does not deserve to die for what, by comparison to loss of the simple lock, seems a terrible act: the murder of an innocent baby. Nancy means well, too. She kills that innocent child, which has not learned the world and thus gives up no passion and suffers none of the world's pain, to bring home a message that saves an entire human family from disaster, disaster which, in this close-knit world, could have the same tragic reverberations as, say, the lost life of Joe Christmas. For if Temple Drake leaves, she leaves a young son whose paternity is falsely put into doubt and a husband confirmed in bitterness and guilt; she leaves a town full of voices, a world forever far more than fifteen dollars short. If she does not leave, if she confesses and understands her past, she can have another baby. Nancy, for her part, accepts full responsibility for her act; she does not try to justify herself any more than the groom does for shooting the horse. She is a "curious tool." Like Reverend Tooleyman, she believes, and her nearly wordless message penetrates Temple's heart. Humanly, Temple stumbles leaving Nancy's cell, but she goes out to start life over again. Let Gavin Stevens talk, try to explain. The world needs men and women who can listen and be changed, who can act, who, whether able to explain it or not, know passion directly, not merely as something they read in books; who have themselves one of those inexplicable passions that are the "firmament of man's history."

If you look at early photographs of William Faulkner, you may think of him as a bit of a curious tool himself, as he may have done, as in the humorous picture of the dark and shabby man in *Mosquitoes*. But he was a genius with a passion for writing, as we know, and a passion for man, too—a true hope based on his own experience, his own sense of himself. He puts it into the fiction quite early, giving the words to Dawson Fairchild in *Mosquitoes*:

Genius. . . . People confuse it so, you see. They have got it now to where it signifies only an active state of the mind in which a picture is painted or a poem is written. When it is not that at all. It is that Passion Week of the heart, that instant of timeless beatitude which some never know, which some, I suppose, gain at will, which others gain through an outside agency like alcohol . . . that passive state of the heart with which the mind, the brain, has nothing to do at all, in which the hackneyed accidents which make up this world—love and life and death and sex and sorrow—brought together by chance in perfect proportions, take on a kind of splendid and timeless beauty (339).

Could a small-statured, quiet-voiced ne'er-do-well from a simple town in a poor state partake of that excitement? Well, I've known the Lord to use curiouser tools.

Faulkner's Short Stories and the Making of Yoknapatawpha County*

JAMES G. WATSON

Nearly always in the best of Faulkner's fictions, there comes a moment when, beyond all willing—or unwilling—suspension of disbelief, Yoknapatawpha County quite simply *is*. At such moments we accede wholly to the rhythms of the land where "everything, weather, all, hangs on too long" and to its people, their legends, and their history. "Opaque, slow, violent," Dr. Peabody calls it, "shaping and creating the life of man in its implacable and brooding image."[1] The scene in which Lena Grove makes her urgent and unhurried way across "the hot still pine-winey silence of the August afternoon" in the early pages of *Light in August* is one such instance.[2] Wash Jones's attack with a scythe on the men he calls "the gallant, the proud, the brave" is perhaps another,[3] and every reader can supply a dozen of his own at call.

I do not mean only that in such scenes we recognize the humanity of Faulkner's flesh and blood characters or that we are moved by his poetry, although living people and poetic language are elements of the spell. Nor do I mean that we recognize Mis-

*The research and writing of this paper were done in part with the assistance of summer grants from the National Endowment for the Humanities and the University of Tulsa Faculty Research Program.
    1. William Faulkner, *As I Lay Dying* (New York: Random House, 1964), 44.
    2. William Faulkner, *Light in August* (New York: Random House, 1932), 5.
    3. William Faulkner, *Collected Stories of William Faulkner* (New York: Random House, 1950), 547. Hereafter cited in the text as *CS*.

202

sissippi realities—as the reader of *Ulysses* recognizes an actual Dublin, for example—though again Mississippi is often bound to such moments. I mean instead that at such times Yoknapatawpha is both a place and a way to tell stories—both a setting and a mode of expression, a place that could not be other than where and what it is because of the way it is made. This enigmatic distinction is one that Faulkner himself made in his retrospective remarks on Yoknapatawpha. Beginning with *Sartoris*, he told Jean Stein in that often quoted interview in 1955, "I *discovered* that my own little postage stamp of native soil was worth writing about," but he went on to say, "I *created* a cosmos of my own."[4] The difference between what was *discovered* and what was *created* is the difference between Lafayette and Yoknapatawpha, actual and apocryphal, life and art. And I mention that difference at the outset because it is the *cosmos* and not the *postage stamp* that I plan to discuss.

From the perspective of the present, with the complete corpus of Faulkner's work before us, it is easy to forget that the making of Yoknapatawpha County was—and indeed had to be—a piecemeal job. It might spring whole to Faulkner's mind in 1955 (a *Be Yoknapatawpha* like the oldentime *Be Light*) but the novelist who made that remark about postage stamps and cosmoses was summing up, not setting out. The year before the *Paris Review* interview, Faulkner had published the essay-story "Mississippi," tracing in his own semifictionalized growth from boyhood to middle age a compressed history of his state. Life mixes there with art, the maker with the making, and the north Mississippi region that he calls "Home . . . his native land"[5] is not Oxford but Jefferson. By 1954 and 1955, Yoknapatawpha County had already been made in the stories and novels set

4. James B. Meriwether and Michael Millgate (eds.), *Lion in the Garden: Interviews with William Faulkner, 1926–1962* (New York: Random House, 1968), 255; my emphasis.
5. James B. Meriwether (ed.), *William Faulkner: Essays, Speeches, and Public Letters* (New York: Random House, 1965), 36.

there. In 1927, it had perhaps not even been named. "I am working now on two things at once," Faulkner wrote Horace Liveright in February of that year, "a novel, and a collection of short stories of my townspeople."[6] The novel was *Flags in the Dust*, the Ur-*Sartoris* in which, Faulkner said, he discovered the necessity of total design in a writer's work and the suitability of northern Mississippi to that scheme. There the setting is Yokona County. The collection of short stories was published four years and three novels later as *These 13*.

Precisely what Faulkner meant by the phrase "of my townspeople" in 1927, I do not know; but he could hardly have meant the same thing that he did three decades later when he spoke of his fictional Jefferson as "home." By then he had added to the Yoknapatawpha stories of *These 13* those in *Doctor Martino and Other Stories* (1934) and *Knight's Gambit* (1949), the story chapters in the novels *The Unvanquished* (1938) and *Go Down, Moses* (1942), and the numerous stories published in magazines, some of which were incorporated with previously collected ones into *Collected Stories of William Faulkner* (1950). The plan for a collection of short stories of his townspeople was one to which Faulkner regularly returned—as he did to other projects in the Yoknapatawpha chronicle—and that plan was not completed until the publication of *Collected Stories*, where the first three sections and significant parts of the three others are devoted to that subject.

In 1927, the long process of creating a world was just beginning. The importance of the short stories to Faulkner's earliest conception of that world is suggested by the conjunction of the first collection with the first Yoknapatawpha novel. Its evolution as a place and a way to tell stories can be charted by comparing *These 13* with *Collected Stories*. The similarities and differences between the two volumes reveal, first, the surprising integrity

6. Joseph Blotner (ed.), *Selected Letters of William Faulkner* (New York: Random House, 1977), 34.

of Faulkner's conception of the project over a period of more than twenty years and, second, the flexibility of the stories themselves to serve as units of structure in extended narratives. If we look, as well, at representative work that preceded the discovery of Yoknapatawpha, we can gauge the extent to which Faulkner's county came to serve as a multifaceted and immensely flexible fictional structure in its own right.

This sprawling subject has a number of important connections both within and without Faulkner's fiction. If the making of Yoknapatawpha County was not an instantaneous act of art and imagination, neither was it accomplished in a vacuum. In 1927 Faulkner had before him as models a substantial body of American small town literature ranging from Mark Twain to Sinclair Lewis and such particular collections as Joyce's *Dubliners*, Anderson's *Winesburg, Ohio*, and Edgar Lee Masters's *Spoon River Anthology*. His own 1925 newspaper pieces reflect that influence: as Carvel Collins has arranged them in *New Orleans Sketches* they almost constitute a Book of the Grotesque in themselves. Of the work done in New Orleans and before, however, two particular pieces suggest themselves for comparison with the Yoknapatawpha stories that were to follow. They are the 1922 sketch "The Hill" and the unpublished 1925 expansion of it entitled "Nympholepsy."[7] These are important apprentice pieces: Cleanth Brooks connects them to Faulkner's pastoral through Wordsworth and Swinburne, and Scott Momberger identifies Darl Bundren and Joe Christmas as the successors of their heroes.[8] To these I would add two other sources, hitherto unmentioned, that tie the sketches directly to the tradition of American

7. "The Hill," published in *The Mississippian* in 1922, is reprinted in Carvel Collins (ed.), *William Faulkner: Early Prose and Poetry* (Boston: Little, Brown Co., 1962), 90–92; hereafter cited in the text as *EPP*. "Nympholepsy" is in Joseph Blotner (ed.), *Uncollected Stories of William Faulkner*, (New York: Random House, 1979), 331–37; hereafter cited in the text as *US*.
8. Cleanth Brooks, *William Faulkner: Toward Yoknapatawpha and Beyond* (New Haven: Yale University Press, 1978), 40–43; Scott Momberger, "A Reading of Faulkner's 'The Hill,'" *Southern Literary Journal*, IX (Spring, 1977), 16–29.

small town portraiture and connect them to the germination of Yoknapatawpha County in *Flags in the Dust* and *These 13*. They are Edwin Arlington Robinson's 1916 volume of poems, *The Man Against the Sky*, and F. Scott Fitzgerald's 1924 story, "Absolution."

Robinson is one of four poets Faulkner identified as being still worth reading in 1925 when he appealed for a poetry "beautiful and passionate and sad instead of saddening,"[9] and there are echoes of his poetry in Faulkner's work as early as *A Green Bough*.[10] Robinson's Tilbury Town is the setting of two poems

---

9. William Faulkner, "Verse Old and Nascent: A Pilgrimage," in Collins (ed.), *William Faulkner: Early Prose and Poetry*, 118.

10. In Poem V, *A Green Bough*, the funereal situation, the graveyard setting, the four-syllable refrain line at the end of each stanza, and specific words and phrases all reflect Faulkner's reading of Robinson's early poem, "Luke Havergal." For example, compare Robinson's lines in stanza two:

> No, there is not a dawn in eastern skies
> To rift the fiery night that's in your eyes;

and these opening lines of Faulkner's:

> There is no shortening-breasted nymph to shake
> The tickets that stem up the lidless blaze
> Of sunlight stiffening the shadowed ways.

Robinson advises his bereaved lover:

> Go to the western gate, Luke Havergal,
> There where the vines cling crimson on the wall,
> And in the twilight wait for what will come.
> The leaves will whisper there of her, and some,
> Like flying words, will strike you as they fall;
> But go, and if you listen she will call.
> Go to the western gate, Luke Havergal—
> Luke Havergal.
> . . . .
> There is the western gate, Luke Havergal,
> There are the crimson leaves upon the wall.
> Go, for the winds are tearing them away,—
> Nor think to riddle the dead words they say,
> Nor any more to feel them as they fall;
> But go, and if you trust her she will call.
> There is the western gate, Luke Havergal—
> Luke Havergal.

significant to Faulkner's sketches: "Flammonde" and the title poem, "The Man Against the Sky." Fitzgerald, of course, was known to Faulkner as the grandly successful author of *The Great Gatsby*. His impact on Faulkner's writing is rather broadly based but includes Faulkner's adoption of the title "Absolution" for a 1932 film script and "An Absolution" for one working title of "The Fire and the Hearth" chapter of *Go Down, Moses*.[11] Like Robinson's poems, Fitzgerald's story is set among his own figurative townspeople, in this case in a clearly drawn farming community in the Minnesota-Dakota country.

In Robinson and Fitzgerald, place is integral to meaning, yet in borrowing from them for his sketches Faulkner apparently made no attempt to create an actual, identifiable, or fully rendered physical setting. In both of his pieces a rural laborer climbs a hill at sunset above a village that might be Oxford or even Jefferson, but the town is described in conventional romantic terms more akin to the gardens of *The Marble Faun* than to Tilbury Town. As if in a scene from Swinburne, the buildings in "The Hill" are "figures rising in a dream" (EPP, 90) and the houses and barns in "Nympholepsy" are "hives from which the

---

Faulkner describes this cemetery setting at dusk:

> . . . shadows crowd within the door
> And whisper in the dead leaves as they pass
> Along the ground.

> Here the sunset paints its wheeling gold
> Where there is no breast to still in strife
> Of joy or sadness, nor does any life
> Flame these hills and vales grown sharp and cold
> And bare of sound.

These last lines transfer to the hills the kiss of death that, in Robinson's poem, "flames upon your forehead with a glow / That binds you to the way that you must go." For these and other quotations from Robinson's poetry herein, see Morton Zabel (ed.), *Selected Poems of Edwin Arlington Robinson*, (New York: Macmillan, 1965). Faulkner's *A Green Bough* is in William Faulkner, *The Marble Faun and A Green Bough* (New York: Random House, 1965).

11. Joseph Blotner, *Faulkner: A Biography* (New York: Random House, 1974), 775, 1037.

bees of sunlight had flown away" (*US*, 331). In the latter sketch the town itself is a "fairy land" (*US*, 336).

In situation, language, and symbolism, however, the influence of Robinson and Fitzgerald is pervasive. Indeed, it is situation and symbol rather than plot and character development that Faulkner seems to have been working for in "The Hill." The sketch presents a tableau: the climber, "mesmerized by a whimsical God to a futile puppet-like activity upon one spot" (*EPP*, 90), stands silhouetted at the hill's crest against "the motionless conflagration of sunset" (*EPP*, 92). Simple and earthy, doomed to labor in the future as he has in the past, he momentarily is made to confront "the devastating unimportance of his destiny, with a mind heretofore untroubled by moral quibbles and principles, shaken at last by the faint resistless force of spring in a valley at sunset" (*EPP*, 92). In Robinson's poem, "The Man Against the Sky," the same situation is presented in the same symbols. Like Faulkner's, Robinson's protagonist is a solitary figure who ascends a hill at sunset "To loom against the chaos and the glare/As if he were the last god going home." In language to which Faulkner seems clearly indebted, the poet speculates that the man against the sky may be doomed to witness there "the conflagration of his dreams."[12] Both the poem and the sketch investigate the limits of human significance and understanding—Robinson is also troubled by what Faulkner calls "moral quibbles and principles"—and both end on a tenuous note of hope by affirming the existence of some superhuman order in the universe. As the glare of fire gives way to darkness, Robinson's protagonist chooses faith over "the cold eternal shores . . . of Nothingness" and Faulkner's has a momentary vision of nymphs and fauns in the dusk "beneath a tall icy star"

---

12. Robinson goes on to describe the sunset as "A flame where nothing seems / To burn but flame itself, by nothing fed." Faulkner may well have had the full passage in mind when he wrote, in "Nympholepsy," "The sunset was a fire no fuel had ever fed" (*US*, 334).

(*EPP*, 92). The theme of both pieces is summarized in another of Robinson's poems from the 1916 volume. At the conclusion of "Flammonde" the poet says that the enigmatic man of fire represents the understanding that guides us through life. Here are the lines:

> We've each a darkening hill to climb;
> And this is why, from time to time
> In Tilbury Town, we look beyond
> Horizons for the man Flammonde.

The sense of mystery with which Robinson surrounds such protagonists is not only due to his symbolism, of course, but to the perspective of outside observer that he characteristically employs. His characters are typically subjects of the poet's informed but inconclusive speculation. Faulkner generally prefers that human enigmas originate in the minds of the characters themselves, but in "The Hill" the rustic protagonist is so inarticulate as to be nearly without thought or feeling. Faulkner's treatment of him here approximates Robinson's objective speculations in "The Man Against the Sky." Understanding is imposed rather than evoked from within. This is less true of the expanded "Nympholepsy," where the influence of Fitzgerald's story is evident not only in the author's language but in the language given the protagonist.

"Absolution" is the story of a Catholic boy, Rudolph Miller, who makes a false confession, fears that God will stop his heart, and discovers through the agency of a tormented priest that "There was something ineffably gorgeous somewhere that had nothing to do with God."[13] Just as Jimmy Gatz becomes Jay Gatsby by an act of imagination in Fitzgerald's novel, Rudolph enters adulthood by becoming his own alter-ego, Blatchford Sarnemington. In Fitzgerlad's story adulthood is charged with sex-

---

13. F. Scott Fitzgerald, "Absolution," in *Babylon Revisited and Other Stories* (New York: Scribner's, 1960), 150.

ual promise, and he describes the adult world in language so close to Faulkner's in "Nympholepsy" that it merits extended quotation.

Outside the window the blue sirocco trembled over the wheat, and girls with yellow hair walked sensuously along roads that bounded the field, calling innocent, exciting things to the young men who were working in the lines between the grain. Legs were shaped under starchless gingham, and rims of the necks of dresses were warm and damp. For five hours now hot fertile life had burned in the afternoon. It would be night in three hours, and all along the land there would be these blonde Northern girls and the tall young men from the farms lying out beside the wheat, under the moon.[14]

In "Nympholepsy" the inner life of the protagonist is also rendered in terms of awakened sexuality: come from the wheat fields at sunset, the laborer imagines that "a girl like defunctive music, moist with heat, in blue gingham, would cross his path fatefully; and he too would be as other young men sweating the wheat to gold, along the moony land" (US, 331). Like the language, the basic situation of Faulkner's sketch follows Fitzgerald. Rudolph's transformation begins when he is lured into "immodest thoughts and desires" by a girl for whom he burns with "whitest flame";[15] he kneels before the priest at Sunday mass with "the ebony mark of sexual offenses upon his soul,"[16] certain that God will kill him. Faulkner's character is lured from his hill by the figure of a woman "like a little silver flame" who turns his "once-clean instincts . . . swinish" (US, 332). In a series of Catholic metaphors that very probably originated in "Absolution," the laborer's pursuit leads him to a figurative confession in a "green cathedral of trees" (US, 332) where he hears "slow orisons in a green nave" and expects "a priest to stop forth, halting

14. *Ibid.*, 151.
15. *Ibid.*, 140.
16. *Ibid.*, 138.

him and reading his soul" (*US*, 333). Like Rudolph he is a "trespasser" at the mercy of "some god to whose compulsions he must answer long after the more comfortable beliefs had become outworn," and he too kneels in fear of "abrupt and dreadful annihilation" (*US*, 334). For both characters reality reverses ominous expectations. In "Absolution" the awful authority of Catholicism is broken when the priest's rosary beads begin to squirm in his hands "like snakes,"[17] and the threatful image of the Church is replaced by an amusement park in a world now "ineffably gorgeous"; within the cathedral-like forest in "Nympholepsy" the woman of flame is transformed into a water nymph whose "startled thigh slid like a snake" (*US*, 335) beneath the laborer's hand, and she leads him through a figurative death-by-water to rebirth in the moonlit wheat fields of a town like a "fairy land."

Again, "Nympholepsy" lacks the distinct dimension of place that characterizes Robinson's Tilbury Town poems and Fitzgerald's Minnesota-Dakota country stories. From 1925, when "Nympholepsy" was revised and expanded from "The Hill," it was two years to Faulkner's discovery and initial creation of his own distinct place in *Flags in the Dust*. Yet just as the conjunction of that novel with his proposed short story collection links *These 13* to his earliest conception of Yoknapatawpha County, so one further echo of Fitzgerald's story links "The Hill" and "Nympholepsy" to them. When Rudolph Miller becomes Blatchford Sarnemington at the end of "Absolution," he experiences one strikingly romantic vision that Faulkner did not pursue in "Nympholepsy," probably because it would have been very far out of character for a rustic laborer. Fitzgerald says of Rudolph, "At the moment when he had affirmed immaculate honor a silver pennon had flapped out into the breeze somewhere and there had been the crunch of leather and the shine of silver spurs and a troop of horsemen waiting for dawn on a low green hill. The sun

17. *Ibid.*, 148.

had made stars of light on their breastplates like the picture at home of the German cuirassiers at Sedan."[18] This epiphany and its association with the protagonist's new name may well have been in Faulkner's mind when he wrote the final paragraphs of *Flags in the Dust*, where he said of the name Sartoris, "there is death in the sound of it, and a glamorous fatality, like silver pennons down-rushing at sunset, or a dying fall of horns along the road to Roncevaux."[19] Given the closely interknit texture of quotation and adaptation in Faulkner's sketches, perhaps it is even possible to say that Fitzgerald's German cuirassiers at Sedan became Faulkner's Roland at Roncevaux by way of another of Robinson's poems, "Mr. Flood's Party." Climbing his own hill above Tilbury Town, Mr. Flood is described in this way:

> Alone, as if enduring to the end
> A valiant armor of scarred hopes outworn,
> He stood there in the middle of the road
> Like Roland's ghost winding a silent horn.

That identification, I am aware, is probably too fanciful. Nonetheless, the presence of Charlemagne's most famous paladin in both an early poetic source and *Flags in the Dust* is one more link between the sketches of the mid-twenties and the novel and stories in which, toward the end of the decade, the making of Yoknapatawpha County was begun. Faulkner knew the literature of the Crusades well enough to write a medieval romance of his own in 1925–1926 entitled *Mayday*, and he incorporated terminology, settings, and names from the Crusades into "Carcassonne," the story with which he concluded both *These 13* and *Collected Stories*. "Carcassonne" appears to be a transitional story. It shares with "Nympholepsy" certain elements of psychological fantasy and an undifferentiated symbolic setting; at the same time the close ties between the language

18. *Ibid.*, 150.
19. William Faulkner, *Flags in the Dust* (New York: Random House, 1973), 370.

and imagery of "Carcassonne" and the Yoknapatawpha stories of *These 13* suggest that the story was either written especially for that volume or revised for it from an early draft.[20]

In particular the symbolism of death and rebirth, presented as an overt fantasy in "Nympholepsy," derives in "Carcassonne" from the stories in the body of the collection. This accretive symbolism is one source of unity in the book. In "Carcassonne" the rat-infested loft where the poet argues his immortality with his mortal bones among "whispering arpeggios of minute sound" (*CS*, 898) recalls the loft in "Red Leaves" where Issetibbeha's body servant awaits the Indian ritual of reincarnation among "whispering arpeggios of rat feet" (*CS*, 329). Ritual death is an issue in several of the Yoknapatawpha stories of this book, and the symbolism of death-by-water in the final story echoes and points up similar imagery in "Red Leaves" (*CS*, 327), "A Rose for Emily" (*CS*, 121), "A Justice" (*CS*, 360) and, most strikingly, in "Dry September." There, in pointed contrast to the desiccated setting, both Captain McLendon and Minnie Cooper are described in terms of water: he panting for breath beneath street lamps "nimbused as in water" (*CS*, 176), she entering the square after the rumored rape "like a swimmer preparing to dive" (*CS*, 180).

Such images help to distinguish Faulkner's characters from the easy stereotypes of White Womanhood, Black Rapist, and White Champion that are described by the mob in the Jefferson barbershop. The physical setting of the story is southern, but the characters and the issues that motivate them are human, even mythic. In this dry September of the soul, McLendon and Minnie are represented as crippled principles of male and female potency who desperately turn for renewal to the symboli-

---

20. Joseph Blotner dates the story 1926–1927 because of its similarities to *Mosquitoes* and speculates that it may have been written as early as 1925 (*Biography*, 502). Noel Polk, in an unpublished essay entitled "A Prolegomenon to a Study of 'Carcassonne,'" argues that the story was written especially for *These 13*.

cally named black icehouse attendant, Will Mayes. In such ways does Faulkner mythologize Yoknapatawpha County. By drawing upon the psychology of sexual identity, on the mythology of seasonal renewal, and on regional legends of black virility, he roots his characters in a particularized place redolent of universal as well as regional realities. That place he called cosmos. "Carcassonne" is pointedly not set there; instead, it gathers and compresses the mythic elements of the stories that are set in Yoknapatawpha into an archetypal tale of transcendence that may be read as a poetic coda to the book. In "Carcassonne" a nameless poet in a lost village imagines his bones slanting into "the windless gardens of the sea" (*CS*, 899) while his soul soars free above "the dark and tragic figure of the Earth, his mother" (*CS*, 900). As he gallops "up the long blue hill of heaven" (*CS*, 899), the poet is like the protagonist of "Nympholepsy" who momentarily strides free of his shadow into ideality. The poet is unlike the protagonist of "Nympholepsy" in that the accretive symbolism of the book ties him by association to a fully rendered place—Jefferson and Yoknapatawpha instead of an enchanted wood or fairy land—and to the fully human community that populates that place.

The six stories in which Yoknapatawpha and its people are portrayed comprise the central section of *These 13*: a keystone flanked by the European war stories of Part I and those in Europe and other settings in Part III. In the Table of Contents to the first edition, the three parts are divided and numbered:

A Justice
Hair
That Evening Sun
Dry September
    III
Mistral
Divorce in Naples
Carcassonne

The war stories depict living death: as a group they can be described by a passage from "All the Dead Pilots" in which the
narrator speaks of his story as a "composite: a series of brief
glares in which, instantaneous and without depth or perspective, there stood into sight the portent and the threat of what
the race could bear and become, in an instant between dark and
dark" (CS, 512). The stories in Part III deal with varieties of
love—spiritual and physical, chaste and unchaste, frustrated
and fulfilled—and they conclude with the transcendent vision of
the poet in "Carcassonne." The Yoknapatawpha stories bridge
that distance; at the structural center of the book, death gives
way gradually to the renewal of life and a way is made for healing
love and self-transcendence.

I disagree with those critics who see *These 13* as a book of
unrelieved darkness constructed on the somber theme suggested by the number thirteen in the title. Two of the most persuasive of these are Professors Millgate and Polk. While I begin
by disagreeing with their conclusions, I obviously am indebted
to numerous of their insights.[21] It seems to me that, instead of a
wasteland as Professor Polk would have it, *These 13* is a book of
subtle transformations through which the collective protagonists
of the stories are drawn steadily into the motion of life. The war
composite in Part I serves the same function that Richard P.
Adams attributes to violence in Faulkner's work, dramatizing by

21. Michael Millgate, *The Achievement of William Faulkner* (New York: Random
House, 1966), 259ff; Polk, "Prolegomenon."

215

indirection the "unquenchable vigor of life by showing it in the act of overwhelming and crushing static obstacles in its path."[22] In Part II collective death in a setting "without depth or perspective" gives way to the broader base of human possibility afforded by Yoknapatawpha County, where the past interpenetrates the present in a structure upon which a variety of futures may be built. The first and last stories of Part II are "Red Leaves," which takes place in the county's Indian past, and "Dry September," which takes place in the present. Set at extremes in time, these portray the ritual deaths of the Negro body servant and Will Mayes as extremes rather than normative conditions of the community. Each is narrated by a third-person narrator. Within this frame the speculative revelations of the four first-person narrators contradict and belie comprehensive death by depicting new beginnings and renewals of life. In a structure where the unexpected analogy is often the rule, not only the protagonists of "A Rose for Emily" and "Hair" but also the peripheral narrators of those stories emerge as counterparts of one another. Hawkshaw's life with the memory of his dead fiancée is as barren, though not so grotesque, as Emily's life with the actual corpse of her murdered lover. Hawkshaw's fidelity is rewarded with a new beginning whereas Emily's is not, but each of their lives is a lesson to the narrator, who acquires understanding of himself and his own frailties thereby.

Where such initiations do not actually take place, they are promised. In "A Justice," Quentin is too young to understand Sam Fathers' story of the overwhelming power of love, but at the end of the story he knows that he will understand when he has passed through the twilight of his childhood. In "That Evening Sun," Quentin's inability to understand the story of Nancy and Jesus when he was nine motivates him to tell the story fifteen years later when he does understand it. And to tell it as he

22. Richard P. Adams, *Faulkner: Myth and Motion* (Princeton: Princeton University Press, 1968), 5.

does from the point of view of a nine-year-old. The child's perspective, with its necessary limitations of knowing, suggests that, in addition to Nancy's infidelities and Jesus's vengeance, Quentin's maturation is also at issue in the story. The narrators of "A Rose for Emily" and "Hair" fail to credit the humanity of their subjects and are forcefully reminded of it in the end; the child Quentin witnesses the humanity of Sam Fathers and Nancy and is moved to powerfully recreate it. Although individual men and women do die or are destroyed in these stories, mankind prevails.

That such overlapping patterns—complementary and mutually revealing—should emerge from a collection of stories written at the same period and set in the same place is hardly surprising. As Professor Millgate has said, "The experience of reading the central section according to Faulkner's scheme is one of continual recognition and awareness of reverberation: the recurrence of characters, setting, situations, and themes provokes the recollection and hence the continuing coexistence of the earlier story or stories and produces a total effect of progressive enrichment."[23] Progressive enrichment and, I would add, progression in time. The process of renewal suggested by the various transformations in the Yoknapatawpha stories is reinforced by the several chronologic dimensions within separate stories and between one story and another. The first story of Part II is set exclusively in the past, the final one in the present. Each of the first-person narratives within this frame employs two time settings: that inhabited by the narrator as he tells his story, and the earlier time in which the major action of the narrator's story is set. As the past gives way to present understanding or the present to future promise within each story, a progressive pattern of renewal from generation to generation is established.

23. Millgate, *Achievement of William Faulkner*, 262.

A similar effect is produced by the arrangement of the six stories in the section. Faulkner alternates them according to three roughly coherent time periods: the far past of the pre–Civil War Indian stories, the near past covering the period from the late nineteenth century to World War I, and the post-war present in the 1920s. In "A Justice," Quentin is twelve and inhabits the near past as he relates Sam Fathers' story of the far past in the time of Ikkemotubbe; in "That Evening Sun" he is twenty-four, inhabits the present, and tells the story of Nancy and Jesus that took place in the near past when he was nine. The stories are so arranged that those set in a past time are paired with those set more recently: the effect is of a past unfolding by steady stages into the present in a progression that approximates the cyclical motion of life. The pattern is this:

"Red Leaves"	far past
"A Rose for Emily"	near past to present
"A Justice"	far past to near past
"Hair"	near past to present
"That Evening Sun"	near past to present
"Dry September"	present

Each with a separate life of its own, the stories are linked in this structure by a shared time dimension or by chronologic sequence, and few as they are, they make of Jefferson and Yoknapatawpha County a place that exists both in space and in time. Because they do, it is perhaps fair to say that *These 13* marks a significant state in the making of that cosmos where, as Faulkner later said, he could move his people around "like God, not only in space but in time too."[24] In 1931 he was creating in his own work the effects he had described, with reference to Robinson's poetry, as "beautiful and passionate and sad instead of sadden-

---

24. Meriwether and Millgate (eds.), *Lion in the Garden*, 255.

ing."[25] At the same time he was learning to live, as T. S. Eliot insisted that the modern poet must live, "in what is not merely the present, but the present moment of the past . . . conscious, not of what is dead, but of what is already living."[26]

In 1944 and 1945, when Malcolm Cowley was putting together *The Portable Faulkner*, he was at some pains to suggest the temporal dimension of Faulkner's work: he dated the stories and excerpts according to their subject matter and arranged them in chronologic order under section headings that run from "The Old People" to "Modern Times" and "The Undying Past." The organization of that important anthology is instructive. Although Faulkner praised it as a splendid job,[27] the chronologic sequence of the pieces is uncharacteristic of the form of Faulkner's own collections. In Cowley's book, time is an unbroken line; in Faulkner's, it is a looping string that shows us characters and situations from a variety of perspectives, uncovers unexpected relationships, and transforms the peripheral issues of one episode into the central concern of the next. It is precisely for this reason that the Easter Sunday chapter of *The Sound and the Fury* is so reduced in beauty and power when it appears as "Dilsey" in the *Portable*. Cowley's book is organized to demonstrate his theory that Yoknapatawpha County stands "as a parable or legend of all the Deep South," and he uses "April 8, 1928" as an instance of Negro dignity and endurance.[28] Faulkner specifically avoided reprinting excerpts from novels in his collections, but even though many of the stories from Cowley's anthology are included in *These 13* and *Collected Stories*, Faulkner arranged them according to artistic rather than critical imperatives.

25. Faulkner, "Verse Old and Nascent," 118.
26. T. S. Eliot, "Tradition and the Individual Talent," in *T. S. Eliot: Selected Essays* (New York: Harcourt, Brace and World, 1964), 11.
27. Malcolm Cowley, *The Faulkner-Cowley File: Letters and Memories, 1944–1962* (New York: Viking, 1966), 90–91.
28. Malcolm Cowley (ed.), *The Portable Faulkner*, rev. ed. (New York: Viking, 1967), viii.

Those imperatives Faulkner set forth in a 1948 letter to Cowley in which he outlined his plan for *Collected Stories*. Dedicating the book to "the uplifting of men's hearts," he told Cowley that "even to a collection of short stories, form, integration, is as important as to a novel—an entity of its own, single, set for one pitch, contrapuntal in integration, toward one end, one finale."[29] That same principle governs the structure of *These 13*, as Professor Millgate has said, and it governs the shape of stories and novels throughout the canon. The book itself culminates Faulkner's plan, stated two decades earlier and tried first in *These 13*, for "a collection of short stories of my townspeople"—a project that finally required him to make not only the people but their town and county too. By the time of *Collected Stories*, the county had become both setting and mode of expression in Faulkner's fiction. It was a place created in the fictions that gave those fictions spatial and temporal form.

Collected Stories is divided into six sections of varying length, each of which bears the name of a place or locale: The Country, The Village, The Wilderness, The Wasteland, The Middle Ground, and Beyond. Given its forty-two separate, sometimes uneven stories, the considerable claims that Faulkner made for the unity and integration of the book are difficult to sustain entirely. But if *Collected Stories* is less a single entity than *Go Down, Moses* or *The Wild Palms* is, it does move clearly toward one end and finale. Working on the principle of counterpoint, Faulkner uses The Country and The Village to establish the present reality of Yoknapatawpha, then presents its past in the Indian stories of The Wilderness. In contrast to the Yoknapatawpha cosmos, the next section, The Wasteland, portrays the spatial and temporal disorientation of war. It is followed by The Middle Ground, where the space-time sense is revived in stories such as "Wash" and "Mountain Victory," and the book con-

29. Cowley, *Faulkner-Cowley File*, 115–16.

cludes with Beyond, where space and time are transcended in a series of fantasies that ends with "Carcassonne." This movement is reinforced from section to section by a sequence of thematic statements on the nature of maturation, individual identity, the ritual past, living death, love, and imagination. To express these themes, Faulkner framed each section with complementary stories.

As in *These 13* the frame stories are units of structure that define the boundaries of a complete action and move the narrative forward by uncovering likenesses in apparent unlikeness and unities in apparent diversity. They also define the theme of each section. In The Village, for example, the first and last stories are "A Rose for Emily" and "That Evening Sun." The limits that a closed society imposes on the identity of the individual are dramatized in the lives of two women, quite unlike, whose dilemmas are nonetheless the same. Both stories involve betrayals of love ending in murder, or the threat of murder; and the aberrations in each proceed from the women's isolation in society. Miss Emily is "a tradition, a duty, and a care" (CS, 119) to the collective town; Nancy "aint nothing but a nigger" (CS, 293) to the Compson children. In the reverberent and accretive context of The Village, it is simply untenable to argue that Emily is a symbol of the antebellum South betrayed by the North, or to find in Nancy's self-imposed agonies an allegory of southern racial guilt. The white spinster and the black washerwoman share the same destiny for the same human reasons; in addition they represent two extremes of the isolated life between which other characters in The Village work out their own destinies with varying degrees of failure or success.

Certainly The Village owes some of its considerable power to the excellence of the first and last stories, which elevate the victories and defeats of stories such as "Centaur in Brass" and "Uncle Willy" and "Mule in the Yard" above their immediate contexts. Nonetheless, the narrative frame can fuse form and

221

meaning even where no such inherent strengths exist. An example of this situation, and of a somewhat different function of the frame tales, is Section I, The Country. Probably every reader would agree that the opening story, "Barn Burning," is superior to "Shall Not Perish," with which the section closes. Yet together they define the boundaries of a complete action: the pattern of initiation begun when Sarty Snopes flees family and society into "the urgent and quiring heart of the late spring night" (CS, 25) is completed when the Grier boy accepts his right relation to family, the South, and the nation. The conflict is between loyalty to self and responsibility to society; phrased in "Barn Burning" as a contest between Snopes and de Spain, it is resolved in "Shall Not Perish" by the reconciliation of de Spain and Grier. In this way both an emblematic life and a book are begun. The single end and theme toward which they move may be seen if the opening and closing sections of *Collected Stories* are considered in light of the framing technique that characterizes each of its parts. It seems significant here that Faulkner ignored Cowley's suggestion that he omit the stories in Beyond or, failing that, transpose the final two sections so that the book would end with The Middle Ground.[30] As it stands, The Country and Beyond constitute a comprehensive frame encompassing the course of life from birth to death. In this regard the suitability of the initiation pattern in the opening section of the book is quickly seen. Collectively the child protagonists of The Country experience the birth of self, and the way is opened for an investigation of the implications for the self inherent in a variety of human situations and experiences. These comprise the thematic focus of the four interior sections of the collection: the individual in society (The Village), the ritual past (The Wilderness), death-in-life (The Wasteland), and love—both sexual and familial—(The Middle Ground). In the final section, Beyond, the self con-

30. *Ibid.*, 119.

fronts death literally and figuratively and finds in death various modes of immortality, among them the immortality of the artist.

To say this is to argue that the theme as well as the narrative form of *Collected Stories* is essentially the same as *These 13*, and it brings me again to the enigmatic story "Carcassonne" with which both collections conclude. In spite of Noel Polk's persuasive, sometimes brilliant explication of that fascinating story, I cannot bring myself to see in it the failed promise that he sees. Remember, if you will, that *Collected Stories* was published in 1950 with, as part of its purpose, "the uplifting of men's hearts." In that year Faulkner delivered his Nobel Prize address, which I will spare you the quoting of except to remind you that that speech ends, too, with a poet, whose privilege, Faulkner said, was "to help man endure by lifting his heart, by reminding him of the courage and honor and hope and pride and compassion and pity and sacrifice which have been the glory of his past."[31] "Carcassonne" is so suitable a tailpiece to *Collected Stories* because it evokes precisely these values: the courage and honor of the Crusaders, Tancred and Godfrey of Bouillon; pity for King Agamemnon, so cruelly murdered by *"the woman with the dog's eyes"* (*CS*, 898); and the compassion of Christ Himself, the *"King of Kings"* (*CS*, 898), through whose sacrificial death we are taught that man will not merely endure but prevail.[32]

The poet of Rincon, so well read in Homeric epic and the literature of medieval romance that he can quote them in his reveries, phrases that essential Christian idea in this way: *"the flesh is dead living on itself subsisting consuming itself thriftily in its own renewal will never die for I am the Resurrection and the Life* Of a man, the worm should be lusty, lean, hairedover.

31. Meriwether (ed.), *Essays, Speeches, and Public Letters*, 120.
32. Cleanth Brooks erroneously attributes the title *"King of Kings"* to Agamemnon rather than to Christ, with the result that he misreads the theme of rebirth in the story. Brooks writes, "Agamemnon, a commander of the Greek host, was a king of kings, but it is Faulkner who has made Clytemnestra knock her husband's bones together" (*Toward Yoknapatawpha and Beyond*, 63).

Of women, of delicate girls briefly like heard music in tune, it should be suavely shaped, falling feeding into prettinesses, feeding. *what though to Me but as a seething of new milk Who am the Resurrection and the Life"* (*CS*, 897). The immortality of the flesh lies in "its own renewal"—through love and birth and maturation and through its capacity, dramatized in these collections of short stories, to withstand isolation and war in a seemingly diminished epoch of human history. The immortality of the soul is promised in "Carcassonne" by Christ and achieved, in imagination if not in fact, in that galloping ascent with which the story and the collections end, *"up the hill and right off into the high heaven of the world"* (*CS*, 899). The poet of "Carcassonne" rejects the bone-bred knowledge that "the end of life is lying still" (*CS*, 899) for that imaginative transcendence to which Faulkner laid claim a quarter of a century after writing "Carcassonne" when he spoke of himself as God, creator of cosmoses.

"Life is motion," Faulkner told Jean Stein in 1955; "The aim of every artist is to arrest motion, which is life, by artificial means and hold it fixed so that 100 years later when a stranger looks at it, it moves again since it is life."[33] The way to arrest motion, he had discovered, was through fictional forms that might approximate, by their complex—their contrapuntal—integration, the very processes they held in fictional suspension. Form might not only capture but create life. Yoknapatawpha County is such a form, both a place and a way to tell stories. The short stories contributed to its making precisely because they invite incorporation into the diverse and multifaceted structures that Faulkner created from them in his collections both early and late. Perhaps no actual place could have held such a conception; actualities, after all, are subject to time and change. And besides, as Faulkner told an audience at the University of Virginia, "because of the barenness of the Southerner's life . . . he

33. Meriwether and Millgate (eds.), *Lion in the Garden*, 253.

had to resort to his own imagination, to create his own Carcassonne."[34] Still, without the dimensions of time and space, one's own imaginary Carcassonne might be equally bare—a flat tableau like "The Hill," perhaps, or an ornate and puzzling dream on the order of "Nympholepsy." Outside the context created by the other stories in *These 13* or *Collected Stories*, the short story "Carcassonne" is such a dream, which may account for the fact that Faulkner apparently never offered it for publication by itself. In the context of those books, where lives are caught and held in the motion of life, "Carcassonne" moves to the rhythms of the stories that it concludes and comments upon. *"I want to perform something bold and tragical and austere"* (*CS*, 899), the poet of "Carcassonne" tells his skeleton. What he performs is a work of art: *These 13* in 1931 and *Collected Stories of William Faulkner* in 1950. The skeleton of each book is its formal structure and the stories that compose that structure, like the poet's bones, have undergone a sea-change by the end of the book, "knocking together to the spent motion of falling tides in the caverns and the grottoes of the sea" (*CS*, 897). Rooted in the mortal lives in stories set in a living time and place, the theme of both collections soars with the mind of the poet beyond its mortal vehicle: "a dying star upon the immensity of darkness and of silence within which, steadfast, fading, deep-breasted and grave of flank, muses the dark and tragic figure of the Earth, his mother" (*CS*, 900). If Faulkner's own imaginary Carcassonne was Yoknapatawpha County, it seems to me no more than fitting that he should conclude the two collections where Yoknapatawpha County is made with the story "Carcassonne."

34. Frederick L. Gwynn and Joseph Blotner (eds.), *Faulkner in the University: Class Conferences at the University of Virginia, 1957–1958* (Charlottesville: University of Virginia Press, 1959), 136.

Watching for the Dixie Limited:
Faulkner's Impact upon the Creative Writer

THOMAS L. McHANEY

Like Percy Adams, who ended one of his informative essays on Faulkner and French literature by reference to the remark,[1] I am also much taken with Flannery O'Connor's interpretation of the southern writer's relationship to Faulkner: "The presence alone of Faulkner in our midst makes a great difference in what the writer can and cannot permit himself to do. Nobody wants his mule and wagon stalled on the same track the Dixie Limited is roaring down."[2] This seems to me a perfect expression of *impact* in at least one of its literary meanings. The passage is an example of what I have looked for in the reactions of other creative writers to Faulkner's work. I have ranged through several languages and literatures, as best I could, finding that creative writers sometimes seem to have more in common with one another, regardless of national or linguistic differences, than with their own native literary establishments. Faulkner is a grand case in point; in fact, the literary establishment, especially in the sense that it constitutes the world of the best-seller and the major reviewing media, did not have as much to do with him in

---

1. Percy Adams, "Faulkner, French Literature, and 'Eternal Verities,'" in *William Faulkner: Prevailing Verities and World Literature*, ed. W. T. Zyla and W. M. Aycock (Lubbock, Tex.: Texas Tech University, 1973), 7–24. See also Percy G. Adams, "The Franco-American Faulkner," *Tennessee Studies in Literature*, V (1960), 1–13.

2. Flannery O'Connor, "The Grotesque in Southern Fiction," *Mystery and Manners* (New York: Farrar Straus & Giroux, 1969), 45.

his own linguistic zones, America and England, as did the other creative writers in English. His impact on them was immediate and sustained, so much that a look back across the years at his reception by fellow artists throws serious doubt upon the often repeated contention that 1939 marks the beginning of serious consideration for Faulkner in the states.[3]

When Malcolm Cowley began corresponding with Faulkner in 1944 about the Viking *Portable* anthology, he reported that New York publishers, the "bright boys among the critics," and academicians neither understood nor appreciated Faulkner, but "when you talk to writers instead of publishers or publishers' pet critics about the *oeuvre* of William Faulkner, it's quite a different story; there you hear almost nothing but admiration, and the better the writer the greater the admiration is likely to be. Conrad Aiken, for example, puts you at the top of the heap." Later in 1945, Cowley reported the opinion of Jean-Paul Sartre, who spoke for a generation of French writers just emerging from their wartime activities: "What he said about you was, 'Pour les jeunes en France, Faulkner c'est un dieu.'"[4] The phenomenon Cowley had noticed was not hatched in the 1940s. More than anyone else, creative writers—novelists, poets, dramatists— showed appreciation and expressed wonderment for Faulkner's work from the beginning of his career.

Among the first to appreciate Faulkner's genius were the literary members of the New Orleans bohemia to which he came in the mid-1920s. They encouraged an apprentice writer, but sometimes they simply marveled at him. Sherwood Anderson saw him as a coming man, with the paradoxical disadvantage of

3. Perrin Holmes Lowrey, "The Critical Reputation of William Faulkner's Work in the United States, 1926–1950" (Ph.D. dissertation, University of Chicago, 1956), 219; O. B. Emerson, "William Faulkner's Literary Reputation in America". (Ph.D. dissertation, Vanderbilt University, 1962), 311ff.; William Webb Pusey repeats the dictum in his article upon Faulkner's reception in Germany to 1940 in *Germanic Review*, XXX (October, 1955), 211.

4. Malcolm Cowley, *The Faulkner-Cowley File* (New York: Viking, 1966), 10, 24.

too much talent,[5] and this seems to me a case of impact, something more than admiration—a hard-working man of letters, who struggled with his art all his life, reeling a little in the face of a young turk. John McClure, the New Orleans newspaperman who conducted the *Times-Picayune* book page and edited the *Double Dealer*, was also a poet and fiction writer. He was the first editor to give Faulkner's prose sketches and tales an airing, but he also reviewed *The Marble Faun* in January of 1925, finding it to be the work of a "born" poet.[6] The following year, along with North Carolina novelist Thomas Boyd and Tennessee poet and critic Donald Davidson, McClure praised Faulkner's first novel.[7] All three writers responded first to Faulkner's style. Boyd's criticism was particularly characteristic of much that was to come. He was himself a popular, not an innovative novelist, and he did not know what to make of Faulkner's experiment in form, but he acknowledged the power of the book—as if the power of the book did not come, in part, from the form Faulkner had given it. As Cleanth Brooks has wisely said, reviewing the frequent misappraisals of Faulkner by British journalistic critics, "Can there be real badness of style if vitality and power inhere in the work that employs such a style?"[8] I would not be like the Freudian critic who pins his subject to the wall, damned if he does, damned if he doesn't, by showing how the presence of an image indicates an obsession while the absence of the same image indicates a *real* obsession. I am most interested in the creative writers who have praised Faulkner;

5. The relationship between Anderson and Faulkner is viewed in the first chapter of my *William Faulkner's The Wild Palms: A Study* (Jackson: University Press of Mississippi, 1975).

6. John McClure, New Orleans *Times-Picayune*, January 25, 1925, Magazine Section, 6.

7. Thomas Boyd, "Honest but Slap-Dash," *Saturday Review*, April 24, 1926, 736; John McClure, *Times-Picayune*, April 11, 1926, Magazine Section, 24; Donald Davidson, Nashville *Tennessean*, April 11, 1926.

8. Cleanth Brooks, "The British Reception of Faulkner's Work," in Zyla and Aycock (eds.), *William Faulkner*, 41–55.

but even opposing him or, as we shall see, resisting his influence, writers (and more "ordinary" critics, too, for that matter) often reveal one form or another of Faulkner's impact.

Mosquitoes did not fare quite as well as *Soldiers' Pay*, but Davidson and McClure both recognized Faulkner's talent and promise. Conrad Aiken, a fine poet and a fiction-writer as well, did not like some of Faulkner's mannerisms, but he had genuine praise for Faulkner's characterization, humor, style, dialogue, and creation of setting, an opinion concurred in, on almost the same grounds, by another poet, Elinor Wylie.[9]

In 1929, *Sartoris* drew high praise from Davidson, who said that as a "stylist and an acute observer of human behavior" Faulkner had few betters. Lyle Saxon, another creative writer from the New Orleans circle, wrote in the *New York Herald Tribune* Sunday book section that *The Sound and the Fury* was "as merciless as anything that I know which has come out of Russia," yet so American that it should not be compared with European work.[10] In a still not widely read pamphlet issued by Faulkner's publisher, the then-popular novelist Evelyn Scott (who was avant-garde herself, though she had won recent success with *The Wave*) expressed her enthusiasm for the uniqueness of *The Sound and the Fury*, too. Her essay sprang from a spontaneous letter which she had expanded at the publisher's suggestion. Four years before the French writer André Malraux was to make his famous remark about *Sanctuary's* representing the infusion of Greek tragedy into detective fiction, and more than two decades prior to Albert Camus's discovery of the modern rebirth of the language of tragedy in *Requiem for a Nun*, Evelyn Scott wrote that the Compson novel had "all the spacious proportions of Greek art," and, like Camus later, she found in

9. John McClure, *Times-Picayune*, July 3, 1927, Magazine Section, 4; Donald Davidson, *Tennessean*, July 3, 1927; Conrad Aiken, *New York Evening Post*, June 11, 1927, Sec. III, 7; Elinor Wylie, *New Republic*, July 20, 1927, 236.

10. Donald Davidson, *Tennessean*, April 14, 1929; Lyle Saxon, *New York Herald Tribune*, October 13, 1929, 3.

Faulkner the paradoxical expression of the spirit of great tragedy in terms of a diminished modern age of disillusion.[11]

British novelists began their public praise of Faulkner chiefly in 1930 and 1931. The successful author of *High Wind in Jamaica*, Richard Hughes, has told the story of his first acquaintance with Faulkner's work and his immediate efforts to get Faulkner published in Britain.[12] In his preface to the English edition of *Soldiers' Pay* in 1930, Hughes praised it as "tragic fascinating and beautiful . . . by a man who is a novelist to his fingertips." As other novelists would do, Hughes assumed rightly that the man who wrote Faulkner's books was possessed of a keen intellect and a wide acquaintance with the best literature—not, as the simple-minded journalistic critics liked increasingly to say, simply *possessed*. Hughes's unassuming and selfless recognition of a fellow writer is touching and exemplary, and particularly so when you compare it with the garbage written about Faulkner during the two decades after Hughes's introductions to *Soldiers' Pay* and, in 1931, *The Sound and the Fury*. Faulkner had demonstrated, he wrote, a "highly and widely educated" mind and a true humanity.[13] Of course he was right; but how long did it take the popular press to find that out?

Hughes introduced *The Sound and the Fury* to a British audience with the assurance that one need only read the book to get its meaning; he himself, he said, had read it three times with increasing pleasure and understanding.[14] Like Evelyn Scott in her pamphlet, he found the Benjy section not a puzzle but a piece of writing that was both fascinating and inevitable in its

11. Evelyn Scott, "On William Faulkner's *The Sound and the Fury*" (New York: Cape and Smith, 1929); reprinted, in part, in *Twentieth Century Interpretations of The Sound and the Fury*, ed. M. Cowan (Englewood Cliffs, N.J.: Prentice-Hall, 1968).

12. Richard Hughes, "Faulkner and Bennett," *Encounter*, XXI (September, 1963), 59–61.

13. Richard Hughes, Preface to William Faulkner's *Soldiers' Pay* (London: Chatto & Windus, 1930), ix-xi.

14. Richard Hughes, Introduction to William Faulkner's *The Sound and the Fury* (London: Chatto & Windus, 1931), vii-ix.

structure. A similar sentiment was repeated in the British journal *Spectator* by the English novelist L. A. G. Strong, another early champion of Faulkner's work abroad. The form of *The Sound and the Fury* worked so well, Strong wrote, one could not imagine how it might have been done otherwise; it repaid the difficulties one encountered on a first reading.[15] Writer Frank Swinnerton, doubtless rushed for time as a frequent reviewer and without Hughes's leisure to reread the book, found it complex, but he admitted that like great music it might become clearer with greater familiarity. "One is conscious of immense power, a terrific drive of creative invention," he wrote—happily handing me an image of my metaphor of *impact*. Without realizing it, perhaps, and all the way across the Atlantic, he had been brushed by the Dixie Limited on one of its early runs. Faulkner, he said—we see him standing there looking down the quickly darkening track at the big red light on the observation car—was the "most powerful and the most enigmatic" of the new American literary figures.[16]

As stated earlier, this recognition would become a commonplace in Faulkner's reception; *impact* is really the better word, because it doesn't necessarily imply that Faulkner was well-received. Professional critics, unless they were writers themselves and thus prepared mentally and emotionally to appreciate the genius behind Faulkner's work, did not have time to appreciate Faulkner, or they couldn't free themselves, very often, from flip judgments that had more to do with where Faulkner lived than what or how he wrote. Faulkner was, as an honest and puzzled reviewer would put it much later, the "bane" of weekly reviewers who found stacks of books around their chairs and deadlines to meet as they hustled the literary buck. Because he did not repeat himself and because he did not compromise his vision,

15. L.A.G. Strong, *Spectator*, April 25, 1931, 674.
16. Frank Swinnerton, "Writers Who Know Life," *London Evening News*, May 15, 1931, p.8.

his struggle to blend material and method, by commercial over-simplifications of psychology, plot, or novelistic form, he was difficult to get a handle on. His work was always demanding because of its scale, its human complexity, its formal innovation, and—almost incidentally, but still importantly in a country of at least two minds—subject matter. The standards by which he wrote were more readily perceived and appreciated by his fellow writers than by the critics.

Nineteen thirty-one brought *The Sound and the Fury* to Britain, and in America it constitutes one of the transition points in Faulkner's literary impact. He attracted an unusual amount of attention in that year; apparently the effect was calculated, even if as second thought and with possibly unexpected results.[17] The Dixie Limited was pushing *Sanctuary* that year. *As I Lay Dying* had appeared in 1930 without attracting much attention; *Sanctuary* did the work of the proverbial two-by-four you are supposed to use to catch the attention of the mule. But L. A. G. Strong, writing in the *Spectator* again, did not recoil; the novel strengthened the evidence that "Faulkner is a writer of the first importance," though the subject matter did not allow it to be generally recommended. The American playwright Robert Sherwood made a specific avowal of impact: it was, he wrote, a great novel which addressed itself directly to the senses.[18]

Sanctuary made waves everywhere, of course, and helped start a good deal of backlash from what Malcolm Cowley would call the "bright boys." A lot of those waves reached the shores of Europe, however, with results that are generally well known. That same year Sinclair Lewis praised Faulkner (and other young American writers) in his Nobel Prize acceptance speech, and there were important essays on Faulkner in Italy and

17. Faulkner's account of writing *Sanctuary* is a good piece of creative writing itself, with a germ of truth; our best perspective upon this so-called potboiler may always be the immediate responses of creative writers who rated it so highly when it appeared.

18. L. A. G. Strong, *Spectator*, September 19, 1931, 362–64; Robert Sherwood, *Scribner's*, LXXXIX (April, 1931), 13.

France that helped bring Faulkner to the notice of creative writers in Europe. Mario Praz and Maurice E. Coindreau, who wrote essays in Italy and France, were not specifically creative writers, but Praz's eminence as an Americanist and Coindreau's zeal and expertise as a translator "from the American" made them perfect conduits to writers in their countries.[19] W. W. Pusey cites the following year, 1932, as the date of the first mention of Faulkner in a German periodical and says that serious consideration did not begin until 1935, when *Light in August* was translated. Hermann Hesse, Gottfried Benn, Bernt von Heiseler, Eckart von Naso, Richard Moering, and Gerhart Pohl are among the writers whom Pusey mentions as commenting upon Faulkner's work. The situation in Germany was of course enormously complicated from 1933 by censorship and the "strangulation of intellectual freedom," but Faulkner received favorable attention.[20] Lino Novas Calvo, novelist, biographer, and translator, receives credit for introducing Faulkner into the Spanish-speaking world in 1933, writing on "El Demonio de Faulkner" in *Revista de Occidente*. Like other writers, he noted that Faulkner hit the reader directly with the experience portrayed in the books.[21]

Mario Praz had told Italian readers in 1931 that Faulkner was not the purveyor of gratuitous violence but a moralist (see note 19 above); we would not hear that until 1939 in America, from George Marion O'Donnell, a novelist and short story writer. But I am getting ahead of the Dixie Limited; that, as we know, can

19. For a discussion of Praz's importance, see Mario Materassi, "Faulkner Criticism in Italy," *Italian Quarterly*, XV (Summer, 1971), 47–85; for Maurice Coindreau, see *The Time of William Faulkner: A French View of Modern Fiction*, ed. and trans. George M. Reeves (Columbia: University of South Carolina Press, 1971).

20. See W. W. Pusey, "William Faulkner's Books in Germany to 1940: Translations and Criticism," *Germanic Review*, XXX (October, 1955), 211–26; for the postwar reception in Germany, see Edith Zindel, *William Faulkner in den deutschsprachigen Ländern Europas: Untersuchungen zur Aufnahme seiner Werke nach 1945* (Hamburg: H. Lüdke, 1972).

21. See Arnold Chapman, *Spanish American Reception of U. S. Fiction, 1920–1940* (Berkeley: University of California Press, 1966), 127–50, 216–20.

be dangerous. In 1932, which is where I want to be, O'Donnell reviewed *Light in August* for the *Memphis Commercial Appeal* and found it more human than *Sanctuary*, a judgment that perhaps no one but a novelist could have made from Mr. Crump's town. L. A. G. Strong continued to praise Faulkner in England, where *Sartoris* was just being published. Almost in wonderment, Strong observed that one must accept a man of genius whole or not at all; he was prepared to accept Faulkner on those terms. Robert Penn Warren, reviewing the story collection *These 13* that same year, began his lifelong appreciation of Faulkner by responding to the work's "most triumphant aspect," the sense of place.[22]

In 1933, the distinguished French writer and intellectual André Malraux published the preface to the translated *Sanctuary* which I have already referred to,[23] and L. A. G. Strong called *Light in August* a "fine, significant and important piece of work" that "burns throughout with a fierce indignation against cruelty, stupidity and prejudice." Both these non-Americans presented views of Faulkner as tragedian and moralist which would have come as news to most American and British critics, who were then busy putting Faulkner at the head of what was called the "cult of cruelty."[24] Their voices were not heard in the corridors of literary power, nor apparently was the reply of Evelyn Scott, she who had responded to *The Sound and the Fury*. When Henry Seidel Canby, editor of *Saturday Review*, went so far as to commission a psychiatrist to analyze *Sanctuary* (among other works), Scott sent in a reply "From a Novelist," raising

22. George Marion O'Donnell, *Commercial Appeal*, October 9, 1932, sec. E, 5; L. A. G. Strong, *Spectator*, February 27, 1932, 296, 298; Robert Penn Warren, "Not Local Color," *VQR*, VIII (January, 1932), 160.

23. *Nouvelle revue francaise* (November, 1933), 744–47.

24. L. A. G. Strong, *Spectator*, February 17, 1933, 226. See Henry Seidel Canby, "The School of Cruelty," *Saturday Review*, March 21, 1931, 673–74; Alan Reynolds Thompson, "The Cult of Cruelty," *Bookman*, LXXIV (January-February, 1932); and the series of pieces by L. Kubie in *Saturday Review* beginning October 20, 1934, 217–18.

questions about the approach, evidence, and conclusions of the hired medicine man.[25]

Despite the silliness in *Saturday Review*, 1934 was another important year in the enlargement of Faulkner's reputation among other writers. Important articles and translations appeared in Italy and France. Italians Aldo Camerino and Emilio Cecchi both discerned Faulkner's moralism, and Cecchi believed the fiction to be "humanly saturated" with compassion.[26] French novelist Eugene Dabit envied American writers their subject matter and style and noted Faulkner's pervasive tragic mode; about *Sanctuary* he said that the problems of the novel's technique were overridden by its power—the reader of Faulkner is exposed directly to a senseless world and drama of high intensity.[27] Valery Larbaud, in the preface to the translation of *As I Lay Dying*, complemented Malraux's remarks about Greek tragedy by discerning epical elements in the story of the Bundrens and a full mythological cast of characters.[28] From England, the Vorticist painter and writer Wyndham Lewis—"A Moralist with a Corncob" was the catchy title coined by the editor of *Blast*—deprecated Faulkner's style but granted the passionate character of the work and its unforgettable characters, once again demonstrating the response that refuses to see the source of the power it feels.[29]

Although as James B. Meriwether has pointed out, the New Critics did not do much toward explicating or helping the sale of Faulkner's works in the 1930s and 1940s, the writers who had begun as "Fugitives" noticed and praised Faulkner's fiction be-

25. *Saturday Review*, November 10, 1934, 272, 280.
26. See Materassi, "Faulkner Criticism," 47–85.
27. Eugene Dabit, *Europe*, April 15, 1934, 599–600; Eugene Dabit, *Europe*, October 15, 1934, 294–96.
28. Valery Larbaud, Preface to William Faulkner's *Tandis que j'agonise*, trans. Maurice E. Coindreau (Paris: Gallimard, 1934).
29. Wyndham Lewis, *Life and Letters*, X (June, 1934), 312–28.

fore they turned to popularizing formalist criticism.[30] In 1934, Robert Penn Warren compared Faulkner with then-popular T. S. Stribling, concluding that the younger writer was more concerned with deeper issues and meanings and was more poetic and contemplative. John Crowe Ransom, in 1935, listed the breadth of Faulkner's subjects and themes and called him the "most exciting figure in our contemporary literature just now." Allen Tate, though he had some difficulties with Faulkner's personal style and was perhaps too busy creating his own career to spend much time helping Faulkner, seems to have regarded the Mississippian all along as "the most powerful and original novelist in the United States and one of the best in the modern world," a quote I pick up from 1945.[31]

Power with impact, and variety, were noted by the coauthor of *What Price Glory?*—Lawrence Stallings—when he reviewed *Pylon*, saying there were three Faulkners: the comic genius of "A Rose for Emily"; the nostalgic, gallant local colorist of the *Saturday Evening Post* stories; and the overheated prose technician of the new 1935 novel, *Pylon*, who fascinated and beguiled.[32] And Lawrence of Arabia himself entered the act that same year in a prefatory letter to a book entitled *The River Niger* by Simon Jesty; Jesty's novel used epigraphs from *The Sound and the Fury* at the head of each of its sections. T. E. Lawrence, apparently praising Faulkner's spontaneity, remarks in his brief preface: "I know that Faulkner began with many of these epigrammatic and seeming-obscure allusive sentences, written in a staccato rhythm, with nouns, adjectives (many) and verbs (few) dancing in measure. But Faulkner shed this mannerism as he

30. James B. Meriwether, "Faulkner and the New Criticism," *Books Abroad*, XXXVII (Summer, 1963), 265–68.

31. Robert Penn Warren, *American Review*, II (November, 1933-March, 1934), 483–86; John Crowe Ransom, "Modern with the Southern Accent," *VQR*, XI (April, 1935), 184–200; Allen Tate, *Essays of Four Decades* (Chicago: Swallow, 1968), 545.

32. Lawrence Stallings, "Gentleman from Mississippi," *American Mercury*, XXXIV (April, 1935), 499–501.

wrote more and more hurriedly. Jesty has been too careful, writing this book."[33] Graham Greene, writing in 1937 in the *London Mercury*, did not like *Absalom, Absalom!* but he did find that Faulkner imparted a "new sense of spiritual evil,"[34] acknowledging the power of Faulkner's vision.

These were opinions which were by no means obligatory. Despite the remarkable fiction which Faulkner had written between only 1929 and 1936, he did not have the kind of fashionable reputation that can roll bandwagons; or, to put it another way, the Dixie Limited was on track, but the tracks didn't go down Main Street as they do in some Mississippi towns. Europe admired his speed—e.g., Lawrence, above—his technology— e.g., Jean Paul Sartre's discussion of *Sartoris* in 1938[35]—as well as his passenger list and the sound of his whistle, if I may burden Flannery O'Connor's metaphor some more. Even the American writer Kay Boyle, writing in 1938, saw two Faulkners: the native southerner and the sophisticated author with European experience, as she called it. Between these two influences, she wrote, Faulkner possessed "the strength and the vulnerability which belongs only to the greatest artists."[36]

Nineteen thirty-nine has been called a turning point in Faulkner's reception, and that may be true in America, but by 1938 the Frenchman Maurice E. Coindreau had established himself as the chief intermediary between Faulkner and his French audience. He had begun to bring Faulkner to the Latin Americans, too, a task which the French influence generally continued over the years, since so many Latin Americans received at least part of their literary taste and education from Paris. Coindreau's essays, translations, and prefaces brought Faulkner to a receptive and influential artistic audience. As far

33. T. E. Lawrence, Preface to Simon Jesty's *The River Niger* (London: Boriswood, 1935).

34. Graham Greene, *London Mercury*, XXXV (March, 1937), 517–18.

35. *Nouvelle revue francaise* (February, 1938), 323–28.

36. Kay Boyle, *New Republic* (March 19, 1938), 136–37.

as the 1939 date for American criticism's turning point goes, there were two substantial articles on Faulkner in prestigious journals, both, as we might by now expect, written by writers: Conrad Aiken in *Atlantic Monthly* and George Marion O'Donnell in *Kenyon Review*. Not only had these two artists already responded to Faulkner in print much earlier, but, as should be clear by now, there had been in America a fairly extensive response to Faulkner by a goodly number of others who took Faulkner seriously, assumed he knew what he was doing and saw that he did it well, and achieved excellent critical results when they applied a serious point of view toward the fiction in their reviews, anticipating many later, more reflectively arrived at, judgments. Aiken, for example, repeats what an attentive and multilingual reader would have already heard from other American, English, Italian, and French authors: Faulkner's style is deliberate and effective and functional; it immerses one in the novel's action. Faulkner's formal experiments are not willful but organic, and music, Aiken suggests, offers an appropriate analogy for discussing the work. O'Donnell, simplistically overstating an allegorical scheme of his own devising, nevertheless uses what he calls Faulkner's mythology to stress the novelist's essential morality.[37]

Two further statements from 1939 will give us an impression of how writers—as opposed to critics—responded to Faulkner. It is worth noting that in this year the public critical reception of *The Wild Palms* was so wildly varied that an important editor felt moved to discuss the relativity of book reviewing.[38] This was at the same time that Jean-Paul Sartre was giving his version of Faulkner's metaphysic, and if his version of that metaphysic is highly debatable now, he was at least revolutionary and unique,

37. Conrad Aiken, *Atlantic Monthly*, CLXIV (November, 1939), 650–54; George Marion O'Donnell, *Kenyon Review*, I (Summer, 1939), 285–99.
38. George Stevens, "Wild Palms and Ripe Olives," *Saturday Review*, February 11, 1939, 8.

compared with popular criticism in America and England, in discovering any metaphysic at all, especially without feeling the need to apologize for doing so. We might close out the responses of this decade with one that is appropriately metaphorical. Novelist Wallace Stegner claimed that no one writing could evoke a violent scene like Faulkner; he found the orchestration of the two plots of *The Wild Palms* justifiable; and he admitted that reading Faulkner was "like taking hold of an electrified fence."[39]

The decade of the forties, despite the claim that it began with serious consideration of Faulkner's work and the fact that it ended with the awarding of the Nobel Prize for Literature, was Faulkner's nadir. After the remarkable period which began the year of the crash on Wall Street and ended almost coincidentally with the bombing of Pearl Harbor, Faulkner lapsed into an uncharacteristic silence, deeply upset by the war, plagued with family problems and responsibilities, spending large amounts of time and energy in Hollywood to earn the money his books did not bring him, despite the continuing admiration of his fellow novelists and poets. His work was not welcome in Fascist countries, but, as Cowley wrote him in 1945, he became a god to the French writers and not to them alone. A survey of articles by writers on Faulkner during the forties shows growing assurance on their part of his greatness. If Donald Stanford, an editor of *Southern Review* along with Cleanth Brooks and Robert Penn Warren, could write that *The Hamlet* was Faulkner's "latest explosion in a cesspool," Stephen Vincent Benet, a creative writer as well as an editor, could find a gentler metaphor: it had impact, but the author of *John Brown's Body* and "American Names" said it was like listening to backwoods gossip: well orchestrated, full of folk humor, and in superb style.[40]

Another writer who championed the Mississippian during

39. Wallace Stegner, "Conductivity in Fiction," *VQR* (Summer, 1939), 446–47.
40. Stanford, *Southern Review*, VI (Winter, 1941), 610–28; Stephen Vincent Benet, "Flem Snopes and His Kin," *Saturday Review*, April 6, 1940, 7.

this decade was Warren Beck, who will now be less remembered for the fiction he has written than for his criticism of Faulkner, recently collected into a volume. In "Faulkner's Point of View," Beck took the critics to task for their naiveté, error, and general inadequacy, including their failure to perceive Faulkner's moral vision. He summarized Faulkner's treatment of southern materials in "Faulkner and the South," pointing out that there is no uncritical nostalgia in Faulkner's work, but, instead, humanity, genius, and a full grasp of the life around him. Beck then demonstrated the diversity, adaptability, richness, and accuracy of "William Faulkner's Style," and, in "A Note on Faulkner's Style," he added the observation that critics who extracted a Faulkner sentence from context and attacked it for obscurity were unfair. The matter was simple to novelist Beck: Faulkner's style depended upon variety, tensions between parts of long passages, the inspired synthesis of diverse elements. Faulkner was simply the most brilliant writer in America; critics could not read.[41] It is worth noting that when Beck sent copies of some of his articles to Faulkner, the reticent private man responded with a fine, uncharacteristic letter of appreciation.[42]

Carson McCullers and Delmore Schwartz both also wrote on Faulkner in 1941, though Schwartz was not to do as well for Faulkner then as he would reviewing *A Fable* in 1955, when he wrote one of the few really perceptive, sympathetic accounts of that book.[43] Robert Penn Warren reviewed *The Hamlet* in *Kenyon Review*, curiously countering in the pages of another journal

41. Warren Beck, "Faulkner's Point of View", *College English*, II (May, 1941), 736–49; Warren Beck, "Faulkner and the South," *Antioch Review*, I (March, 1941), 82–94; Warren Beck, "William Faulkner's Style," *American Prefaces*, VI (Spring 1941), 195–211; Warren Beck, "A Note on Faulkner's Style," *Rocky Mountain Review*, VI (Spring-Summer 1942), 5–6, 14.
42. Warren Beck quotes the letter in "Faulkner: A Preface and a Letter," *Yale Review*, LII (Autumn, 1962), 157–60.
43. Carson McCullers, "The Russian Realists and Southern Literature," Decision, II (July, 1941), 15–19; Delmore Schwartz, "The Fiction of William Faulkner," *Southern Review*, VII (Summer, 1941); 145–60, Delmore Schwartz, review of *A Fable* in *Perspectives USA*, X (Winter, 1955), 126–36.

the devastating attack by Stanford in Warren's own *Southern Review* and tooling up, in effect, for his substantial treatment of Faulkner in the 1946 reply to Malcolm Cowley's Viking *Portable* introduction.[44]

The postwar era saw Faulkner's own self-willed reemergence. By 1948 he was publishing on his own again and, until his death in 1962, he performed another prodigy like the one with which his career began, neatly balanced as to numbers: from 1926 to 1942, he published almost a book a year, and between *Intruder in the Dust* and *The Reivers* he did not do much worse. During this period his impact becomes, as well, influence. As Reynolds Price has expressed it, "Faulkner is a special and enormous case. All Southern writers who have written in the last twenty years have had to bear the burden of being called Faulknerian. . . . Reviewers who lament the 'influence' of Faulkner are really only asking that all other Southern writers arrange to be born outside the South."[45] Like Joyce, Faulkner has changed the face of the modern novel, and everyone writing novels, practically, including non-southern Americans and Europeans as well, has had to face his work and decide, positively or negatively, their posture toward it. Impact can, in fact, become both influence and disdain, or at least deliberate avoidance. Some writers simply have had to run from Faulkner, to get off the tracks, in order to develop voices and materials of their own.

I don't have a mule and wagon—to get back to Flannery O'Connor again—and maybe what I represent, as the author of a couple of dozen short stories, is more like a goat cart or a penny slipped on the rail, but I am still an example too, a conscious one, for while I spent as much time absorbing the material of fiction in northern Mississippi as I did anywhere, I set

44. Robert Penn Warren, "The Snopes World," *Kenyon Review*, III (Spring 1941), 253–57; Robert Penn Warren, New Republic, August 12, 1946, 176–18, and New Republic, August 26, 1946, 234–37.
45. Reynolds Price, *Kite-Flying and Other Irrational Acts*, ed. John Carr (Baton Rouge: Louisiana State University Press, 1972) 75.

everything I do in my other simultaneous home, Arkansas. Shelby Foote once said, a bit disconsolately, I think, and expressing his own experience more than any certain truth, "I think the Southern novel has run its string. . . . Maybe Faulkner used it up." Then he pointed out how impact can be a little pernicious:

We in the Delta have been strongly influenced by Faulkner [despite the fact that he is a "hill country" writer] and so we were raised where we were and also reading Faulkner, which is a tremendously persuasive thing to encounter. It had an influence on us similar to the influence of the Delta itself. . . . So that writers since Faulkner have tended to make Delta people sort of like hill people, under the Faulkner influence, but they are very different people.[46]

Joyce Carol Oates has revealed that in her earliest attempts at fiction there had been "a bloated trifurcated novel that had as its vague model *The Sound and the Fury*,"[47] a demonstration of impact, too, I believe—that poor maimed novel obviously was on the tracks when it shouldn't have been. Under the same influence, William Styron was able to bring off *Lie Down in Darkness*, proving, at least, that being knocked into the middle of next week by the Dixie Limited can also have its advantages. Eudora Welty expressed her pleasure and awe this way: having Faulkner living in and writing about Mississippi as she made her own career was "like living near a mountain, something majestic—it made me happy to know it was there, all that work of his life. But it wasn't a helping or hindering presence. Its magnitude, all by itself, made it something remote in my own working life. When I thought of Faulkner it was when I *read*."[48]

Even Hemingway couldn't escape Faulkner's impact—in more ways than one[49]—and he was forever shadowboxing the

46. Shelby Foote, *Kite-Flying*.
47. "The Art of Fiction, LXXII," *Paris Review*, 74 (1978), 218.
48. Eudora Welty, *Paris Review*, 55 (1972–73), 82.
49. See McHaney, *Faulkner's The Wild Palms*, chap. 1.

champion he never met, as in *Death in the Afternoon*, when the author has the following dialogue with the inquisitive old lady who interrupts the bullfight narrative:

Madame . . . as age comes on I feel I must devote myself more and more to the practice of letters. My operatives tell me[this was not long after *Sanctuary*] that through the fine work of Mr. William Faulkner publishers now will publish anything rather than to try to get you to delete the better portions of your works, and I look forward to writing of those days of my youth which were spent in the finest whorehouses in the land amid the most brilliant society there found. . . .

Old lady: Has this Mr. Faulkner written well of these places?

Splendidly, Madame. Mr. Faulkner writes admirably of them. He writes the best of them of any writer I have read for many years.

Old lady: I must buy his works.

Madame, you can't go wrong on Faulkner. He's prolific too. By the time you get them ordered there'll be new ones out.

Old lady: If they are as you say there cannot be too many.

Madame, you voice my own opinion.[50]

How far Hemingway had his tongue in his cheek here we can't know: he was, however, clearly intimidated by the creator of "Anomatopoeio County," as he once called it, and more than once, in his cups, admitted to other writers that Faulkner was a better writer—"I would have been happy just to have managed him."[51]

I hasten to emphasize that not every twentieth-century novelist after Faulkner has admired him, though in an odd way, since Faulkner's presence could not be ignored, there is an element of *impact* in the negative attitude, too, a kind of deliberate looking away. Both sides are represented in a recent discussion between John Hawkes and John Barth published in the April, 1979, *New York Times Book Review*. Hawkes asks, "Something

50. Ernest Hemingway, *Death in the Afternoon* (New York: Scribner's, 1932), 173.
51. Carlos Baker, *Ernest Hemingway: A Life Story* (New York: Scribner's, 1969), 656.

I've never been able to understand is why you have such strong feelings for Borges, Beckett and Nabokov, but not for Faulkner. Do you really think that Faulkner's comic visions are so terribly different from those of the other three writers? I love Faulkner and I'm disappointed that you seem not to." Barth replies that all his "literary fathers" are foreigners, though he "read Faulkner with proper astonishment and instruction" when a graduate student. He goes on to say that "there's a wonderful thing about Faulkner—the way European and South American writers learn from him. The most incantatory mumbo-jumbo in Faulkner— 'the outraged wagonwheels going down the immemorial something or other'—taken far enough south, below the Rio Grande, comes to interest me. I watch Gabriel Garcia Marquez learning from Faulkner, and all the things that bother me in Faulkner I admire when I see them in Marquez."[52]

As you may know, in many Latin American towns they are still operating the electric trollies taken—perhaps prematurely, it now seems—from American streets. Repainted, run with Latin style, they catch an American tourist once in a while, and not merely with nostalgia—that unexpected bump has more than a little relationship to our own Dixie Limited, as we can see from John Barth's remarks. Faulkner's impact upon the French and Latin American writers has been as strong as anywhere; the repercussions, the shock waves, the reflected forces often come back to carry Faulkner's impact, half-disguised, into his own country again. There has been a near complete synthesis of Faulkner's impact and influence in France, and the postwar era in Europe has seen both Italian and German response to him, inhibited first by fascism and then by war, catching up. Faulkner's world is apparently sufficiently large and rich for many different writers to find something of themselves and for

52. Thomas LeClair, "Hawkes and Barth Talk About Fiction," *New York Times Book Review*, April 1, 1979, p. 31.

themselves within it. Thus the young French writers of the so-called New Novel have been most taken by his techniques: manipulation of point of view and time and exploration of style. Michel Butor and Claude Simon both sometimes sound like Faulkner, while a writer as different in sound as Robbe-Grillet still accounts the Mississippian an influence too. According to Robbe-Grillet, "The New Novel will in any case have the merit of bringing to the awareness of a rather large (and continually growing) public a general evolution of the genre, whereas there has been a persistent attempt to deny it, relegating Kafka, Faulkner, and all the others to vague marginal zones, when they are, quite simply, the great novelists of the first half of the century."[53] Simon has said, "The Sound and the Fury . . . truly revealed to me what writing could be. . . . [Faulkner] rediscovers all the literary culture of the West. Faulkner is the Picasso of literature."[54]

Latin American writers, who, as noted, received large amounts of their literary educations through France, also inhabit a world much like Faulkner's, with changing agrarian societies, plantation aristocracy, racial problems and generational conflicts, latent violence and civil war. The Colombian Gabriel Garcia Marquez, author of the remarkable *One Hundred Years of Solitude*, plays down literary influence when he speaks of Faulkner, talking essentially of impact: "What I owe to Faulkner is . . . that his whole world . . . was very like my world, that it was created by the same people. . . . What I found in him was affinities between our experience"; and, reportedly, "When I first read Faulkner, I thought, 'I must become a writer.'"[55] The Cu-

---

53. *For a New Novel*, trans. Richard Howard (New York: Grove Press, 1965), 136.
54. Simon is quoted from a review in *Nouvelles litteraires* by V. Mercier, *The New Novel from Queneau to Pinget* (New York: Farrar Straus & Giroux, 1971), 27.
55. *Seven Voices: Seven Latin American Writers Talk to Rita Guibert*, trans. Frances Patridge (New York: Knopf, 1973), 327; *Into the Mainstream: Conversations with Latin-American Writers*, by Luis Harss and Barbara Dohmann (New York: Harper & Row,

ban Vargas Llosa has said, "I have Faulkner in my blood."[56] Miguel Angel Asturias, Carlos Fuentes, Ernesto Sabato, Jose Revueltas—most of them, I shamefully hasten to admit, only names to me as far as their fiction is concerned—and many others in Latin America have written or spoken of Faulkner's impact. As the authors of *Into the Mainstream: Conversations with Latin-American Writers* point out, Faulkner is the "single greatest influence" in Latin American literature of the last twenty years.[57] Jorge Luis Borges, who translated Faulkner's *The Wild Palms*, admits beginning the work simply because he was paid for it, but he admits that he became involved as his work progressed, and in his short introductory history of American literature, he moves to Faulkner after considering Dreiser, Sinclair Lewis, Sherwood Anderson, and John Dos Passos by saying, "we have spoken of writers of unquestionable talent; now we reach a man of genius. . . . Faulkner's hallucinatory tendencies are not unworthy of Shakespeare."[58]

In 1959, the *New York Times Book Review* published a series of short essays on "The Worldwide Influence of William Faulkner,"[59] and in the two decades since then a growing body of criticism, commentary, literary history, bibliography, and recorded conversation has testified to the growth of this influence, the spread of interest in Faulkner. However, nothing gives Faulkner back to us as plainly but sharply as the evidence of his literary impact upon other writers. His fiction has had physical force—called a jolt of electricity, a movement in the blood, an intellec-

1967), 322. See also Florence Delay and Jacqueline de Labriolle, "Marquez est-il le Faulkner colombien?" *RLC*, XLVII (1973), 88–123.

56. Quoted in Robert G. Collmer, "When 'Word' Meets *Palabra*: Crossing the Border with Literature," *William Faulkner*, in Zyla and Aycock (eds.), 161.

57. *Into the Mainstream*, 24.

58. Ronald Crist (ed.), "Borges at NYU," in *Prose for Borges*, ed. Charles Newman and Mary Kinzie (Evanston, Ill: Northwestern University Press, 1974), 406; Jorge Luis Borges, in collaboration with Esther Zemborain de Torres, *An Introduction to American Literature*, trans. and ed. L. Clark Keating and Robert O. Evans (Lexington: University of Kentucky Press, 1971), 48–49.

59. *New York Times Book Review*, November 15, 1959, pp. 52–53.

tual shock—and it has constituted revelation, giving young writers elsewhere the sudden knowledge that they must write, that what they see and feel is legitimate material for fiction. As criticism, the *cri de coeur* and the statements of praise that accompany the shock of recognition are not always useful: they do not explain anything, they simply say that something is there. Perhaps, however, that is enough. It is a certification of authenticity when one honest man of letters responds unselfconsciously to another. Such response is a reminder of what is important in art, and a reminder, too, of the essential difficulty, loneliness, mystery, and passion of creation. If we learn nothing else from Faulkner, we have learned a great deal when we have glimpsed that.

The Sources
of Faulkner's Genius

JOSEPH BLOTNER

Not long ago I received a two-page, single-spaced letter about my biography of William Faulkner from a lady born and raised in Mississippi. Her letter made good reading, full of generous comments that pleased me very much. But in her next-to-last paragraph she wrote, "I will never understand how anyone could survive his combination of hard drinking and hard riding." I could share her wonder on that score, but then she went on to say, "However, what puzzles me most is that I see no real explanation of his peculiar genius." Though again I felt that I understand her perplexity, I couldn't help feeling some disappointment that the book she had liked so much had not given her more insight into its essential subject. But I was not unfamiliar with such puzzlement.

Malcolm Cowley had written a good review of the biography, and he did another of my edition of Faulkner's letters. In the course of the latter he mentioned particularly Faulkner's work between 1926 and 1941, and he wrote, "There is nothing in his life or letters, nothing in heredity or environment, to explain the extraordinary fecundity of those earlier fifteen years. The reader, like Faulkner himself, can only accept the fruit of them with puzzled gratitude."

The puzzlement that Cowley referred to was also there in the mind of the artist himself. Looking back, in his middle fifties, he wrote Joan Williams, "And now, at last, I have some perspective on all I have done. I mean, the work apart from me, the work which I did, apart from what I am. . . . And now I realise for the first time what an amazing gift I had: uneducated in every formal sense, without even very literate, yet alone literary, companions, yet to have made the things I made. I dont know where it came from. I dont know why God or gods or whoever it was, selected me to be the vessel. Believe me, this is not humility, false modesty: it is simply amazement. I wonder if you have ever had that thought about the work and the country man whom you know as Bill Faulkner—what little connection there seems to be between them."[1]

I have spent a good part of my professional life thinking about his genius in one way or another. And I am not sure that it *is* possible finally to say, It came from this talent and from that grief, from this part of his mind and that part of his heart. This is, of course, a problem shared by other biographers. I think particularly of the comments of two of my former colleagues, historians, at the University of Virginia. After finishing the first of his volumes on Thomas Jefferson, Dumas Malone wrote, "In my youthful presumptuousness I flattered myself that sometime I would fully comprehend and encompass him. I do not claim that I have yet done so, and I do not believe that I or any other single person can."[2] Twenty years later, after publishing his noteworthy political biography, Merrill Peterson wrote, "Of all his great contemporaries Jefferson is perhaps the least self-revealing and the hardest to sound to the depths of being. It is a mortifying confession, but he remains for me, finally, an impenetrable man."[3] With Faulkner, even with our awareness of these difficulties and uncertainties, we still find ourselves trying to formulate answers in scholarship and in criticism. And so, even

1. Joseph Blotner (ed.), *Selected Letters of William Faulkner* (New York: Random House, 1977), 348.
2. Dumas Malone, *Jefferson the Virginian* (Boston: Little, Brown Co., 1948), vii.
3. Merrill Peterson, *Thomas Jefferson and the New Nations* (New York: Oxford University Press, 1970), viii.

knowing that the effort may leave us still searching, I should like to try again to suggest a few answers to that question Faulkner posed when he meditated "where it came from." Though he was a reticent man, he left us a number of clues.

They involve his heredity, his immediate background of parents and environment, his physical makeup, his emotional patterns, his intelligence and education (formal and informal), and his attitude towards his art. No doubt, as we explore each of these qualities, we will be able to think of others who possessed some very like Faulkner's and yet were not great writers. And this comparison may provide a partial answer to our central question, perhaps simplistic, perhaps obvious, but yet true: that his genius resided in this rare and complex combination of all of them.

He once told his friend Phil Stone that he thought that though people generally speaking did the best they could, they were pretty much governed by heredity. For himself he claimed Scottish ancestry. His people, he said, were from the Highlands. He did not overvalue family background and may have shared something of the view of Colonel John Sartoris (the character modeled on his own great-grandfather) about family pride: "In the nineteenth century chortling over genealogy anywhere is poppycock. But particularly so in America, where only what a man takes and keeps has any significance, and where all of us have a common ancestry and the only house from which we can claim descent with any assurance, is the Old Bailey. Yet the man who professes to care nothing about his forefathers is only a little less vain than he who bases all his actions on blood precedent."[4] But Faulkner was proud of his Scots lineage, of the tartan and claymore he said the family owned, and of the great-grandfather who spoke Gaelic. Thinking of the way Faulkner later mastered the use of dialect, the way he wrote sagas of families, one can

4. William Faulkner, *Flags in the Dust*, ed. Douglas Day (New York: Random House, 1973), 82.

speculate that something of a cultural if not a racial inheritance descended to him from artists such as Robert Burns and Sir Walter Scott. One thing he certainly did have was a coherent sense of his past, a sense of family and of clan loyalty and responsibility. Though there appears to be no evidence that he ever traced the Falkners and Murrys and the other collateral family lines back to Scotland, he could trace those who had come to America just before the midpoint of the eighteenth century. The ones whose lives were most important to him were in the generations of his great-grandparents and their descendants.

Colonel William C. Falkner was many things in his lifetime, from penniless waif to affluent railroad builder, but one of the careers he pursued most consistently was that of writer. A largely self-educated genius, he published an amazing variety of work from his late adolescence virtually to the end of his life: from the memoir of an ax-murderer (he wrote as an amanuensis only) to narrative verse. He wrote novels and a play and also travel sketches which were not much different in kind from those of other writers such as Mark Twain. One sees, of course, that the difference between these two is like the difference Twain perceived between the almost right word and the right word: the difference between the lightning bug and the lightning. But even so, the writing was a remarkable and very profitable achievement for a man who had a half-dozen other major occupations in his life. And it was enough to make his great-grandson say, in reply to his teacher's questioning, "I want to be a writer like my great-grandaddy."

The Colonel's adoptive father, John Wesley Thompson, like himself, was given to both violence and poetry, leaving behind him verses which declared eternal love in spite of looming disaster, verses with something of a Miltonic flourish about them. The poetic strain apparently bypassed the Colonel's son and, one thought until recently, his grandson, the father of William Faulkner. Murry Falkner was a railroad man, a merchant, a college administrator, and a frustrated cowboy. But not long ago I was permitted to read through a scrapbook Murry Falkner kept, in which I found a short humorous essay in typescript and a series of diary entries that revealed something of a poetic sensibility if not poetic practice. Murry Falkner's wife and mother-in-law possessed a talent for painting and sculpting. Of his four sons, three displayed talent at painting and drawing, and three of the four also became published authors. Though William Faulkner's work is of a different order from that of the other Falkners and the Butlers, it does seem clear that there is a distinct pattern of inheritance here.

The physical inheritance was a different matter. The eldest turned out, in maturity, to be the shortest. But if he was the runt, 5'6" at full growth, he was agile and well coordinated, a shortstop and a quarterback, a good tennis player, and a good shot. And even if in maturity, when horseback riding was his favorite form of exercise, he had such a bad seat that one injury followed hard upon another, he was still a rugged man. Even in his sixties, when he had developed Anse Bundren's complaint, the male equivalent of "dowager's hump," he was still deep-chested and strongly built, a man whose dignity of movement derived from good bones and muscles, a sturdy frame. But as my Mississippi correspondent observed, he punished it severely, from early manhood onwards, not just with the exhausting demands of the profession to which, like Thomas Mann's Gustave von Aschenbach, he consecrated his best hours, but also with the sprains and strains, the bruises and fractures, and the lost weekends and weeks and months that, incidentally, gave him the material for one of his most painful stories, the posthumously published "Mr. Acarius." But the body saw him through in spite of all, saw him through until the sixty-fifth year of his age. It sustained him in a way that suggests the maxim of that other strong and self-abusive genius, Ernest Hemingway: *il faut (d'abord) durer* (it is necessary first of all to last).

252

It seems to me that there is one quality that is sometimes ignored or slighted in assessments of writers. We assume as a given that they possess imagination, a special capacity for empathy, and a facility with language. But even with those writers—if they are great writers—who are not systematic thinkers or who seem not much interested in ideas, there is another factor present: a powerful intelligence undergirding all the other attributes, an intelligence that covers much of the spectrum of human activity. One quick example comes to mind—Robert Frost writing to his daughter in November, 1945: "With things like the atomic bomb I pride myself on putting them in their relative place a priori without ever having been in a physics laboratory. I said right off uranium was only a new kind of fuel. Wood will rot down to ashes in a few years."[5] He went on with a long paragraph of speculation that might have been a gloss on a poem he had written thirty years earlier, "The Wood-Pile," with its stacked cord of maple abandoned in the woods to what he had called "the slow smokeless burning, of decay." Faulkner had this kind of intelligence. No Stanford-Binet test was administered to him and his classmates, but his almost straight-A record tells us something. He lost interest and quit before he was out of high school, but his education continued, fueled by curiosity and that keen intelligence. He was aware of what he had. Years later, with characteristic assurance—it would have been arrogance or bravado to some—he put it to the mother of one of his New Orleans friends. "Mrs. K.," he said, "I'm a genius." Before pursuing the form which that education took after he left the Oxford High School, there is another gift, and a related gift, that we must mention: the faculty of memory.

His memory was extraordinary, not just for the schoolroom tasks of childhood, but for most of what he saw and read. His nephew Jimmy thinks he had something close to total recall. If

5. Lawrance Thompson and R. H. Winnick, *Robert Frost: The Later Years, 1938–1963* (New York: Holt, Rinehart and Winston, 1976), 132–33.

he made small errors in reciting some things he prized, such as John Philpot Curran's words on liberty, he would amaze listeners with fluent renderings of Shakespeare: all, for instance, of "The Phoenix and the Turtle." He had favorite poems of Housman and Yeats and Joyce by heart. When he was working at Warner Brothers in 1942, the writers at lunch would sometimes play a game of quotations, and the only one who could match the prodigious memory of Tom Job, playwright and sometime drama teacher at Yale, was William Faulkner. When asked if he had a phenomenal memory, he said that the artist was like a packrat, a magpie, that he had something of kleptomania, that, in his words, "he misses very little." To one he said, "As far as I know I have never done one page of research. Also, I doubt if I've ever forgotten anything I ever read too."[6] He remembered what he read in books and what he heard on boardinghouse porches and upland farms, and so it was all there, in his "lumberroom," as he called it, when he needed it. Comparing the rapture of writing *The Sound and the Fury* with the labor of writing *Light in August*, he said, "now I was deliberately choosing among possibilities and probabilities of behavior and weighing and measuring each choice by the scale of the Jameses and Conrads and Balzacs. I knew that I had read too much, that I had reached that stage which all young writers must pass through, in which he believes that he has learned too much about his trade."[7] Of course he worked all his life at learning his trade, and memory was one of his chief aids. By the time he reached his late fifties, details of stories he had written fifteen years earlier would elude him (the poker-playing strategy in "Was," for instance), but his recall of favorite classics and of events in the lives of his own creations would remain sharp to the end.

6. Frederick L. Gwynn and Joseph Blotner (eds.), *Faulkner in the University* (Charlottesville: University of Virginia Press, 1959), 203, 251.
7. Joseph Blotner, *Faulkner: A Biography* (New York: Random House, 1974), 703.

To return briefly to his education, what was it like? Scholars have studied the reading that constituted its major part—and some months ago I read for a publisher an entire monograph devoted to the subject. His reading began in his childhood, fostered in his lawyer-grandfather's capacious library and encouraged by his mother's love for the classics: for Shakespeare, for Conrad, and for others he would read all his life. In essays for the University of Mississippi newspaper he would describe his early love for Swinburne and Housman, for Shakespeare and Keats. The range of his reading in classic writers was extraordinarily wide. And after his friendship blossomed with the erudite young Phil Stone, when Stone would bring home from Yale with him books he would give to Faulkner, the course in literature broadened to include the avant-garde: Pound and Joyce and Yeats and Cummings. It would go on, from the Greek tragedians to the *commedia dell' arte*. Even in his sixties his memory would range from the miracle and morality plays to the poet Djuna Barnes. His advice to young writers was, "Read, read, read. Read everything—trash, classics, good and bad, and see how they do it. . . . Then write. If it's good, you'll find out. If it's not, throw it out the window." As for himself, he said "I read everything I could get my hands on."[8] The evidence bears him out. Before we talk about the way he did his writing and why he did it, there are other qualities we should mention.

He was both a dreamer and an observer, one for whom the world of imagination could be more vivid than that around him, yet one on whom little of the outer world was lost. In adolescence he had changed, it seemed, from a doer to a dreamer. But often when he seemed to be dreaming, or at least quietly aloof, he was observing closely with those keen brown eyes, so dark they could seem almost black. The writer's insight came from reading, he said, but there was something else the writer had to

8. James B. Meriwether and Michael Millgate (eds.), *Lion in the Garden: Interviews with William Faulkner, 1926–1962* (New York: Random House, 1968), 55–56.

do: as he put it, "to watch people . . . to never judge people. To watch people, what they do, without intolerance. Simply to learn why it is they did what they did."[9] Actually, he himself went further than that. Although inevitably he did make judgments, he had an extraordinary sensitivity, a capacity for sympathy, particularly for the weak and the handicapped, for the very young and the very old. One man who treated Faulkner during a period of suffering saw in him an intense emotional responsiveness exceeding that of ordinary people, such a capacity for receptiveness to others that their problems hurt him. That was one reason, his nephew would say, why he normally would not let others get close to him, because he knew that in this way his own vulnerability was increased, that their hurt would become his.

There were times, of course, when this sympathetic observer, sitting motionless or walking with eyes straight ahead, *was* dreaming, times when he had withdrawn into the inner world of imagination so vividly populated by the hundreds of characters who were intensely real to him. Their existence did not end with the story or the book. "They are still in motion in my mind," he said. "I can laugh at things they're doing that I haven't got around to writing yet . . . the characters themselves are walking out of that book still in motion, still talking, and still acting."[10] To Malcolm Cowley this was the central quality of Faulkner's work. "Faulkner's imagination," he wrote, "was a treasure house stored with many sorts of images, persons, events, not to mention patterns, motives, dreams, and compulsions."[11]

So he had this world to draw upon—these worlds to draw upon: literature and life. Phil Stone shared them, trying cases at

9. Gwynn and Blotner (eds.), *Faulkner in the University*, 192.
10. *Ibid.*, 197–98.
11. Malcolm Cowley, *—And I Worked at the Writer's Trade* (New York: The Viking Press, 1977), 224.

the courthouse and telling his friends, "You can never practice law in Lafayette County until after you've read *Pere Goriot*." Faulkner could read the books, often Stone's books, and he could go out into the country, sometimes on his own, sometimes strolling with Stone, and sometimes electioneering. "I don't go out with a notebook," he said, "but I like these people. That is, I like to listen to them, the way they talk or the things they talk about. I spent a lot of time with my uncle, he was a politician, and he would have to run every four years to be elected judge again. And I would go around with him and sit on the front galleries of country stores and listen to the talk that would go on, with no notebook, no intention to put it down, I just—it was interesting and I remembered most of it, and I have known them in farming and in dealing with horses and hunting, things like that, but without carrying a notebook at all, just to remember."[12] It was from just such a situation, he confided to his brother John, that he got the material for the most hilarious part of his story "Spotted Horses." And so he could mine the riches of this region, not just its history but its tradition of oral narrative, and this would become one of the hallmarks of his art: a distinct voice telling what happened, often to be succeeded by another unique voice, weaving together to form a pattern and to give a sense of experience as rich as life itself. And he would see that Mississippi could be for him more than just his homeland. As he said Sherwood Anderson told him, "It's America too; pull it out, as little and unknown as it is, and the whole thing will collapse."[13] And his apocryphal county, as he came to call Yoknapatawpha, would become, in his words, "a kind of keystone in the universe."[14]

We know how he prepared himself to create that world: read-

12. Gwynn and Blotner (eds), *Faulkner in the University*, 233.

13. James B. Meriwether (ed.), *William Faulkner: Essays, Speeches and Public Letters*, (New York: Random House, 1965), 8.

14. Meriwether and Millgate (eds.), *Lion in the Garden*, 255.

ing and observing, and then writing—moving from poems to stories to novels. We think of the dedication of John Milton, leaving Cambridge to spend the better part of a decade in the quiet of his parents' home; of Nathaniel Hawthorne, leaving Bowdoin and returning to Salem to pursue the nurturing of his art in much the same manner. William Faulkner once wrote of "my father's unfailing kindness, which supplied me with bread at need despite the outrage to his principles at having been of a bum progenitive."[15] Like Milton and Hawthorne, Faulkner was patiently learning his trade, and spending a quiet and rustic apprenticeship longer than either of theirs.

So he worked through that apprenticeship, drawing, he would say, upon the triad of imagination, observation, and experience. But there is another area we must explore, another layer, deeper and more complex, more difficult to know, than any of those we have already mentioned. *Why* did he write? One thinks of Milton listening to "sweetest Shakespeare, Fancy's child,/Warble his native wood-notes wild." One could say Faulkner wrote as the bird sings, because he had to, because it was his most natural response, his total response to life. But we know how he worked at his painting and drawing as a young man with something of the same devotion he gave to his writing. He would say that the writer was "demon driven." He told one man, "If a story is in you, it has got to come out. If you have something to say—you can write it—in fact, you have got to write it."[16] When Joan Williams was concerned about her work he told her, "You will write, some day. Maybe now you haven't anything to say. You have to have something burning your very entrails to be said . . . writing is important only when you want to do it, and nothing nothing nothing but writing will suffice, give you peace."[17] But for all of this, he was selective, negotiating, as it

15. William Faulkner, *Sanctuary* (New York: Modern Library, 1932), v.
16. Meriwether and Millgate (eds.), *Lion in the Garden*, 10.
17. Blotner (ed.), *Selected Letters of William Faulkner*, 312.

were, with his demon, whose nature we can attempt to determine later. He wanted to paint and write poetry and he realized that neither would be first-rate. In poetry, he said, you tried to distill the essence of the human condition into fourteen lines. If you couldn't, you took the next most demanding form and tried to do it in three thousand words in a short story. And if you couldn't do that, you took one hundred thousand and wrote a novel. So he wrote because he had to, yet he could choose his form.

What were the elements, in his case, beyond the fact of being doomed, as he sometimes said, to the writer's trade? What of his volition and motivation? He once wrote, "I read and employed verse, firstly, for the purpose of furthering various philanderings in which I engaged."[18] Though the word he chose smacked of youthful cynicism, it points toward a real and valid motive. Increasingly shy and withdrawn as he moved into adolescence, he was keenly conscious of his shortness, as he was of his brother Jack's height. And as for his looks, he felt that he was unattractive if not downright ugly. He may have felt some social insecurity as well. An early unpublished and unfinished piece called "And Now What's to Do?" was clearly imitative of Sherwood Anderson but showed autobiographical elements too. It described a boy whose father ran a livery stable, as Murry Falkner did, a boy whose classmates were the children of "lawyers and doctors and merchants—all genteel professions with starched collars." The boy, wrote Faulkner, "was sixteen and he began to acquire a sort of inferiority complex regarding his father's business."[19] So his gifts would have to compensate. He wrote to gain love and acceptance. Recent studies have employed modern psychoanalytic concepts in analyzing his characters, and be-

18. Carvel Collins (ed.), *William Faulkner: Early Prose and Poetry* (Boston: Little, Brown and Company, 1962), 115.
19. William Faulkner, "And Now What's To Do?," in *A Faulkner Miscellany*, ed. James B. Meriwether (Jackson: University Press of Mississippi, 1974), 146.

tween their lines I thought that I read an attempt to apply some of the same techniques to the author, in search of the processes which led to the creation of the characters. Well, what do we know in this area?

He never got along well with the father who thought he had been of "a bum progenitive." Faulkner seems to have felt very little love for his father but rather anger and hostility. His mother he loved very much, as did his brothers. Phil Stone thought that all the Faulkner boys were too close to their mother, and it seems clear that the women they married did not have an easy time with their mother-in-law. (Shortly after Dean, the youngest, married, he told his bride, "Mother and Bill will always come first.")[20] Jack, the second brother, recalled Billy and his mother in one clear vignette out of childhood: "He looked up at her with steady, open affection as I have seen him do a thousand times."[21] She loved him and was proud of him, and she was always at pains to say she was proud of all her boys. When a psychiatrist unwarily asked Faulkner directly if he had received enough love from his mother, the response was stony silence. This should not be overvalued: it was exactly the response *anyone* would have received on thus violating the privacy of this most private of men. But most of the women he loved resembled his mother in some way: in stature, in features, or in temperament. (I wrote this paper six months ago. I was interested to hear for the first time, this past Sunday night, Jill Faulkner Summers say, in the NEH documentary film *William Faulkner: A Life on Paper*, "I think that probably Pappy's idea of women, ladies, always revolved a great deal around Granny. She was just a very determined tiny old lady that Pappy adored. Pappy admired so much in Granny and he didn't find it in my mother and

20. Dean Faulkner Wells, "Dean Swift Faulkner: A Biographical Study" (M.A. thesis, University of Mississippi, 1976), 165.

21. Murry Falkner, *The Falkners of Mississippi*, (Baton Rouge: Louisiana State University Press, 1967), 58.

I don't think he ever found it in anybody. I think that maybe all these, including my mother, were just second place.")

For several of these loves, these other women, Faulkner made gifts of his work, verses and stories beautifully lettered, illustrated and bound, with titles such as *Mayday* and *Vision in Spring*. One hand-lettered poem, which may well have been written about the time his first love was preparing to marry another, sounds like more than just a poetic exercise. It was vain to implore him, he wrote, to forget her face and her smile:

> It is vain to implore me
> I have given my treasures of art
> Even though she choose to ignore me
> And my heart.[22]

Frustrated love, both early and late, evoked gifts and laments, in poetry and in prose.

Sometimes he wrote to assuage the grief that love brought. He once told Maurice Coindreau that he wrote *The Sound and the Fury* when he was troubled by difficulties of an intimate nature, and he told another friend that he wrote *The Wild Palms* to stave off what he thought was heartbreak. With only rumor and conjecture to go on, we may never know what the difficulties were, as he began to write about Caddy and Quentin Compson in the late winter or early spring of 1928, the year before his marriage, at long last, to the sweetheart who had married another nearly a dozen years before. A recent confessional memoir does tell us, however, something about his anguish ten years later, in the fall of 1938, as he began to write about Harry Wilbourne and Charlotte Rittenmeyer.[23] What we do know is that anguish, deprivation, and desire could be productive. Hemingway, among others, observed that the energy that fueled the sex

22. Blotner, *Faulkner*, 195.
23. Meta Carpenter Wilde and Orin Borsten, *A Loving Gentleman: The Love Story of William Faulkner and Meta Carpenter* (New York: Simon and Schuster, 1976).

drive also fueled the writing. Faulkner once commented to his friend Ben Wasson, "When I have a case of the hots, I can write like a streak." There seems a kind of assertiveness, perhaps even pride here, perhaps something of amusement very different from the emotions that must have accompanied the sublimation, during the unhappy love affairs and the unhappy years of his marriage, when the force of his libido was directed toward paper, pen, and ink rather than a living woman.

Apparently he wrote out of a more generalized grief as well. A young romantic and a dreamer who created fauns and nymphs in delicate verse, he came to see a shocking contrast in the outer world. "Billy looks around him," his mother once said, "and he is heart-broken at what he sees." But these emotions, which could produce word shapes like the chaste glass shapes of his creation Horace Benbow, could be expressed in another way, in a book as violent as *Sanctuary*. We remember Swift's epitaph, how he lies where "Savage indignation there / Cannot lacerate his breast." As Swift's Yahoos owed something of their creation to that savage indignation, so did Faulkner's Snopeses to his. He could create for himself—and for others to see—a world which rendered vividly man's bestiality, and thus imply its obverse, the kind of world of which he sometimes dreamed. Once he put it explicitly. He used degradation and violence, he said, "as tools with which I was trying to show what man must combat, and specific instances in which he has been strangled by degradation and violence, when he has hated the violence he participated in."[24]

He said that sometimes he wrote something for himself and then sent it off to his publisher almost without realizing that someone else would read it. Even granting that this is metaphor, or perhaps hyperbole, it does reflect that private part of himself, that aspect of his motivation or his gift which prompted him to

24. Meriwether and Millgate (eds.), *Lion in the Garden*, 206–7.

write to please himself. It might be a private image of beauty, like Caddy Compson, or it might take a more generalized form: "To take man's dilemma," he said, "the old familiar things in which there's nothing new and can't be anything new, and by the light of my own experience and imagination and a great deal of hard work, to make something which was a little different which wasn't here yesterday."[25] This reflects the shy, the private, the withdrawn man. He once told a French graduate student, "I find it impossible to communicate with the outside world."[26] It seems to me that one must allow here for some sort of distortion in transmission, although anyone who sat with Faulkner in one of his characteristic silent moods might well have agreed that he had put it exactly right.

There was another element stronger than grief. As a boy Faulkner was something of an exhibitionist, wearing his grandfather's clothes on the square, sporting dress suits and English-cut clothes with a handkerchief tucked in his sleeve. He sought attention in dress and he sought it in his writing, though he once told Phil Stone in discouragement that he thought he would gain neither money nor recognition from his work. He wrote out of pride in his gifts. He recorded Sherwood Anderson's admonition: "You've got too much talent. You can do it too easy, in too many different ways. If you're not careful, you'll never write anything."[27] A haughty fatal pride, he wrote, was the mark of the Sartorises, that fictional family modeled after his own. His own bearing was prideful, like that of his forebears. Phil Stone once said that the Faulkners could stand adversity, but that in success they would "ride you down with boots and spurs." This was true of the Old Colonel, it seems, and there was a streak in his great-grandson that could come very close to cruelty. A proud man, a master artist proud of his gifts, he said (as did Joyce and many

25. Gwynn and Blotner (eds.), *Faulkner in the University*, 258.
26. Meriwether and Millgate (eds.), *Lion in the Garden*, 71.
27. Meriwether (ed.), *Essays, Speeches and Public Letters*, 7.

others) that the artist was godlike. He said it smiling, but he said it: "I'm convinced I can improve on the Lord."[28] He was not only prideful; he was competitive, as much as Hemingway. Said Faulkner, "You want to be better than Shakespeare."

The sense of pride, the sense of self, comes up against the strongest shock in contemplating death. "Some day," Faulkner said, "we must all pass through the wall of oblivion." For him there was no sense of the Beatific Vision to be achieved, of being at one with the All, of the drop of rain reuniting with the sea—none of those consolations at the loss of individual identity. Faulkner spoke of leaving a scratch on the wall of oblivion to show that you were here for a while. Sounding something like that artist he admired so much, Joseph Conrad, Faulkner said, "The aim of every artist is to arrest motion, which is life, by artificial means and hold it fixed so that 100 years later when a stranger looks at it, it moves again since it is life. Since man is mortal, the only immortality possible for him is to leave something behind him that is immortal since it will always move."[29] Sounding something like Shelley in "Ozymandias," he said that a man "can build a bridge and will be remembered for a day or two, a monument, for a day or two, but somehow the picture, the poem—that lasts a long time, a very long time, longer than anything." The boy who wrote poems to further what he called youthful philanderings also wrote, said Faulkner, "to complete a gesture I was then making, of being 'different' in a small town."[30] Later he was still writing to be different, to achieve immortality.

The elements I have been discussing have related, most of them, to the self, to the demands, if you like, of the ego. There is another element which deserves to be mentioned in Faulk-

28. Gwynn and Blotner (eds.), *Faulkner in the University*, 123.
29. Meriwether and Millgate (eds.), *Lion in the Garden*, 253.
30. Collins (ed.), *Early Prose and Poetry*, 115.
31. Meriwether and Millgate (eds.), *Lion in the Garden*, 56.

ner's motivation, in his view of his craft and its status. Calling on
Shelley again, one can recall his famous "Poets are the unac-
knowledged legislators of the world." Faulkner always said he
thought of himself as a "failed poet," yet he has rightly been
called an epic poet in prose. (He said, "My prose is really poetry.")[31] And even if we conclude that some of the most elevated
and inspiring passages in his Nobel Prize acceptance speech
came primarily from a sense of what the occasion required,
there are in it echoes of views he apparently held all of his life.
He recalled that as a child he had read a book by the Polish
Nobel laureate, Henryk Sienkiewicz, and also Sienkiewicz's
foreword to that book about writing to uplift men's hearts.
Faulkner would realize later that this was a part of his own motivation, one component of it, at any rate. And the writer had
another responsibility: "The writer is the person that will record
man's endeavor, the course over the years, the centuries, by
which man has improved his lot to get rid of suffering, injustice.
The writer's responsibility is to tell the truth."[32] As he grew
older, became more the public man with a vast body of achievement behind him, this theme came up more often. Apparently
this responsibility seemed more vital to him, now as he turned
outward more than he had earlier done, as he saw more of the
world, as he felt an increasing sense of responsibility beyond the
boundaries of his apocryphal county. If the arts decayed, he told
a Japanese audience, man was finished. The French graduate
student recalled a more aphoristic statement: "Art is not only
man's most supreme expression; it is also the salvation of mankind."[33] This too, presumably, requires interpretation. If man
could survive atomic warfare and all it would destroy, he might
be expected to survive the loss of art as well. But he would have
ceased to be man in losing this essence of his humanity.

32. *Ibid.*, 201.
33. *Ibid.*, 71.
34. *Ibid.*, 239.

Having looked at some aspects of the Why of Faulkner's achievement, we should turn to a related question, the How of it, and the two are here closely related. He embraced what he called the writer's solitary task. He accepted the isolation it imposed with dedication and even with ruthlessness. He told Jean Stein, "The writer's only responsibility is to his art. He will be completely ruthless if he is a good one. He has a dream. It anguishes him so much he must get rid of it. He has no peace until then. Everything goes by the board: honor, pride, decency, security, happiness, all, to get the book written. If a writer has to rob his mother, he will not hesitate; the 'Ode on a Grecian Urn' is worth any number of old ladies."[34] Again, in the context of his own life, there is something of metaphor or hyperbole here. But his daughter remembered, "When we lived at Rowan Oak and Pappy was working, he didn't like to talk much at all. He was always thinking about his stories, getting the characters arranged in his head, storing up energy for his next bout with the typewriter. Pappy would become so involved in his writing that his nearest, his dearest weren't accepted."[35] His wife once told an interviewer, "There are times when Billy will go into his workroom and stay for hours. He hasn't any key, so he takes the doorknob off and carries it inside with him. No one can get in and he is quite secure."[36] And there were times when, miserably unhappy, he worked at home through long periods of depression. When he felt that he needed to do so, he left his home in the hope that he could write elsewhere, and his family felt that if it ever came to an absolute choice between his home and his art, he would not hesitate to make it. His drinking—part family pattern, part escape mechanism, part postscript to creative la-

---

35. Jill Faulkner Summers, as quoted in Paul Gardner, "Faulkner Remembered," *A Faulkner Perspective* (Franklin Center, Pa: Franklin Library, 1976), 14.
36. *Ibid.*, 26.
37. Gwynn and Blotner (eds.), *Faulkner in the University*, 194.

bor—was of course an integral part of that complex psyche which produced his art. Once the drinking produced a further insight into his view of himself and his art. His daughter saw a siege of it coming on; she asked him not to do it, for her sake. His answer was a chilling nonsequitur, but his meaning was perfectly clear. "Nobody remembers Shakespeare's children," he told her.

He called the writer demon-driven. Once he said, "the writer works in a kind of an insane fury."[37] He also remarked that he had no fixed rules for writing though he generally worked early in the day. "I write when the spirit moves me," he told one, "and it moves me every day."[38] From time to time here I have mentioned motivation and achievement. My oldest friend is the leading authority in this field. He put some of his work and thought in layman's terms for me. "Time spent is the key," he told me. "Great talent times time spent equals a very productive life." To my mind Faulkner's achievement provides a striking example of this formulation. Nearly three dozen books bear his name. The volume of his unpublished early work, much of it verse, is very large. He said that he destroyed two novels which did not suit him, and he left another unfinished for the same reason. He said that the craftsman's task was to try and to try and to try, to make the work match the dream, though it never did. Though he sometimes dashed work off, hard-pressed for money as he was for his first thirty years as a published writer, he also showed a capacity for almost endless patient revision. "Spotted Horses," for example, exists in nearly a dozen versions, both published and unpublished, and it is very likely that there were other attempts he destroyed. This, he thought, was the way the writer should work. Then, having done the best he could, he should not look back but rather go ahead to the

38. Meriwether and Millgate (eds.), *Lion in the Garden*, 24.
39. *Ibid.*, 234.

next one. The writer's obligation, he said, was "to get the work done the best he can do it; whatever obligation he has left over after that he can spend any way he likes."[39] If what my friend told me is the key—great talent times time spent—Faulkner would seem an embodiment of that axiom. Poor Hawthorne, and poor Melville in the Custom House, happier Twain on the steamboats—but each of them spending years at vocations other than writing. Faulkner was in the university post office for nearly three years, but he was kicked out of it partly because he spent more time writing poems than handling letters. During his brief months in the university power house, he apparently spent almost as much time writing fiction as watching gauges. His other jobs—selling books and painting houses—took possibly even less time out of his productive life. And even in Hollywood, years later, he was writing. Recalling Billy Faulkner's brief, abortive career in the First National Bank of Oxford, his Uncle John said, "he just *wouldn't* work." Summing it up better than he knew, he said, "he never was nothin' but a writer."[40]

In trying to explore these wellsprings of Faulkner's art, I have not dealt with the ways in which he contradicted himself. The demon, he said, was inherent. "You are born with it."[41] It was crucial in his case, and I suspect he thought that it was a hallmark of all great writers, an essential ingredient of their talent. But a few days after making that remark, he would say, "At one time I thought the most important thing was talent. I think now that the young man or the young woman must possess or teach himself . . . infinite patience." Then in the next breath he said, "The most important thing is insight . . . curiosity . . . and if you have that, then I don't think the talent makes such difference."[42] Perhaps this is the moment to remember Whitman:

40. Robert Coughlan, *The Private World of William Faulkner* (New York: Harper & Brothers, 1954), 58, 43.
41. Gwynn and Blotner (eds.), *Faulkner in the University*, 159.
42. *Ibid.*, 192.
43. Blotner, *Faulkner*, 1789.

Do I contradict myself?
Very well then I contradict myself,
(I am large, I contain multitudes.)

We might remember Emerson too. Faulkner was never one to
concern himself with what seemed to him foolish consistency in
matching the facts of one of his books to those in another. He
doubtless felt the same in commenting about his art.

Thinking back now to Faulkner's own puzzlement about this
discrepancy between himself and his work, it seems to me that
one of the reasons others often thought they perceived a discrepancy was because of the way he spoke, usually simply and
directly and often ungrammatically. Not always: once when we
were talking about Matthew Brady's battlefield photographs, he
suddenly mentioned the unbearable stench from all that car-
nage. He went on: "The Confederate corpses didn't have
enough meat on them to produce it; it was the effluvium from
the Yankee corpses that permeated the circumambience."[43]
More typical was Harvey Breit's experience. Standing at the
window of his Hotel Algonquin room, Faulkner said, "Harvey,
come over here and look down." Breit did, half expecting some
profound observation from the creator of Yoknapatawpha County.
Faulkner said, "Don't all them people look like bugs?"[44]

I don't know that I am much closer now than I was at the
beginning to answering Faulkner's questions or our own about
the sources of that genius, much closer to determining what, in
that brain and in that spirit, produced the work. Perhaps we are
finally forced back to an old formulation. Faulkner had it in mind
when he told a questioner, "James Joyce was one of the great
men of my time. He was electrocuted by the divine fire. He,
Thomas Mann, were the great writers of my time. He was
probably—might have been the greatest, but he was electro-

44. *Ibid.*, 1628.
45. Gwynn and Blotner (eds.), *Faulkner in the University*, 280.

cuted. He had more talent than he could control."[45] Perhaps we should rest there, acknowledging that talent as a divine gift, rejoicing in the fact that he received it and used it and provided the fruits of it to enrich us all.

Contributors

JOSEPH BLOTNER was among the lecturers who inaugurated the Faulkner and Yoknapatawpha conferences in 1974. He was also William Faulkner Lecturer and visiting professor of English at the University of Mississippi in the spring of 1977. Among his books are *Faulkner in the University*, edited with F. L. Gwynn; *William Faulkner's Library: A Catalogue*; *Faulkner: A Biography*; and *Selected Letters of William Faulkner*. He is a professor of English at the University of Michigan.

MERLE WALLACE KEISER for her doctoral dissertation at New York University made a comprehensive study of the novel *Sartoris* as it was published in 1929, with particular emphasis on characters, structure, themes, and style. She has taught courses in English and American literature at Norwalk Community College in Connecticut.

THOMAS L. MCHANEY is a professor of English at Georgia State University. He has published two books on William Faulkner— *William Faulkner's "The Wild Palms": A Study* and *The PRO Reference Guide to Faulkner*. He has also published numerous articles about Faulkner and other figures in American literature and more than a dozen short stories. In 1972, he lectured and read from his fiction at the University of Mississippi Writer's Conference.

Contributors

MICHAEL MILLGATE, who was guest lecturer for the 1976 Faulkner and Yoknapatawpha Conference, is author of *The Achievement of William Faulkner* and coeditor of *Lion in the Garden: Interviews with William Faulkner, 1926–1962*. Among other distinguished books he has written are *American Social Fiction* and *Thomas Hardy: His Career as a Novelist*. A native of England, Millgate has taught in England, India, the United States, and Canada. He is presently professor of English at the University of Toronto.

JOHN PILKINGTON is Distinguished Professor of English at the University of Mississippi. The author of *Francis Marion Crawford* and *Henry Blake Fuller*, editor of *Stark Young: A Life in the Arts*, and a contributor to many scholarly journals, Professor Pilkington is now engaged in writing a biography of Stark Young and a book on William Faulkner.

NOEL POLK, professor of English at the University of Southern Mississippi, has done a book-length study of Faulkner's *Requiem for a Nun* and has edited Faulkner's *The Marionettes*. He has written many articles on Faulkner and other southern writers and is coeditor of *An Anthology of Mississippi Writers*.

JAMES G. WATSON is the author of *The Snopes Dilemma: Faulkner's Trilogy* and numerous articles about Faulkner and other American writers. He has chaired panels on Faulkner at the national Modern Language Association meetings, and he is now working on a book about Faulkner's short stories. He is a professor of English at the University of Tulsa.